Custodians of Salvation

Custodians of Salvation

Last Rites and Cremation in Banaras

Sarita K. Kashyap

B L O O M S B U R Y
NEW DELHI • LONDON • OXFORD • NEW YORK • SYDNEY

BLOOMSBURY INDIA
Bloomsbury Publishing India Pvt. Ltd
Second Floor, LSC Building No. 4, DDA Complex, Pocket C – 6 & 7,
Vasant Kunj, New Delhi, 110070

BLOOMSBURY, BLOOMSBURY ACADEMIC INDIA and the Diana logo are
trademarks of Bloomsbury Publishing Plc

First published in India 2025
This edition published 2025

Bloomsbury Academic India
An imprint of Bloomsbury Publishing Plc

ISBN: HB: 978-93-61315-61-9; eBook: 978-93-61313-21-9;
2 4 6 8 10 9 7 5 3 1

Typeset by Integra Software Services Pvt. Ltd.
Printed and bound in India by Replika Press Pvt. Ltd

To my husband Ashish, who has walked every step of this journey with me

Contents

Illustrations

Figures

Tables

Foreword

Banaras, the sacred city, is the final destination for the Hindus who want to attain *moksha* or salvation, which means freedom from the cycle of birth, death and rebirth. This is the most sought-after place for those who are at an advanced stage in their lives and seeking *moksha*. The last rites are performed on the banks of the River Ganges, and cremations are carried out by members of a caste called Dom. Except for a few sociological studies, our knowledge about this caste in the cremation ground of Banaras is still very limited. I welcome the publication of this book which I am sure will contribute to our understanding of last rites, *moksha*, and those who perform the cremations. The author has conducted extensive fieldwork in the cremation grounds of Harishchandra Ghat and Manikarnika Ghat. This book explores why for centuries Dom have been regarded as the custodians of salvation. A detailed and rich description has been provided on their everyday lives, their living and working conditions. This book explains the changes that are taking place with regard to cremation, occupational hazards that Dom encounter in situations like pandemic and issues pertaining to the environment, and why they migrate in search of new occupations. The author has analysed at length how the Covid-19 pandemic influenced the traditional rites and rituals in the cremation grounds, and posed risks to those who had to perform cremations at the *ghats* during this critical time. Besides rites, rituals, castes and the pandemic, the author raises some important issues pertaining to the environment and draws our attention to the fact that tradition and modernity are incompatible in a city like Banaras as far as last rites are concerned. Environmental issues have to be addressed keeping this in mind. In short, this will be a worthy addition to the existing sociological literature on the sacred city and salvation. It is a highly readable, theoretically astute ethnographic account that we have been looking for.

Abhijit Dasgupta,
Retired Professor,
Department of Sociology,
Delhi School of Economics,
University of Delhi,
Delhi

Preface

The idea to work in this area sprouted in 2017 at Jawaharlal Nehru University, Delhi. As I watched the documentary *Children of the Pyres*, the sight of young children running in the middle of cremation ground filled with ashes, dead bodies and high flames of pyres left me shocked. It was astonishing to see those children, from the age group of eight to fifteen years, working and sleeping at the cremation *ghat*. At a later stage, after reviewing available literature, it was decided to initially focus on the Dom community due to the lack of sufficient information.

My first fieldwork in Banaras was undertaken in June 2017 followed by November–December 2017. Then for my doctoral study, I decided to re-work in the same area to investigate many unexplored areas. Ethnographic fieldwork was conducted at Harishchandra *Ghat* starting from November 2019–March 2020, November–December 2020, March–April 2021, to July–October 2021.

Intervals in field visits were due to the coronavirus pandemic. Though the effect of the pandemic seems not to have withered away soon enough, as a way out, the masses accepted the 'new normal' after the disturbing phase of normlessness. Data was collected after 'normal' situation was relatively resumed. The pandemic provided a different perspective and reality of the cremation grounds which would not have been possible otherwise. The Covid-19 pandemic provided an excellent opportunity to understand the position of the Dom in the present times. This book provides a detailed account of what actually unfolds at the cremation *ghat* of Banaras, when the world was in shock and people were trembling with the fear of infection and excessive death rates. The pandemic provided a scope to understand how people had adapted to the 'new normal' in death rites.

The works of Robert Hertz (1960), Veena Das (1977), Meena Kaushik (1979), Jonathan P. Parry (1994), Dev Nath Pathak (2018) and Ravi Nandan Singh (2022) provided specific insights into this area and served as guiding lights for this book. These works helped to a detailed understanding of cremation, rites and rituals in Hinduism and the division of mortuary labour. These works provided specific insights such as (i) death is assimilated into the process of cosmic regeneration and the act of cremation is a cosmogony (Parry 1994:31), (ii) due to the sacredness of Kashi, cremations are performed continuously keeping it as the navel of the universe (Parry 1994:32), (iii) the role of Brahmin and the lower castes is not limited to removing impurities but to also act as a mediator between forces of good sacredness and bad sacredness (Kaushik 1979), (iv) the lower castes just like the Brahmin stand on the threshold of sacred and profane and act as a ritual intermediary between the individual and liminal categories (Kaushik 1979:6–18) and (v) there is a continuum with traditional practices on one end and technological practices linked with the environment on the other at both local and global levels but in a different way (Singh 2022:114).

However, all these focused studies did not examine how the Dom understand permanent and temporary pollution related to their work. Though the Doms are scattered across India, their engagement in death rites is not mandatory, as a few are undergoing social mobility in other parts of India. The role of the Dom in different places is somehow limited to arranging the pyre or staying as keepers of the cremation ground. But the religious aspect, firm belief in the idea of salvation and the role of Kashi in bestowing salvation provide an important position to the Dom, and their role becomes important in the performance of last rites which requires an ethnographic understanding. This book is an anthropological exploration into the lives of Dom who have been engaged in handling dead bodies for many centuries, yet remain unseen. It addresses the dilemma of providing the status of 'custodian of salvation' to the Dom who are considered outside the varna hierarchy. Another focus of this book is on the division of labour within the death industry of Banaras, with special reference to the Dom.

Further the book investigates issues like environment pollution due to the unregulated cremation practices performed adjacent to the Ganges River and the ways traditional beliefs are leading to the degradation of the environment. It also explains the potential changes in old beliefs and practices related to death due to advancing modern technologies.

The book further provides insights into the continuous strife between the technological aspect of modernity, that is, crematorium and the traditional belief system in regard to the performance of last rites.

Acknowledgements

I take this opportunity to express my humble gratitude to everyone who became part of my research journey. Thanks must first of all go to the large number of friends and informants on the *ghats* of Banaras who patiently put up with my sometimes intrusive presence, went out of their way to instruct me and offered me hospitality in their homes. I am forever grateful to the Dom community for accepting me and providing insights into their unexplored lives. I received extensive support from my respondents especially Bandevi and Vikram. Both of them supported me during my entire stay in Banaras. I am indebted to them.

Secondly, I am thankful to the librarians and staff of the institutions from which I gathered data and completed research: Ratan Tata Library of the University of Delhi, Central Library of Jawaharlal Nehru University, Central Library of Banaras Hindu University and Prime Ministers' Museum and Library, Delhi.

I use this space to thank Professor Abhijit Dasgupta without whom this work would not be in this form. No words are enough to express my gratitude to him. He not only acted as a mentor and stood by my side, but simultaneously always took my challenges into consideration. He carefully read and commented in detail on every single draft of my chapters. His continuous suggestions on every draft led this book to its final form. As my mentor, he provided me with a space to explore and engage with my ideas. He always reminded me to think about what new my research could contribute in the academics. His minute observations helped me greatly, from improving my reading skills to penning down my arguments. His guidance and support motivated me to finish this work on time. My thanks to Prof. Dasgupta for being an enthusiastic supporter of this book, a sympathetic yet critical reader, and for helping keep my spirits up whenever I was overwhelmed preparing the manuscript.

Words will not be enough to thank Dr Sunil Babu for his immense help. He generously gave his time and crucial insights and always pushed me to refine my arguments. I learned a lot from his useful feedback about methods and language. Both of which made my work a learning and enjoyable process.

Dr Vikas Bajpai originally motivated me to pursue this study during our initial discussion at Jawaharlal Nehru University. I owe him thanks for his kindness and encouragement.

I take this opportunity to thank my friends and colleagues for listening my ranting during the writing phase. I cannot express my gratitude enough for their help in continuously providing me with important ideas and works of literature.

Lastly, this journey began with a series of challenges. In all these years of struggles, one thing that had never left my side was the love and support of my family. If it had not been for my family, this journey would not have been completed. They always stood by my side in every situation. In the end, this whole process has been a learning experience for me, and with it, I also grew slowly step by step. This research and fieldwork were supported by the University Grants Commission, Junior Research Fellowship from 2019 to 2023.

Abbreviations

BHU	Banaras Hindu University
BOD	Biochemical Oxygen Demand
FCC	Faecal Coliform Counts
GAIL	Gas Authority of India Limited
GAP	Ganga Action Plan
IIT	Indian Institute of Technology
MBD	Mother Brother Daughter
MLD	Million Litres a Day
PHC	Primary Health Care
PPE	Personal Protective Equipment
WHO	World Health Organization

Glossary

achhuth untouchable

agni sacred fire

akaal mirtyu/ alp mirtyu untimely death in youth

anna measurement of money. One rupee is equal to 16 *anna*

asprisyas untouchable

bageecha garden area

bhaiya brother

bheek turn when coins are jingled in alms

boli system verbal claim

chamar the caste handling leatherwork

chandal the caste handling dead bodies

charan paduka spot at the cremation *ghat* where God Vishnu is claimed to perform austerities

damru dal groups playing pellet drums

darshan 'seeing' God

dev deepawali festival of deepawali for Gods celebrated in Banaras by lighting thousands of lamps on the *ghat*

dharma code of conduct

dhol/ dholak musical instrument

gaddi throne, used here for ancestral property

gamchha towel often red in colour

ghar ki baithaki resting time period for family members as *pari* of other families are in the process

ghar ki pari turn of family members for ownership of cremation *ghat*

ghat segment of river frontage

ghat chekhna capturing of *ghat*

ghee clarified butter

grahak pakadna catching customer

havan samgiri ingredients for offering in fire sacrifices

kapal-kriya rite of breaking skull with a bamboo shaft during cremation

kar tax, payment given to Dom for the sacred fire

karma doctrine of compensation

kashi khanda eulogistic text on Banaras

kashi-labh profit of Kashi; promise of salvation for those who die in Kashi
kashi-vaas residence in Kashi from different places seeking salvation
khand division of section
kund sacred pond
linga symbol of divine, a phallus as symbol of Shiva
madhi an open space under a shed/roof, where the sacred fire is kept burning
mahakaal/ mahadev Lord Shiva
mahapatra funeral priest
malik owner/ boss
mantras hymn
massan cremation ground
massan holi playing Holi with ashes at cremation ground
massan nath Lord of cremation ground
mati refers to dead body, after a person dies, the normal terms to refer to it are *mati* or body. It is due to Hindu belief that human body is made of earth and in the end, it will mix with the earth
mazdoor labourer
moksha salvation
mukhagni rite of placing sacred fire in the mouth of a dead body
mukti liberation from the cycles of life and death
mumukshu bhavan shelters for dying person to attain salvation
naukar servant working under the Dom-Raja
panchak a set of five lunar asterisms in which it is inauspicious to die or cremate a dead body
panchkrosi the pilgrimage which circumambulates the entire sacred space of Banaras
pari turn/ the system of allocating rights to perform on rotation basis
pari-ghat management of working of cremation *ghat*
patidar partners/shareholders
pinda-dan balls of rice offered to the dead
prasad offering to God
pravaha immersion of dead bodies which are not considered suitable for cremation such as pregnant women, infants, sadhus, persons who died due to small pox or by snake bite
preta ghost, spirit

puja worship
putla-vidhan last rites of an effigy made of flour for the deceased, in case the corpse is not available for cremation
raja king
roli red-coloured powder
samsara cycle of birth and rebirth
shamshan cremation ground
shastras religious texts
shastrik scriptural
shiv baraat marriage procession of Lord Shiva
shraddha offering to ancestor
sona turn to sieves ashes for jewellery
tahel turn of ownership of *ghat*
tarak mantra sacred chant that helps the seekers cross over the ocean of worldly existence
theka contract; the Dom caste make different kind of contracts with the mourners for cremation
tirtha crossing ford pilgrimages
trishul trident associated with Lord Shiva
varna theoretical division of the caste system as Brahmin, Kshatriya, Vaishya and Shudra

Introduction

One fine afternoon, during the peak of June 2017, many bodies were cremated through the prescribed traditional mode of open pyre near the bank of the Ganges at the cremation ground[1] of Harishchandra Ghat. As the sun appeared higher in the sky, the increased frequency of heatwave, accompanied by intolerable heat from the blazing flames of open pyres emanating plumes of dark smoke, led to an increase in the temperature, hence making it arduous for the Dom to burn these dead bodies.

A skinny man in his mid-thirties with a dark complexion and a bare chest had a red *gamchha*[2] tied around his waist. He was trying to pick up a fallen half-burnt body mass from the ground with the help of a temporarily made bamboo shaft to place it back on the pyre. The Dom has to deal with polluted substances, the death impurity, and due to the ascribed nature of this occupation, he has been assigned an inferior status.

Meanwhile, a group of mourners who brought a dead body to the *ghat,* after placing it near the bank of the Ganges, went upstairs to take the sacred fire from the Dom-Raja. They had to pay the demanded tax, which is the fee for the fire.[3] *Madhi*[4] is where the negotiation for the charge of sacred fire and the cost of cremation takes place between mourners and the Dom-Raja. Here, the Dom-Raja sits on *gaddi*[5] while the mourners are provided space on the ground, an indirect way of emphasizing the higher status of the Dom-Raja at the time of death.

This fire is crucial because, as per myth, taking it from the hands of the Dom helps the soul in attaining salvation. Here lies the contradiction of considering the Dom as lower[6] in caste status because of the polluted nature of their ascribed work, yet simultaneously mandatorily taking the sacred fire from them after paying the demanded fee. In other words, a caste whose position lies outside the *varna* system has been provided with the status of custodian of salvation in Hindu society.

The Dom predominantly settled in the holy city of Banaras in India.[7] They have been indulged in the practice of arranging and burning dead bodies for generations and are attendants of the cremation ground. The colonial literature described the Dom as 'the representation of uncleanness, where humanity finds extreme degradation' (Sherring 1872:400). These people are often stigmatized due to their caste status and derogatory terms such as 'Chandala' and '*achhuth*' (untouchable) are used to refer them by other castes in Banaras. They are victims of various discriminations, including what Erving Goffman conceptualizes as stigma. Locating the interactive situation at a micro level, Goffman (1963) attempts to locate his stigma theory of perceiving people within the ideology and points out that 'we construct a stigma theory, an ideology to explain his inferiority and account for the dangers he represents, sometimes rationalizing an animosity based on other differences, such as those of social class' (Goffman 1963:15).

The stigma associated with this occupation and their caste status undermines their contribution to society. They are referred to as those '*earning from the dead*'. Not only does the caste-based society, but even the State, fail to give them the due importance and respect they deserve.[8] Weber (1958) argued that caste has been a fundamental institution of Hinduism, comprising two significant principles: *Samsara* (belief in the transmigration of the soul) and *Karma* (doctrine of compensation). The notion of salvation places tremendous emphasis on the caste system, as it is believed that people are born into a specific caste not by 'accident of birth' but because of *karma* in their prior lives (Weber 1958:118–21). Hence, as caste and Hinduism are closely linked, one cannot be studied without considering the other. This book attempts to understand how a sacred place is negotiated by making the Dom, who have been marginalized as a lower caste for centuries, the custodian of salvation and involving them in the last sacrificial rites of Hindus.

Death and Dying

Banaras holds an apex position in Hinduism. The presence of *Jyotirlinga*[9] in the Kashi-Vishwanath temple, along with one of the fifty-one *Shaktipeethas*[10] in the Vishalakshi temple, increases its importance. Moreover, Kashi is known for its historical cremation grounds. *Kashi Khanda*[11] mentions the promise of Lord Shiva to provide instant liberation to those dying in Kashi. It is believed that he whispers the *tarak mantra* (sacred chant that helps the seekers cross over the ocean of worldly existence) into the ears of dying people. Due to the mythological importance of Kashi in bestowing salvation, Hindus from across the world prefer it as their destination for performing last rites to attain the fruits of *Kashi-vaas*[12] and *Kashi labh.*[13] Thus *Kashi-vaasis* are the seekers of salvation. Their social and emotional life is governed by the strict philosophy of *Kashi-vaas* as they adhere to the basic principle of practising detachment from all forms of social, material and emotional bonds (Pal 2021:63). Because these are considered as entrapments for the souls that make its liberation difficult. Thus they rigorously follow rules that will facilitate in their desire of attaining liberation.

Parry (1994) argues that Kashi has been understood as a microcosmic representation of the universe. He equates the universe with the body (Parry 1994:31). As the universe is destroyed during the conflagration, the body is similarly destroyed in the cremation process. But, neither the universe nor the body is completely destroyed, as cosmic dissolution represents the beginning of the universe, and the destruction of the physical body represents an 'act of regeneration'. Hence, death is assimilated into the process of cosmic regeneration, and the act of cremation becomes a cosmogony (Parry 1994:31–2).

In Hinduism, the death ritual provides a link between two realms of reality: the social and cosmic worlds. Rituals separate the sacred from the profane and, at the same time, provide a mediating category between them. Thus, rituals associated with death place the whole event within a wider area—the all-encompassing reality of the cosmic world—thereby validating the social world (Kaushik 1979:4-1). These rituals also facilitate the movement between the cosmic and social categories. Here, a merger occurs between the cosmic and social categories, regenerating and recharging the cosmos. Thus, the bounded auspicious (marriage and worship) and bounded inauspicious (*pinda-daan* to ancestor) deal with the cosmos as integrated with the social world, and the rituals within these domains are important symbolic acts which recharge the cosmic universe using social categories (Kaushik 1979:4-2).

Funeral ceremonies involve rites of transition, as suggested by Van Gennep (1960), whereby mourners and the soul of the deceased travel a path running parallel to each other. The unburied dead, or those who have died "bad deaths," hinder the proper performance of these rites, sustaining themselves as ghosts at the expense of the living. Thus, there is a symbolization of unresolved fears of death (Gennep 1960:164). Turner (1974), extending Van Gennep's analysis of rites of passage, emphasized that during the liminal period of mourning, social order becomes fluid and creative (Turner 1974:47). Furthermore, relationships become more egalitarian, and the hierarchies and rules that govern normal social conduct may be broken more readily. Clive (1998) mentioned that this is because such marginal situations involve what phenomenologists have called 'world-openness', which is at once a source of danger and stimulation, where people are thrown back upon themselves and forced to become more reflective: what was once dirty may become clean, and vice versa (Clive 1998:65).

Thus, dying is not an act in isolation, as argued by Pathak (2018) in his work *Living and Dying: Meanings in Maithili Folklore*. The phenomena of death and dying should not be merely reduced to cosmogony or thanatology, as its imagination utilize metaphors from events of life, thus assuming an art form. In his analytical understanding of Maithili folk songs, Pathak (2018) argued that the expression pertaining to death and dying in everyday life situations is 'emotional truthfulness', a hinge concept behind the art of dying (Pathak 2018:213). He elaborated that emotional truthfulness

> alludes to the folk tendency to be spontaneous in expressions, indulge in the mundane, discharge everything expedient, fulfil the needs of all kinds, perform ritual as well as non-ritual actions, and engage with the divine and seek transcendence. It is by the virtue of 'emotional truthfulness' that folk life becomes a narrative fraught with contradiction, ambivalences, and polyphony, and a premise for the dissolution of the binary oppositions of living and dying.
>
> (Pathak 2018:213)

The death of a close one often leads to a feeling of normlessness and chaos. The performance of the last rites becomes crucial here, as death threatens society by questioning the continuity of human relationships and undermining the basic assumption of order on which society rests. Society helps individuals by providing some belief in performing rites that lead to its proper functioning during the chaos. The performance of the final ceremony includes burial, cremation or immersion of the last remains of the deceased. These rites ensure the soul's peace and a place in the realm of ancestors, which finally frees the living from the obligation of mourning (Hertz 1960:54).

In modern times, there has been a shift in these ceremonial practices. Ravi Nandan Singh's (2022) work *Dead in Banaras* shows that nowadays the use of existing and new cremation technologies finds a hybrid presence in modern India. This can be understood as a 'continuum on one axis, which is the dominant traditional practice, and on the other end is the technological practices that are inextricably linked to the environment at both local and global levels but in a different way' (Singh 2022:114). Thus, with the advent of technologies, certain changes are emerging in different parts of the world in response to environmental challenges. For instance, in Denmark, crematoriums have already been using heat energy generated during the cremation processes for civil use. It is argued that there is a difference between this energy and the corpse, as a 'person has a corporeal substance and organic signature in death, energy is devoid of these, and thus this recirculation must be accepted on this ground' (Singh 2022:112). Thus, there has been a shift in Denmark in adopting technology, moving from the burial practice to the cremation of the dead and filtering the recirculated heat energy for public use. Yet, the aesthetic of burial is maintained by preserving the ashes of the deceased in an urn.

In the context of Banaras, this shift could be understood by looking at the Ganga Action Plan 1986, which focused on the ecological and environmental preservation of the Ganges River. Along with this, the launch of an electric crematorium at Harishchandra Ghat also helped. Even the set-up of the iron grill at the cremation ground, which consumes less wood to cremate bodies, is another initiative undertaken with the environment in mind (Singh 2022).

Thus, keeping these crucial aspects in consideration, this book seeks to understand how the technological aspect of modernity has been intervening in the old tradition of wood cremation, and whether the former has succeeded in replacing the existing religion-based ritual aspects. If so, it examines its impact on the livelihood of the Dom community.

The Dom have been engaged in this ascribed occupation of death for generations. But there is dearth of literature on this caste. This book provides detailed ethnographic information on them and also seeks to understand the process of consciousness formation among them, besides analysing other contributing factors. Subaltern consciousness consists of opposing elements: an autonomous one (which unites the individual with all their fellow workers in the practical transformation of the real world) and a borrowed one (a superficially explicit element inherited from the past and uncritically absorbed) (Gramsci 1971:333). Gramsci argues that 'this group does have their own conception of the world, which could be even in an embryonic form. But this group, due to reason of submission and intellectual subordination, adopts borrowed conceptions from the other dominant group, which they verbally affirm and believed to be the ones which are followed in normal times' (Gramsci 1971:327). Hence, this caste 'continuously recreate[s] a microcosm of the larger system in their own cultural system'; they 'complement and replicate' the same hierarchal caste differentiation based on the transaction of food and service providers from which they have been excluded (Moffatt 1979:5).

Caste has also been understood as a cultural construction of power (Dirk 1987:401). It tends to change continuously and reflect the actual power relationships in society. This leads to a constant process of formation and disintegration of caste identities through fusion and fission (Bandyopadhyay 1997:10). Thus, one's consciousness has been continuously shaped and developed by the process of interaction between the dominant and the subordinate (Chatterjee 1989:206).

The presence of the Dom in Banaras, an urban religious space, also contributes to their consciousness formation. In this case, religion is an important parameter that demands the presence of the Dom in death ceremonies. Religion provides a universalist code for society, offering ideological justification to the dominant group to ensure social division, while simultaneously, for the subaltern group, it is perceived as an element that could provide them access to a powerful cultural code (Chatterjee 1989:172). Consciousness formation needs to be understood as a process involving various forms of consciousness, such as caste, class, gender and religion, which coexist and engage in complex interactions (Sarkar 1984:274). Still, caste continues to be its central element (Chatterjee 1989:169). Furthermore, consciousness formation can be influenced by factors such as one's residence in an urban or rural setting and accessibility to resources, which can lead to awareness and affiliation with power.

Urban spaces facilitate a few changes in the rigid structure of the caste system. Here, the availability of opportunities to work in different areas, in addition to the presence of vast populations, leads to a shift from collectivity to individuality, and anonymity can easily be maintained, thus providing the scope for hiding the visual caste markers evident in rural areas. The better economic capacity of an individual allows possession of economic goods and thus momentarily shifts the visual status markers from caste to class. However, in these spaces, caste communities live separately in a spatial dimension surrounded by their own caste members (Chatterjee 1989:170). Urban areas closer to rural regions often observe higher migration for employment, and people in unfamiliar places prefer to stay within their own caste communities. Thus, the urban spaces 'fit the communication pattern of a traditional town. The persistence of this pattern in the modern part indicates the particularity of caste' (Lyche 2017:249). Simultaneously, they provide a scope for hiding one's caste identity from strangers, as only closer groups with whom one has face-to-face interactions are aware of each other's caste.

Yet, lower castes that shift to the urban sector find it 'hard to make headway beyond the margins of urban economy in its informal sector' (Jodhka and Manor 2018:7). This is because, in the urban economy too, affluent castes and their kinship groups continue to maintain their monopolies in trade and business, due to which marginalized groups face inequalities (Jodhka and Manor 2018).

In recent days, modernity accompanied by technological advancements has led to tremendous changes, and upward mobility in the domain of occupation has become possible for caste groups that have been marginalized. For instance, these days, hair stylists perform the work of barbers, and gynaecologists perform the role of midwives. However, as this book reveals, it is quite interesting that no one has replaced the work of the Dom in cremating dead bodies, even though technological aspects have modified the ritual performance of cremation and people have begun investing in the business of death. In the performance of the death ritual, the barber still tonsures the hair of the mourner, the Dom cremates the dead body and the *Mahapatra*[14] performs the last rites. Furthermore, another point that differentiates the work of the Dom from other castes, such as the Chamar,[15] is the ritual aspect linked with the former. In short, these caste groups are still trapped in their traditional occupation when it comes to the death business because here both religion and caste act as contributing factors. So, caste dynamics in the social sphere[16] of the death industry needed to be explored,[17] the ways these ritual specialist castes of the death industry interact in the cremation *ghat* social sphere and share the subjective meaning of salvation.

The caste system is an undeniable reality in Hindu society, attributing a position to the individual in the hierarchy based on the concepts of purity and pollution attached to one's occupation (Dumont 1970:107). Many writers have identified occupation as the sole criterion for the caste system, including Ibbetson (1883) and Nesfield (1885). Ibbetson provides a descriptive definition of caste as a group of people who practise a 'hereditary occupation, seek preservation and support of the principle by the elaboration from the theories of the Hindu creed or cosmogony of a purely artificial set of rules, regulating marriage and intermarriage, declaring certain occupations and foods to be impure and polluting, and prescribing the conditions and degree of social intercourse permitted between the several castes' (Ibbetson 1883:10).

The main characteristics of the caste system are hereditary specialization, hierarchy and mutual repulsion (Bougle 1971:143). The structural definition of the caste system can be exhibited in a society with divided groups that are closed, ranked, exclusive and exhaustive. These groups cooperate rather than compete with each other, along with relations that are organized by roles (Bailey 1993:121). The division of labour in the specialization of caste occupation is considered different among Hindus, as differentiation is present not only in the final product but also in the instruments used to produce the object (Bougle 1971:157). In addition, the question of the continuity of the division of labour in India is explained by the fact that Hindus have 'grafted religious obligation into a material necessity' (Bougle 1971:163).

Nesfield (1885) attached the greatest importance to occupation in the caste system. He arranged the myriad castes into an order of their dignity or rank, showing the castes performing activities known in the primitive phase, such as fishermen and hunters being ranked the lowest. Those working in metallurgy and with prestigious metals like gold and silver hold more prestige.

> Throughout the whole series of Indian castes, a double test of social precedence has been in the active force, the industrial and the Brahmanical; and these two have kept pace together almost as evenly as a pair of horses harnessed to a single carriage. In proportion as the function practised by any given caste stands high or low in the scale of industrial development, in the same proportion does the caste itself, impelled by the general tone of society by which it is surrounded, approximate more nearly or more remotely to the Brahmanical ideal of life.
>
> (Nesfield 1885:116)

Dumont (1970) distinguished traditional, holistic societies from modern 'individualistic' ones. India was incorporated into the category of traditional societies, as it stresses the holistic domain by ranking its individuals into different caste groups within a hierarchical structure based on the religious principle of purity and pollution.

Brahmins stand at the apex with ritual purity, in opposition to lower castes, who are allocated an inferior position at the bottom of the caste pyramid. The maintenance of one's purity requires the separation of castes, yet different castes must live together, for Brahmins cannot do without the services rendered by lower castes. Hence, Dumont's description combines the idea of interdependence with that of the repulsion of castes towards each other. This repulsion has manifested in the form of endogamy, communal restrictions and the division of labour based on one's caste, which leads to stronger interdependence.

Dumont (1970) viewed hierarchy as a system based on the dichotomy of pure and impure, and in social organization, this opposition is reflected in the roles of Brahmins and the lower castes. He understood caste ranking as essentially a ritual matter emerging from notions of purity and impurity rather than power (Dumont 1970:66). The origin of social order among Hindus is traced back to *Rigveda*,[18] which mentions four groups known as *varna*.[19] These groups are arranged in a hierarchal structure, in which Brahmins occupy the topmost position, followed by Kshatriyas, next comes the Vaishyas and last is the Shudras. Although there is no mention of any fifth group, sociologists and anthropologists included another group known as 'untouchables' (*asprisyas*), who are better known as Dalits[20] in the Hindu social order (Kumar 2014:36). The word *asprisya* means un-touchable, appeared between the third and sixth centuries of the Christian era, when the word '*Chandala*' was constituted as the fifth varna (Bandyopadhyay 1997:13).

Moffatt defined an 'untouchable' as a 'person of a discrete low caste, excluded for reasons of their extreme collective impurity from particular relations with higher beings' (Moffatt 1979:4). The material deprivation and the stigma of pollution are the major reasons behind their lowest position (Beteille 1972:414). They are subjected to 'cumulative domination' at the socio-cultural, economic and political levels (Oommen 1984:45). This leads to their deprivation from these domains while relegating them to a lower position (Beteille 1969; Mencher 1974).

The upper castes use the idea of *dharma* (code of conduct) to rationalize the caste system, which acts as a tool for the repression of the lower castes (Mencher 1974:476). Deliege (1999) argues that untouchability cannot be just reduced to ritual aspects and uses the concept of 'cumulative deprivation' to describe lower castes as those who have lower ritual status, poor economic conditions and lack of political power (Deliege 1999:50). Thus, defining lower caste as 'economically dependent and exploited, victims of many kinds of discriminations and ritually polluted in a permanent way' (Deliege 1999:2).

Considering the above-mentioned definitions, the Dom can be understood as a caste that has been allocated a degrading and lower position in Hindu society, as they are engaged in ritually polluted occupations that have led to their exclusion, exploitation and discrimination, further depriving them of economic and political power.

This caste identity of being permanently polluted led to their marginal and inferior status, due to which they are set apart from the rest of society and are forced to shift to areas away from the centre, but they do not constitute a separate society. They are integrated into society to remove the filth of society (Deliege 1999:8). Hence, simultaneously, they act as an intermediary between the higher beings (upper caste) and malevolent ghosts (Moffatt 1979; Quigley 1993). This is evident during an eclipse when the shadow of planets (Rahu and Ketu) falls on the sun, which is treated equivalent to the shadow of Dom's funeral attendant falling on a Brahmin; thus, by offering a gift to the Dom, people hasten it to end and return to their purity and auspiciousness (Parry 1991:271). In exchange for their services to the upper caste, the Dom receives the dead person's belongings, such as shrouds, bamboo biers, clothes and pieces of jewellery of the deceased, and a funeral feast cooked by the bereaved family. It seems these gifts are an effort to remove the inauspiciousness of death pollution and transfer the danger to the receiver. Through this transaction, the Dom accept their lowness to the people they offer their service (Marriott 1968; Moffatt 1979).

Dumont (1970) pointed out that hierarchy and separation are two basic aspects of the categorical opposition between pure and impure in the caste system (Dumont 1970:109). He further argues that birth and death are seen as harbouring danger in other parts of the world, whereas in India, the same events are associated with impurity rather than danger. But Das (1971) criticized him by providing evidence from Sanskrit texts and other literature to show that there is no exclusive segregation between impure events and procedures in which only polluting castes are involved, or pure events in which only Brahmins participate. In addition, the function of those who perform rituals is not limited to removing impurity but also extends to protecting pure ritual events from certain mystical forces of negative sacredness surrounding them. Hence, Brahmins are seen as mediators between man and the forces of positive sacredness, whereas impure castes are seen as mediators between man and negative sacredness (Das and Uberoi 1971). She further clarified, 'It seems problematic to treat birth and death impurity as identical with caste impurity' (Das 1976:259). Moreover, there is a difference in the semantic discourse, as birth pollution is termed *sutaka*, death pollution is *maranasauca* and 'untouchable' is referred to as *achhuth*. Thus, specific terms exist for birth and death pollution, but the same is missing for caste pollution. She further added that the theory of variations in birth and death pollution should consider those categories of people who are not affected by pollution (priests, kings and ascetics) and those categories of people who are doomed to be permanently polluted (those who had committed five great sins) (Das 1976:261).

Primarily, this study seeks to explore the status of inferiority imposed upon the Dom and the disjunction by assigning them the role of custodians of salvation, making it mandatory to take fire from their hands in exchange for a fee. As works of literature reveal, Hindu life revolves, to a large extent, around the notions of purity and pollution (Laungani 1997:191). The presence of ascribed occupations within a hierarchical arrangement of the *varna* system serves as evidence of this (Dumont 1970:108). This hierarchical arrangement of the pure and the impure underscores the superiority of the pure over the impure; both must remain separated. The same principle is reflected in the division of occupations, which are also distinguished as pure and impure and, therefore, must be kept separated (Gokhale 1993:2). The ubiquitous caste system places lower castes in a degrading position by involuntarily engaging them in traditional occupations that are permanently fixed as polluted. The upper castes require them to clean their filth to maintain their 'purity'. This made the latter a carrier of such pollution (Parry 1980:42).

As an outcaste, the Dom belong to one of the marginalized sections of Hindu society. By virtue of their birth, they are expected to undertake jobs seen as permanently polluting, such as dealing with animal and human waste products. Being treated as inferior, they seldom enter the homes of the upper castes, as doing so could defile the latter's house. However, the deceased's family members must perform the rites related to preparing the corpse and its funeral. In doing so, they enter into a state of pollution themselves, which is considered temporary pollution. Attending to and burning corpses, however, is a fixed degrading occupation for the Dom, relegating them to the status of permanently polluted. This contradiction between temporary pollution and permanent pollution needed to be studied as the primary aim of the research.

With the arrival of philologists and later missionary ethnographers such as Cohen, caste has become an area extensively researched. While colonial ethnographical knowledge production was primarily for administrative and governance purposes, post-independence India produced literature on caste studies that mainly focused on discrimination and exclusion, followed by the role of rites and rituals and the notion of purity and pollution. However, there is a paucity of literature on funeral workers. I began this work for my M.Phil. project (Kumari 2018), which focused on the implications of the Dom's traditional occupation on their health status.

When I began to explore and understand the Dom community and the intersectionality of temporary pollution and permanent pollution, the works of Meena Kaushik (1979), Jonathan P. Parry (1994) and Ravi Nandan Singh (2022) provided specific insights, such as: (i) death is assimilated into the process of cosmic regeneration, and the act of cremation is a cosmogony (Parry 1994:31), (ii) due to the sacredness of Kashi, cremations are performed continuously keeping it as the navel of the universe (Parry 1994:32), (iii) the role of Brahmins and the lower castes is not limited to removing impurities but to also act as a mediator between forces of good sacredness and bad sacredness (Kaushik 1979:6:12), (iv) lower castes like the Brahmin stand on the threshold of sacred and profane and act as a ritual intermediary between the individual and liminal categories (Kaushik 1979:6:18) and (v) there is a continuum with traditional practices on one end and technological practices linked with the environment on the other at both local and global levels but in a different way (Singh 2022:114).

However, all these focused studies did not examine how the Dom understand permanent and temporary pollution related to their work. Though the Dom are scattered across India, their engagement in death rites is not mandatory, as some are engaged in the process of social mobility (Lillelund 2009). The role of the Dom in different places is often limited to arranging the pyre or serving as keepers of the cremation ground. However, the religious aspect, the firm belief in the idea of salvation and the role of Kashi in bestowing salvation provide an important position to the Dom, making their role significant in the performance of last rites, which requires an ethnographic understanding.

The works of Parry (1994), Das (1977), Hertz (1960) and my research provided me with a preliminary view of domains crucial for understanding the Dom lives. Although 'death is a big business in Banaras', as argued by Parry (1980:4), in which different caste groups are involved for their livelihood. The presence of technology at the *ghat* itself marks a shift from traditional practices to modernity. Further, the social sphere of the cremation *ghat* of Banaras has been the domain of different sections that earn livelihood directly or indirectly through the death business, indicated by the presence of their kiosks.

However, the meaning of death and salvation cannot be solely reduced to the economic aspect because this process involves a spiritualized landscape (Kashi), specific ritual specialists and sacred fees linked with rituals. Here, different service castes are engaged based on their respective turn systems. The spectrum of these service caste workers is broad, including the Mahapatra to perform the last rites, the Dom for arranging and burning the pyres, barbers to perform the tonsure ritual and the Mallah to ferry those corpses for immersion in the Ganges that were not sanctioned to be cremated according to Hindu beliefs. Hence, interaction on a daily basis among these service castes is an important aspect to explore the structure and dynamics of the cremation *ghat*.

Ever since anthropologists and sociologists began a systematic study of India, they have approached the question of caste from a colonial perspective, even to the modern day. In the works of Kaushik (1976) and Parry (1994), there is a continuity in the conceptualization of Dumont's purity and pollution, which needs to be critically analysed through an ethnographic understanding of the marginalized Dom.

This study investigates how the ritual aspects methodologically and theoretically constructed as a kind of discourse, and how the caste question in their everyday life reproduces the same circumstances whereby they are unable to understand the way it has been acting upon them. The Covid-19 pandemic provided an excellent opportunity to understand the position of the Dom in the present times. This study provides a detailed account of what actually unfolded at the cremation *ghat* of Banaras, when the world was in shock and people were trembling with the fear of infection and rising death rates. People were struggling to perform the last rites for their loved ones as numerous bodies were waiting in queue at the cremation grounds, and technology, that is, the electric crematorium, failed to cremate these bodies because of a technical snag. The only hope was the arduous toil of the Dom.

1

Experiencing the Field

The sight of young children running in the middle of a cremation ground filled with ashes, dead bodies and high flames of pyres left me shocked. These boys were attempting to escape angry mourners after snatching shrouds from lying corpses. 'Children of the Pyre',[1] beautifully captures the real and challenging lives of seven male Dom children who stole shrouds from dead bodies – in exchange for one rupee per shroud – in the extreme conditions at the cremation ground of Manikarnika Ghat. It was astonishing to see those children, in the age group of eight to fifteen years, working and sleeping at the cremation *ghat,* consuming intoxicants and using abusive language.

After watching the documentary and reading available literature, I left Delhi for my first visit to Banaras City for my M.Phil. project during the first week of June 2017. I took a bus and reached Banaras the next day. I stayed in a hotel room at Godowlia Chowk and sought directions from local shopkeepers to reach Manikarnika Ghat. While passing through many narrow lanes for which Banaras is famous, I saw men carrying the biers of dead bodies for their final rites, wrapped in a shining golden shroud and chanting *Ram Naam Satya Hai.*[2] I followed some of the mourners. The lanes were narrow, and it was difficult to walk, given that there were milling crowds, vehicular traffic and cows blocking the roads. Mourners were making their way through these narrow lanes, carrying biers on their shoulders.

While experiencing these lanes, with a constant stream of mourners for the first time, it became a difficult situation to decipher. Moving further, I saw different colours of shrouds and funeral items displayed in shops for sale. I then realized that, perhaps, the cremation *ghat* was closer. After walking some distance, I came across a vast area where large piles of wood logs were stocked for cremation. Shirtless men, mostly thin and weather-beaten, off-loaded logs from boats and carried them to designated spots. They were transporting them depending on where cremations were held. I moved further and saw the temple of *Mahakaal*,[3] around which many workers sat and relaxed, to avoid the scorching sun. There were many men, some selling funeral items, others dealing with customers, and a few were mourners. At a distance, barbers were tonsuring heads of mourners. Among these men, I needed some help to locate the Dom. I tried to enquire about them from a man standing there. I asked, 'Where can I find Dom caste? I want to understand the challenges in their work.' He instantly replied dismissively, 'Oh, madam! They do not face any problems. In fact, they trouble other people.'

I was taken aback and decided to move forward as some people pointed towards the *madhi*, from where mourners were taking the sacred fire. It was an old structure where the sacred fire was kept, and some men sat while a few rested there. The Dom-Raja was not present; his nephew was managing his *pari*. I sat with them and noticed that there were no other women around. I enquired whether females were forbidden to come to the cremation *ghat*. The response was that there is no rule; generally, *females are soft-hearted and do not dare to visit the cremation ghat.*

Though I came to Banaras to see the involvement of Dom's children at the cremation *ghat*, during my interaction, I gained insights into other aspects, such as the importance of the sacred fire from the hand of the Dom, their role in cremation rites, and their living and working conditions. During our interaction, they informed me about another important cremation *ghat* in Banaras, the Harishchandra Ghat.

Next, I left for Harishchandra Ghat; it was different from Manikarnika Ghat as the roads here were broader, with saree stores and restaurants lining both sides. After following the directions from locals to find the Dom locality, I reached the street. As I entered it, I noticed it was extremely untidy, with garbage and biological waste strewn about. I enquired of a passer-by about the house of the Dom. He then pointed me to an old house with a broken wooden door. I knocked on the door, and a woman in her late thirties opened it. I asked her if this was the house of the Dom; she stood there in silence for a few seconds and then told me, in a rather unpleasing manner, to go to the *ghat* and shut the door. I was a bit disheartened by her reluctant approach. Moving ahead, as I walked through the garbage, I saw some men sitting under a tarpaulin and smoking marijuana. They were Dom men. They were ready to talk to me; however, I felt uncomfortable being surrounded by strangers in this environment.

During the interaction, a man, who appeared to be in his late fifties and was drunk, said, 'Girls should not roam like this and should stay at home.' He added, 'only a particular kind of girl roamed like this'. I was uncomfortable hearing that, so I immediately left the place and walked further to find a spacious area—the cremation ground of Harishchandra Ghat. The brief conversation with those men further disappointed me, as I felt I won't be able to do my research. However, moments later, I came across some children and an old man from the Dom community who made me feel comfortable and spoke to me enthusiastically. It was then that I gathered the courage to undertake this research.

On the bank of the Ganges, numerous pyres were burning using traditional methods, and simultaneously, from a large chimney, plumes of smoke were released from the bodies cremated in the gas crematorium. The presence of a mechanized crematorium at a place where traditions have a firm grip highlights the idea of conflict and convergence between technology and tradition (see figure 1.1).

This *ghat* was different from the Manikarnika Ghat. It was not crowded, and even at the base of the gas crematorium, younger Dom children, aged three to five years, were playing. This *ghat* was relatively spacious and cleaner, as fewer dead bodies were brought here. Another difference was that at Harishchandra Ghat, Doms stayed near the cremation *ghat* itself, whereas Doms working at Manikarnika Ghat stayed at Meer Ghat (another *ghat*). After this, I returned to Delhi to plan my next trip. The ethnographic fieldwork

Figure 1.1 Cremation ground of Harishchandra Ghat.[4]

began in November 2019. The initial task was to build rapport with respondents. I was not sure how many months would be enough to be accepted as an insider.

Ethnographic fieldwork can be a challenging and unanticipated journey. While the researcher is immersed in the exploration of the field, the field simultaneously reveals many unexpected facets, leaving an everlasting impression on the memory of the individual.

The circumstances influencing an ethnographic journey largely depend on the nature of one's field. In order to discover, describe and represent the world of the research, ethnographers have traditionally committed themselves to the first-hand exploration of research settings with naturalistic field methods (Atkinson and Coffey 2002; Hammasley and Atkinson 1995; Li 2008).

My field site was the Harishchandra Ghat in Banaras, where, on a daily basis, around thirty bodies are cremated. The work of handling dead bodies is a gendered and ascribed occupation performed by Dom men for centuries. They are stigmatized and treated as inferior because of the 'impure and polluted' nature of this work. This chapter is a reflection of an unexplored journey as a female ethnographer on the cremation ground of Banaras. Cremation grounds are considered to be forbidden for females in Hindu society. Rarely are females visible on these *ghats*. However, its location in Banaras, a religious place and emerging tourist spot, facilitates an opportunity for females to visit it. These cremation grounds, unlike those in other places, are not located in secluded areas; instead, they are situated in the centre of the city near the bank of the Ganges River. Furthermore, the position of Banaras as a provider of salvation increases the importance of its cremation *ghats*.

Involvement and Detachment[5]

I revisited Banaras on 3 November 2019 to begin my ethnographic study. The boundary of Harishchandra Ghat starts from the crossroads. Here, the Dom men stand and verbally claim their right over the dead body by uttering the word *matti* for the dead body reaching the cremation *ghat*. When I reached the crossroads, I started receiving a warm welcome as those people recognized me.

Proper accommodation, drinking water and safety are some of the crucial factors in the field (Srinivas 1976:7). In the beginning, I rented a room located at some distance from the *ghat*, as I was unable to find one near the Dom locality. After some months, I shifted to another room closer to the *ghats*. The primary reasons for this were the considerable distance of my previous room and the sudden upsurge of the coronavirus pandemic. A close respondent arranged a room for me in his friend's house, belonging to the Mallah caste. This room was located near Harishchandra Ghat. Ideally, I should have stayed with the Dom community, but it was not feasible in this case because they already face space constraints due to their larger family size.

In the Dom community, female movements are restricted within their locality. Being housewives, they stay within their houses and do not have chances or any specific requirement to interact with outsiders. However, the gossip about an unknown city girl interacting at the *ghat* with men of their community reached them. One of my close informants took me to his house and introduced me to his mother.

Slowly, I grabbed opportunities to build rapport with women. On several occasions, after my formal questionnaires were over, the ladies began their gossiping. Being present among them provided me with some hints of what was unfolding in their everyday lives. It pointed towards unwritten rules that were followed, set boundaries for females, marriageable age, possible spouses. Even if a good deal of the gossip was untrue, it provided valuable leads in my quest for information. The individuals and themes that were regarded as worthy of gossip would help in understanding their local culture (Srinivas 1976:23).

In the field, my primary concern was rapport building with these families. In the beginning phase, I had ample time for breaking the ice, building rapport, and gaining the informants' trust. This period offered the opportunity to get acquainted with informants, and gradually they began to accept my presence as a normal phenomenon. This introductory stage of fieldwork provided scope for collecting relevant information on non-sensitive areas (Srinivas 1975:1392). I began by collecting information on genealogical details through household surveys, as in the initial days, their kinship linkages were quite confusing. Later, I noticed that Dom families residing at Harishchandra Ghat were in affinal relationships as they practised cross-cousin marriages. This helped me get acquainted with everyone at the *ghat* and also proved to be an effective way to interact, as people were reluctant in the beginning. The activity of gathering genealogies made their faces familiar to me and vice versa. This is among the easiest ways of establishing social bonds with the people an ethnographer wishes to study (Srinivas 1976:21). It was a tedious but beneficial exercise in gaining unrestricted entry into male working spaces as well.

Meanwhile, I strictly adhere to the practice of regularly maintaining a field diary to record observations and conversations, and to reflect on the positive and negative experiences encountered during research. After reviewing the field notes, I noticed that detailed and quantifiable information on Dom families had been collected on various aspects such as occupation, kinship patterns, poverty, health hazards and the challenges of their everyday lives. Some respondents were resistant to direct questioning; in those cases, small pieces of information were acquired gradually through regular interactions maintained over a period of time. These pieces of information were recorded in detail in the field diary, which consists of everything I heard, saw, smelled and even the expressions of speakers during conversations. Thus, ethnographic techniques were employed as a deep venture into 'thick description' (Geertz 1973:20).

In the initial phase of my fieldwork, I was more curious to discover what I intended to study than apprehensive. I was psychologically unprepared for challenges and unaware of the things that were about to unfold until I encountered problems in the field. The next section discusses those in detail.

Female Researcher in a Male Domain

I often reached the cremation *ghat early* in the morning and stayed there until sunset to gain glimpses into the lives of people dealing with death. The stairs of the cremation *ghat* and the nearby tea stall were perfect spots to observe interactions among people and the performance of cremation practices. Men from different sections of society sat on these stairs to relax, have a cup of tea or wait for the completion of the cremation procedure. I engaged in conversations with these people who were willing to talk, after explaining the purpose of my study, particularly emphasizing their right to privacy and confidentiality.

Research is often conditioned by researchers' personal characteristics—gender, age, caste and class. These factors may limit or determine what an ethnographer can accomplish, as women can sometimes accomplish what men cannot and vice versa. Similarly, young people can sometimes accomplish what older individuals cannot and vice versa (Wax 1979:513–14). In Indian context, the researcher caste background plays a crucial role and people can often be seen making rough estimation about their caste status. Initially, for introduction I often reveal my first name. But it is not enough to understand my caste position, so without any hesitation, they enquire about my surname. As my surname is 'Kumari' which does not hint directly to any caste group, they have to directly enquire about my caste.

Further, that a stranger from Delhi was visiting them to research their lives provided a sense of pride to them, and they often boasted about it in front of other caste groups.

But my age, gender and unmarried status turn out to be problematic, as people often enquire about my marriage plans and even suggest suitable partners for me. They are uncomfortable with the idea of a woman in her thirties remain unmarried and staying alone in a different city. However, my close informants often stand by my side and put forward their argument that 'these days, late marriages have become a normal phenomenon in cities as people prefer to study for better lives'. Thus, the status characteristics of a researcher affect the process of gaining access to, establishing and maintaining rapport with informants in a setting (Gurney 1985:42). Female researchers have to work harder to achieve an impression that combines the attributes of being non-threatening with those of being a credible, competent professional (Gurney 1985:43).

Recently, there has been a steep increase in the number of tourists visiting Banaras due to its emergence as a religious and tourist spot. Local people encounter many different faces on a daily basis, with visitors seeking information, and clicking pictures and leaving. However, in my case, I had to stay there for a longer duration. The quality and quantity of time spent proved to be the best method for rapport building and gaining people's trust. My entry into a male-dominated realm was uncomfortable in the beginning. I noticed that I was being thoroughly scrutinized for the way I talked with men and the kind of information I sought. This was done to examine whether I could be a possible threat.

Further, attire is an important aspect in the field, especially for female researchers. I was more conscious because my work was largely focused on men, and any act that could be termed inappropriate in their view could hamper my research. So, I wore culturally accepted attire that consisted of a kurta, salwar, and dupatta (common Indian wear). Respondents often enquired if I smoked or drank, as women in cities do. Rapport building over a period of time helped clear their doubts. Gradually, the eldest members of the Dom community, who often sit at the cremation *ghat,* began calling me for chit-chat and, slowly over time, provided pieces of relevant information.

After spending a few months, I noticed that some Dom men were exhibiting a different attitude towards me. These men were from better-off families in comparison to the rest of the Dom community, as they owned kiosks and were employed at the gas crematorium. Their non-welcoming attitude was probably due to my age, gender and being a stranger. One day, I went to the municipal corporation to get permission from the executive officer to access data on the number of bodies cremated in the gas crematorium in past years. One of the staff members accompanied me into the room where the records were kept. While passing by, I noticed those Dom men involved in an argument with the office staff. They were shocked to see me. Later, when I was sitting with the executive officer, one office staff member accompanied those five Dom men into the office. The executive officer shouted at them for engaging in a fight with the staff of the municipal corporation. The Dom men were shocked to see me sitting there, while they were standing and seeking an apology. After that day, there was a positive change in their attitude towards me.

While studying marginalized groups, researchers should tailor their data collection methods to both the sensitivity of their topic and the vulnerability of research subjects (Li 2008:101). This aspect was taken into consideration while collecting data. It was discovered that among Dom men, there were numerous cases of death at a younger age, and the prevalent reason was liver damage due to excessive consumption of alcohol (Kumari 2018:137). The nature of this ascribed occupation of dealing with dead bodies compels workers towards the intake of substances to cope with the work amid the burning smell of flesh and rotting bodies (Kumari 2018:134). Some of these men could be spotted at the *ghat,* engaged in smoking marijuana or drinking alcohol. These deaths at an early age result in an increased number of widows at a younger age in the community (Kumari 2018).

To check the authenticity of gathered information, data was triangulated through different sources. Ethnography is suitable for investigating sensitive issues because it can provide rich, detailed descriptions about the unknown or little-known (Li 2008:101).

In the field, I encountered 'multiple complex conceptual structures' superimposed and knotted into each other. We have to contrive those structures to understand and then render them (Geertz 1973:10). Hence, the data from the field itself provided various areas which, when arranged together, formed a different picture altogether, one that is non-identical to the normal view. While analysing the genealogies, various interesting aspects became overt, such as the prevalent differences in social and economic status of the Dom, the emerging trend of migration from rural to urban areas and vice versa. A few Dom families that had migrated and settled at Harishchandra Ghat from rural areas often visited their native places during their ownership of the cremation *ghat*. I seized the opportunity and accompanied them to these places. This was helpful, as through their contact, people at those cremation *ghats* interacted warmly with me, and I was able to observe their living and working conditions up close. We travelled through any means of transport that was feasible, such as boats, buses and motorcycles. These journeys were quite exhilarating and different.

One of the primary difficulties as a female ethnographer in a male-dominated space is being aware of uncomfortable gazes following you. As a researcher, I tended to ignore those gazes and focus on my work. Safety also becomes important, as travelling to unknown places was a tricky endeavour. I only went with my close informants and made sure that their families were aware of it.

Further, in the beginning, seeing and smelling the burnt odour of flesh while being surrounded by plumes of smoke and ashes were unbearable. The smoke and ash particles suspended in the surroundings often got stuck on hair and clothes. One of the most chilling experiences occurred during the flood season, when bodies were cremated in a congested space within the Dom locality. As I was trying to capture photographs, something cold suddenly touched my feet. I looked down and saw that a female corpse had just been placed near my feet. Its face was pale white and wrapped in a plain white shroud. That particular face and the felt coldness have been stuck in my memory ever since.

At Harishchandra Ghat, I mostly sat on the stairs, talking and observing people. This was a public space for studying social phenomena by listening, observing, questioning, reading, operating and reflecting, which constitute six cognitive modes (Gobo 2008:23). Three months had passed by then, with the beginning of February 2020. With the coming of summer, it became difficult for me to sit on the stairs without any shade. Men working at the *ghat* were either engaged in their work or, in between, relaxed in their small kiosks.

The fact that I was the only woman now seemed to be more problematic. My two key informants allowed me to sit in their kiosks, but it was uncomfortable as they were stuffed with funerary items stored for selling purposes. There was space left for only one person to sit, and I was an outsider creating trouble for them. As in the field, researchers have to sit, stand or lie in any place, so 'space has to be found, made, or negotiated for the body-thereness of the ethnographer' (Coffey 1999:73). It became essential for me to 'carve out a space'. I was feeling guilty and wanted to repay them for their act of kindness. As my informants were illiterate, I took the initiative of teaching a few of them to read and write when they were free from work or waiting for customers to purchase funerary items. This helped me, as I could stay at the *ghat* and observe people working and interacting.

After a few days of noticing my discomfort in the small kiosk, they proposed to create a space for me in the *ghat* so that I could teach and continue my research. They swept an area on the stairs and cleaned it up by fetching water from the river. They constructed a temporary shed using bamboo as poles, bedsheets as walls and bedding to spread on the floor. These materials generally belonged to the deceased who were cremated at this cremation *ghat*. The Dom have rights over these belongings. As I was aware of this, I hesitated for a few seconds, but noticing their effort and respect towards me, I could not have been happier. This shed was located adjacent to the tea stall, thus providing an opportunity to interact with other Dom men who came there to relax. When people became aware that I was teaching their children, the whole community developed a sense of respect for me and was wholeheartedly willing to provide me with the information I sought.

In the initial stage of the fieldwork, the researcher is provided with a forced role that gives meaning to their presence in the community (Gobo 2008:23). Given that I was a stranger to them initially, there was a sense of suspicion, and they hesitated to share things with me. Gradually, after building rapport over time, I could see a change in their perception towards my presence. Slowly, my identity also changed after constantly constructing and shifting. However, 'this transition from gaining access to the field to actual observation is not a linear and uninterrupted process. This shift is intermittent, changing from being strangers to being familiar'. (Gobo 2008:126).

The camera contributed to my popularity as people loved being photographed (Srinivas 1976:20). After getting their picture taken, they often asked for a hard copy. One day, an old man in his late sixties, who was uneducated and cremated bodies as a means of livelihood, requested me to take a picture of him. Generally, he wore a cotton *dhoti* with a vest and a *gamchha* around his neck. But for the photograph, he wore a white-coloured shirt and pants and completed his look with his *gamchha*. When I handed over his picture, he had a wide smile on his face and safely kept it in his shirt pocket. He revealed that this photograph would act as his identity proof, to show people in the village that he is the Dom-Raja from Harishchandra Ghat of Banaras.

From being a stranger and a 'city girl', I was now a familiar person to them. The newly earned respect as 'madam ji' helped me in several instances during my stay. Slowly, they accepted me as their sister, and for the older members, I was now their daughter. Staying alone away from family, it became their responsibility to take care of me. This turned out to be problematic when I had to interact with males from another caste, especially mourners, as younger informants engaged in arguments with those who tried to start a conversation with me. Later, I explained my research target groups and the need for my study, and slowly, things went smoothly.

During our preparatory phase as ethnographers, we were taught that during fieldwork, while it is important to stay in proximity to the community under study to participate in its social life, researchers should also ensure that they maintain a cognitive distance to avoid any biases while conducting the study. Thus, there remains a need to strike a 'difficult balance between two opposing situations' (Srinivas 1976:7). Is it possible to bring about such a balance? Can a researcher perform these distinctive roles, at once, of being an 'insider' and an 'outsider'? As 'total empathy is professionally and practically impossible. It is precisely the constant reflecting, taking notes, asking questions, completing questionnaires, taking photographs, recording and then transcribing, translating and interpreting imposed upon us by our profession that prevent us from getting completely "inside" the culture which we want to study' (Gobo 2008:8). But it is also 'true that full objectivity in the social science is beyond attainment' (Beteille 1965:12).

Doing ethnography in sensitive research is like walking a tightrope, as such fieldwork requires ethnographers to maintain mindful awareness of ongoing relationships and to make frequent adjustments accordingly (Li 2008:109). There were many occasions when I was highly disturbed as things were going against what I had planned for collecting information and managing impressions with respondents. In those times, I preferred to walk along the bank of the river and sit alone on a distant *ghat* from Harishchandra Ghat. I would often immerse my feet in the flowing water of the Ganges, lost in my thoughts. This solitude of sitting and watching the flowing water restored my spirit and prepared me for another bout of intense socializing. But this was not easy, as my informants often took this route to reach Asi Ghat to have a cup of tea. After spotting me on the bank of the river, they would ask me to join them. I was not in a position to deny their humble request, and this could provide an opportunity to extract more information. Sometimes it became the desire to be a good field worker who could collect all the relevant required information, and for this, I felt I was eliminating all my naturalness to become an actor playing this role (Srinivas 1976:7). I tried hard to make myself liked by everyone, and I found that this meant I had to support views frequently against my own. These attempts to play an unfamiliar role all day long, constantly attempting to react in ways that would be acceptable to my hosts instead of ways that came naturally to me, and unremittingly keeping alert to cues that would tell me whether or not I succeeded were exhausting. These were attempts to maintain an appearance of quiet and even cheerfulness (Briggs 1970:23).

Generally, I stayed on the *ghat* until 6 p.m., and then left for my room. The separate room at the end of the day provided rest and a separation from the community for the time being. I made sure that no male members from the community came to my house, as it would create a negative impression. In addition, the solitude at night was a respite from the efforts of the day spent trying to collect information and maintain a good impression. My room provided me with a space to rethink and plan my next day—for instance, how to proceed, which questions should be asked—in addition to completing my diary entries.

Moreover, the endless struggle to understand their flow of speech in their native language was exhausting. Though the males were well-versed in Hindi, as they often interacted with different people, even when a question was asked in Hindi, they would respond in their native language, which is *Khadi Boli.* So, I began to learn it. However, the problem arose when informants responded to my queries while chewing betel nut. There was hardly any occasion when they were not chewing tobacco or betel nuts. Left with no choice, it proved to be difficult to understand what they were saying while consuming betel nut. I often ended up clarifying again and again, and they would regularly spit and continue the conversation.

Unforeseen Field Circumstances

In the field, researchers should be able to extract correct, relevant and in-depth information. While sitting at the *ghat*, I noticed many tourists and researchers often seek information from natives. People working at the *ghat* have become accustomed to this and use it as an opportunity to earn money in exchange for information. They were always ready with a few short answers to frequently asked questions. To gather correct information, it was crucial to probe deeper, and their trust was a necessary requirement. This is one of the instances where ethnographers have to situationally solve on-site problems they encounter in the research process (Clarke 1975; Ellis 2007; Etherington 2007).

Further, there are five recurring themes encountered by females in fieldwork: protection, conformity, initial suspicion, reciprocity and cultural shock (Golde 1970:70). I encountered all of these in my fieldwork. Sharing one of the instances, while I began teaching Dom children and succeeded in building good rapport with them, I had an unsettling experience. During that time, I met a man in his late 30s talking at a tea kiosk. He initiated a conversation with me and, in the process, mentioned that he was a government employee in the

Indian Air Force. After finishing my tea, as I was about to leave, he offered to drop me off. I was shocked and politely declined his offer. Rather than taking the main road, I often preferred to walk through the stairs of the *ghats, as* it was the shortest route to my room. On my way, while I was about to reach my destination, I saw him again, waiting at a distance on his bike. I was scared but determined to act normally. He once again offered to drop me off. I quickly made up some excuses and left the area immediately.

The next evening, a woman at the tea shop informed me that he had been asking for my mobile number and was looking for me. I was scared because I was staying alone in Banaras. I decided to inform my close contacts about this. They were very supportive and waited for him at the *ghat,* but he did not return, and days passed. Meanwhile, I also left for my hometown for a break.

On my way home, I received a call from my informants. They informed me that a person came to the *ghat* and engaged in an argument with Sujeet,[6] who in anger slapped him. The man shouted that 'Sarita is a spy working in Banaras to gather information', and threatened my respondents of filing a case in Allahabad High Court for harassing an Air Force personnel.

My respondent got scared, called me and asked, 'Sarita, Are you a spy?'. Luckily, my father, who was an army officer, talked to them and calmed down the situation. He even managed to gather details about that person and confronted him, after which that person never came to Harishchandra Ghat, and the matter was closed. However, I was anxious about returning to the *ghat*, wondering whether people would think of me as a spy and whether it would impact my impression management with them. But with time, everything went back to normal.

Literature suggests that rapport with respondents is maintained through exchange relationships (Gurney 1985; Wax 1971). Respondents may ask researcher to perform tasks or do favours for being allowed to conduct research. In some case female fieldworker reciprocity may be problematic such as if powerful males in setting expect sexual favours in return of research access (Gurney 1985:43). In my opinion, this kind of situation can be handled easily if researcher is involved with whole community for collecting information rather than a few individuals. Because then community members are aware of researcher's whereabouts. Making a better rapport with the community provides a sense of responsibility for them too. In my case, regular visits of my family members to my field site, in addition that my father being in army acted in my favour.

After gathering relevant data from the community, it was time to move towards mourners. I was a bit nervous initially, as it constituted an ethical question of whether or not to interview those who had just lost their relatives and were performing their last rites. To tide over this problem, I interviewed distant relatives rather than chief mourners. It was easier to spot distant relatives as they sat far from the dead body, while the chief mourners sat or stood at a proximal distance from the burning body. Whenever a newly dead body arrived at the *ghat*, I started looking for possible distant relatives. To interact with mourners, my key respondents helped me in the initial phase. Rajiv Bhaiya had his tea kiosk at the cremation *ghat*. Whenever I reached the *ghat*, I could sit and talk with people at his tea stall. Sometimes, mourners joined in conversations. While some were attentive listeners to our discussions, others used to put their points of view across. Many were surprised to see a woman sitting among men. So, initially, Rajiv Bhaiya requested mourners to talk with me while having tea. Then slowly, after gaining specific insights and ways of dealing with mourners, I began interviewing them myself. It was generally a group discussion because mourners sat in groups; only one or two people gave answers. Only when the primary respondent could not recall the facts did another person intervene to provide the reply.

It was more challenging to interview mourners accompanying the deceased to the gas crematorium, as in this case, fewer mourners joined the cremation procedures, and generally, only close relatives were present. Also, these people were devastated by their loss and unwilling to converse. Moreover, most bodies that had died unnatural deaths, such as suicide or murder, were brought here. Even the duration of cremation played a crucial role, as people waiting for three to four hours were willing to converse. However, in the case of the gas crematorium, the cremation rites were completed in an hour.

In the last phase, I interviewed people from different caste groups who work at the cremation *ghat* to understand the caste dynamics.

After completing my doctorate in 2023, I went to Banaras to meet my respondents. My informant began crying upon seeing me and said, 'We missed you. You were like a daughter to us. Food is not suiting you as you are getting weaker. Come and stay with us. We will search for a guy for you here only, get married, and settle in Banaras with us'.

Looking back at my journey, it seems true that ethnographic fieldwork contributes to the identity construction of the researcher, as it is often spoken of as a 'rite of passage', a ritual of initiation into a mature professional identity (Coffey 1999; Ferguson & Gupta, 1997:17).

2

In Search of the Dom at Cremation *Ghat*

'Untouchable's Complaint'

Day and night, we are suffering.
We will share our grief with the ruler.
Even God is not listening to our problems.
Don't know how long will we suffer,
You shattered the pillar and saved Prahlad
Rescued the elephant King from the jaws of the Crocodile
Duryodhana's brother was pulling it off
You appeared and extended the end of the sari
You killed Ravan and protected Vibhishan
On the little finger, you lifted the mountain
Where are you sleeping now and not hearing to us
Are you too scared of a Dom touch?

Heera Dom[1]

The poem illustrates the plight of these outcastes during the colonial era, a condition that still holds true in contemporary times. The word 'Chandala' serves as a metonym for the Dom, who were grouped with *Apapatrah*, which means that a 'vessel used by them should be thrown away' (Briggs 1953:30). There was a common saying that the presence of a 'Chandala' or even his gaze could defile a funeral feast; they were considered equal to dogs and were given the clothes of the dead (Briggs 1953:30).

In the previous administration records, the Dom were generally considered to represent a Dravidian menial caste, which was found scattered throughout northern and eastern India (Kaushik 1979:1:30). In the first organized census of colonial India, 1881, the Dom were classified as a 'casteless tribe, and there was lack of efforts to draw any distinction among different branches of the original tribes' (Clarke 1903:10). Clarke argues that though in the census of 1901, the Dom were classified as Hindu but were never embraced by Hinduism (Clarke 1903). This chapter examines who the Dom are and how Dom of Banaras differ from the rest, who spread across India. This chapter begins with the historical context of the Dom across India and then narrows down to the present context of Banaras. Here primary focus is on the everyday lives of the Gotakhor Dom of Banaras residing at Harishchandra Ghat.

Colonial Knowledge

With the arrival of Orientalists to India, who were mainly philologists, and later following them, the colonial knowledge production often drew from ancient Brahmanical texts such as the *Vedas* and *Puranas* to provide a better understanding of the culture of India. In these texts, the Dom have been portrayed as 'aboriginal' and were viewed with abhorrence for what society considered filthy habits, ugly features, and their unsettled, nomadic life (Briggs 1953:4).

Different scholars, such as Sherring (1872), Nevill (1909), Risley (1915) and Briggs (1953), mentioned the Dom as the last surviving members of the Dravidian caste, treated lowly by Aryans and known to indulge in menial occupations (Risley 1915). In Hindu society, a Dom represents lack of cleanliness, while Sherring (1872) added, 'he is loathed and avoided as scum and filth; in short, no language can properly designate the social degradation of his position' (Sherring 1872:400). The Dom also referred to as habitual criminals, where they were claimed to be the chief offenders in the matter of thieving (Nevill 1909:155). Hence, the Dom have been treated as outcastes, criminals and representatives of a degrading position for centuries.

There is no agreement on the actual origin of the Dom, as there are many debates regarding their origin. According to Sherring (1872), in the past, they held certain power and importance, which can be testified by the fact that there was a view suggesting they formerly occupied the country beyond the Ghaghara River and were neighbours of the Bhar caste, who lived in the vicinity of the Rohini River in Uttar Pradesh. Several old forts testify to their importance, as they still retain the names of their founders, such as Domdiha and Domangarh (Sherring 1872:402). Sherring further argues that the degradation of the Dom is similar to that of the Bhar caste, who were conquered and subjected to ill-treatment by Hindus. The Hindus deal with them with caste prejudice and pride, reducing their position to extreme abjectness, which continues to this day (Sherring 1872).

In the Indian context, according to Clarke, the available knowledge of that time suggested that among the jungle tribes that inhabited the wild districts of Gorakhpur and Champaran, there was no particular unity. These were classified under the general name of Dom by the invaders. The word has since been used for a class of basket makers, menial workers, and scavengers who execute tasks that any 'purest' caste members would not perform due to the perceived defilement involved in such work (Clarke 1903:3). In *The People of India,* Risley (1915) provides a brief account of them, stating that they were engaged in various occupations such as basket making, scavenging, execution, burglary and music making. They were also described as vermin eaters. The Dom are known by different names across the northern region of India. The Maghiyas Dom are the main group from which two branches sprung, known as Maghiyas Dom and Bansphor Dom. The former was categorized as thieves, while Bansphors were involved in weaving baskets and cultivation. The Maghiyas were found in the eastern parts of Uttar Pradesh, Bihar and Bengal (Briggs 1953:83). The name 'Bansphor' signified bamboo splitters and was found in northern India. Crooke notes that, besides the occupations mentioned above, they were also sweepers, musicians, and involved in preparing hide for drum heads (Briggs

1953:84). Briggs mentioned the Dom in the southern region of India to be possible descendants of northern India (Briggs 1953). Table 2.1 provides information about the Dom division within northern India.

In the next table (Table 2.2), there is a column representing the names of different authors who have provided details about the Dom in various regions of India along with their traditional occupations. This reference to the Dom, with different names and varieties of occupations across areas, can be understood by the fact that it is possible, in the absence of one lower caste, another caste performs its work (Srinivas 1984:164).

In Banaras, there are two main branches of the Dom: Banarasi[2] and Maghiya Dom. The Banarasi Dom owned the burning *ghats* and do not marry or eat with other settled Dom. They claim no links with the Maghiya Dom (Briggs 1953:82). These Dom had around fifty

Table 2.1 Divisions among the Dom in North India.

Uttar Pradesh	Bihar	Bengal
Bansphor	Bansphor	Ankhuriya
Dharkar	Chapariya	Bajuniya
Domra	Dharkar	Dai Dom
Harcanni	Hari	Dhola
Jallad	Gadahiya	Desia Dhakal
Litta	Dhapra	Bisdeliya
Maghiya	Dakhina/Turi	Banukiya
	Harkar	Ghasera
	Lorhora	Kalindi
	Pacainya	Kaura
	Supara	Madarona
	Tirhutiya	Murdafarash
	Raut Mihtars	Sanci
	Maghiya	Taliabona
	Uttariyas	

Source: Risley (1915), *The People of India*; Briggs (1953, *The Doms and Their Near Relations*.

Table 2.2 Occupations of the Dom across India.

Author	Name of Dom	Occupation and Region
Risley (1915)	Bansphor	Bamboo splitters in North India and manual scavengers in Patna
	Basor	Basket makers and musicians in North India
	Chandala/ Namasudra	Boatmen and cultivators in Bengal
Cape (1924)	City Dom	Dispose off dead bodies, perform menial work, sweeping, and cleaning
	Village Dom	Settled outside villages
	Gipsy Dom	Nomad
Briggs (1953)	Harischanni/ Diving Dom	Attendants of burning *ghat*
	Maghiya	Thieves, basket makers, musicians, and cultivators in Uttar Pradesh, Bihar and Bengal
	Bansphor	Basket makers and cultivators in Uttar Pradesh, Bihar and Bengal
	Baror	Makers of string in Jhansi
	Domra	Executioners and corpse burners in Punjab
	Dharkar (subcaste of Basor)	Makers of cane baskets, winnowing fans, keepers, and sellers of pigs in Bihar
	Domb/Dombo	Weavers and menial workers in South India
	Dommare	Pole performers, musicians, and thieves in Tamil Nadu
	Madiga (corresponds to the Dom of North India)	Leatherwork in Telangana and Andhra Pradesh
	Mala	Musicians and grave diggers in Andhra Pradesh and Telangana
	Medara	Bamboo workers in Telangana and Andhra Pradesh
	Matang/Mang	Chandalas in Maharashtra

Author	Name of Dom	Occupation and Region
Moffatt (1979)	Vettiyan (Paraiyan)	Removers of carcasses, cremation ground attendants, and players of the *parai* drum at funerals in Tamil Nadu
Berreman (1963)	Dom	Blacksmiths, carpenters, drummers, and basket makers in Sirkanda Village, Lower Himalayan Region
Deliege (1999)	Dom	Corpse burners in Orissa

Source: (Risley 1915: *The People of India*); (Briggs 1953: *The Doms and Their Near Relations*); (Moffatt 1979: *An Untouchable Community in South India: Structure and Consensus*); (Deliege 1999: *The Untouchable of India*); (Berreman 1963: *Hindus of the Himalayas*).

families residing at both the famous burning *ghats* of Banaras (Briggs 1953). Supach Bhagat is their claimed ancestor (Cape 1924:36).

This draws a line showing that although the Gotakhor Dom (Harischanni Dom) deny any linkages with the Maghiya Dom, their narratives indicate a shared common ancestor (Supach), as will be discussed next. There are many ways in which the relationship between the Doms in Banaras and their links with Supach can be demonstrated, but it is difficult to obtain an authoritative statement on the matter. According to Briggs (1953), the following narrative appears to be closer to the truth, based on the account provided by the Banarasi Dom.

Myth 1

> Supach, a ghatwala, used to burn dead bodies on the bank of the Ganges. He had two wives; the first one was a Telin woman from the oil-pressing caste. She was a reanimated corpse. She had one son named Telrup, from whom came the descendants of the Raj Dom of Benares. Supach, the second wife was a Candwa, who had two sons, Kalu and Hela. From Kalu arose the Maghiya Dom and the Rahadari Dom. Among Hela's descendants are the Benarsi Doms, the Bansphors and the Dharkars. It is stated that Doms while providing the above information informed that it was Supach who took Raja Harishchandra as his servant. But it is generally claimed that Kalu was the master of that Raja Harishchandra.
>
> (Cape 1924:36)

The Kalu Dom figure prominently in the Dom traditions of the sacred city of the Hindus. The Harischanni Dom of Banaras derive their name from the famous King Harishchandra to mark their superiority (Fisher 1884:53). From his name, cremation *ghat* is also known as Raja Harishchandra Ghat. The Harischanni Dom control the *ghat* at Banaras (Briggs 1953:49).

Sherring (1872) elaborated on the conditions of the Dom of Banaras, noting that only two to three of their families were in better circumstances. They occupied a significant place in the fabric of Indian society because without their assistance the burning of the dead could not take place in Banaras and perhaps even in other cities of India. The Dom is regarded as 'The Lord of Death', he provides the five logs of wood required for the funeral pyre and, as his prerequisite, he takes the clothes of the dead bodies in return. He collects fees for three things: first, for the five logs given by him on which the pyre was built; secondly, for a bunch of straw; and thirdly, for the fire (Sherring 1872:401). Risley (1891), in *The Tribes and Castes of Bengal*, mentioned that in the funeral ceremonies of Banaras, '[T]he Dom is the only person who can furnish the light for the purpose; and if from any circumstances the services of one cannot be obtained, a great delay and inconvenience are apt to arise' (Risley 1891:249).

Myths of the Dom

Myths are prominent narratives that are often recalled by people while explaining their origins, beliefs or the continuation of any practices. Claude Lévi-Strauss (1968) warned against using these myths as a 'representation of empirical facts', whereas Das (1977) argues, 'the mythical reality is a transformation of observed reality, but it is precisely the alchemy which needs to be investigated' Das (1977:17). This study uses myths mentioned by people to ascertain reasons behind their beliefs and the performance of ritual practices, and to grasp an understanding of the continuation of these traditions, instead of comprehending the structure of these myths, because 'rituals reveal values at their deepest level ... men express in ritual what moves them most, and since the form of expression is conventionalized and obligatory, it is the values of the group revealed' (Wilson 1954:241).

Following M.N. Srinivas (1952), myths can be categorized into three parts[3] namely dominant myths, regional myths and local myths. Dominant myths refer to those widely accepted and spread all over the country, such as the worship of the River Ganges for removing one's sins. Regional myths refer to myths limited to a geographical region, and lastly local myths are limited to specific subgroups.

Myths play a crucial role as these 'fulfill a psychological function in offering *Harijans* a prideful claim to former precedence' (Kolenda 1964:123). However, Moffatt (1979) argues that often the downfall of the lower caste in myths is understood as a result of 'foolishness or greed of the lower caste rather than merely accidents' (Moffatt 1979:122). Below are many myths that explain the origin of the Dom. The first myth is common among the Dom of central and western Bengal, who trace their origin to a common ancestor called Kalubir, the son of a *Chandala* woman by her *let*[4] caste husband.

Myth 2

> Kalubir had four sons – Pranbir, Manbir, Bhanbir, Shanbir. From these sons, subcastes: Ankuria, Bisdelia, Bajunia and Maghiya are said to be descended. The two eldest sons, Pranbir and Manbir were, it is said, sent out to gather flowers for a sacrifice. Pranbir, who was lazily inclined, tore the flowers from the trees with a bamboo hook and picked them up as they fell on the grounds. While Manbir climbed the trees and gathered flowers carefully from branch to branch. The flowers brought by Manbir were accepted and he received the title of Bisdelia ('*Bis*' – twenty and '*Dalia*' – branches), as he climbed 20 branches in the service of God. The elder brother's offering was rejected as unclean, and he and his descendants were named Ankuria in reference to the hooks of Bamboo. On hearing this decision, the third brother was greatly pleased and drummed

> on his stomach in token of satisfaction. He and his offspring were therefore entitled Bajunia or Musician Dom. The Dhakal Dhesia or Tapasuria Doms, who remove dead bodies and dig the cross trench, which forms the base of the funeral pyre, also claim descent from Kalubir. One of his sons, they say was sent by Mahadeva to fetch water from the Ganges. At the riverbank, he found a dead body waiting to be burned and was tempted by offers of money from friends of the deceased to dig the necessary trench. On his return, Mahadeva cursed him and his descendants to minister to the dead for all time.
>
> (Risley 1891:242)

The above myth explains the origin of different subcastes of Dom and their rightful hereditary claim over the cremation *ghats*. Another crucial myth, which is important for the present study, features the Gotakhor Dom as the fallen Brahmin as mentioned below.

Myth 3

> Shiva and Parvati were involved in playful dalliance in heaven. Parvati, during the course of the game, dropped her earring, and it fell to the earth. Shiva descended to the earth to retrieve the ornament. While searching, he encountered a Brahmin who had found the ornament and decided to keep it. When Shiva, disguised as an old man, enquired about the ornament, the Brahmin lied, saying he knew nothing about it. Shiva was, however, aware of the theft, and in his rage, he cursed the Brahmin to the life of a *Chandal*. He was doomed to make a living at the cremation *ghats*. The Brahmin begged for mercy and asked Shiva to save him. Shiva relented and assured the Brahmin that his saviour would come in the form of Raja Harishchandra, who, by serving the *Chandal,* would redeem him. Thus, the Doms considered themselves as fallen Brahmin, but nevertheless the custodian[s] of *moksha.*
>
> (Kaushik 1979:1:30)

The main ingredients in the origin of lower caste myths can be categorized as: an original group of brothers, dead carcasses, collective decisions, non-intervention of God, a fall due to trickery, misunderstanding or cheating, the beginning of time characterized by equality, and a hierarchy based on ritual pollution is legitimized (Deliege 1993:544–5). But, in the context of Doms, there is a direct intervention of the God. The above myth highlights that the curse was a punishment by Lord Shiva due to Doms' greedy nature resulting in their downfall from the Brahmin caste, and simultaneously the coming of Raja Harishchandra to be their saviour. Myths illustrate that their ancestors' wrongdoings offended God, and as a punishment, they were allotted menial occupations.

Contemporary Context

The above section provided a general idea about the Dom in the historical context and the presence of different subcastes, which are possible offshoots of the Dom. The next section discusses the present conditions of the Dom in Banaras.

Gotakhor Doms,[5] the subject of this study, resides at Harishchandra Ghat, Meer Ghat, Domri Ghat and Barna/Varuna Ghat in Banaras City. The Dom of Harishchandra Ghat are the focus of this study as it is considered the oldest cremation *ghat* of Banaras, and its name is based on the mythological figure Raja Harishchandra (Kaushik 1979:1:32).

Myth 4

> Raja Harishchandra, due to excessive munificence was so reduced into circumstances that he possessed no money and could not discharge his debt. Due to this, he sold himself to Supach, the owner of the cremation ground. The outcaste Supach, sent him to help at the burning *ghat,* where he was given the duty to collect shrouds and charge taxes from the mourners. One day, his wife came to the burning *ghat* with their only dead son. She did not have money to pay the tax. Raja Harishchandra refused to burn the dead body because he was a servant of a Chandal who had ordered him not to burn the body without taking tax. She tore her garment and gave it as a tax, there came a voice from heaven, and God appeared. God

> restored their son to life and took both of them to heaven along with the Supach.
>
> (Cape 1924:34)

The myth mentioned above is a pan-India myth often recounted by people. It emphasizes the importance of paying a fee for the sacred fire to the Dom. People from across India come to Banaras to receive this sacred fire from the hands of the Dom. This sacred fire burns uninterruptedly in the *madhi* and is worshipped daily by the person who has the *pari.* As one *pari* begins at 6 a.m. and continues until 6 a.m. the next day, the person with the *pari* worships the sacred fire along with the idol of Raja Harishchandra and Kalu Dom. The latter is the ancestor of the Dom, who purchased Raja Harishchandra in the mythical story.

For *puja,*[6] the daily ingredients are sweets, three bottles of alcohol, one *chillum* (clay pipe to smoke, mostly Marijuana) and fruits. Three bottles of alcohol each for sacred fire, Raja Harishchandra and Kalu Dom. The clay pipe is placed in the hand of the idol of Kalu Dom. The diary in which the record of earnings from the *ghat* is maintained is also kept there. During *puja*, half alcohol from these bottles is poured over the sacred fire as an offering. The leftover alcohol is served in three clay cups that are offered as *prasad*[7] to elders and aged members of the Dom's community. In the end, the person having the *pari* is handed over the dairy after applying a mark of vermillion on it.

In the *madhi,* idols of Kalu Dom, Raja Harishchandra and Tara Devi are kept beside a large wall painting that depicts the mythical story mentioned above. The painting shows Raja Harishchandra refusing to cremate the dead body of his son, while his wife pleads with their son's body in her lap. The relevance of this painting and the idols, accompanied by the worship of the sacred fire, is to glorify this myth and subtly remind the mourners of the importance of taking the sacred fire from the hand of a Dom after paying the demanded fees.

One day, I was sitting in the *madhi*, and some mourners came to get the sacred fire. Initially, they were shocked to see me, as I was the only female and, moreover, was sitting with Dom males in the area of *gaddi*, whereas mourners were asked to sit on the floor. At that time, one *naukar* named Raju Chaudhary[8] was working under his *malik*. Since the *malik* was not present at that moment, he negotiated with the mourners.

He first began by asking for some basic information about the deceased person, such as the region the body came from, the reason for death and the age of the deceased. Since the deceased person was an old man, Raju insisted to the chief mourner that *their father had lived a good life and, as a dutiful son, they should provide a grand farewell to him so that his soul could attain salvation in Kashi*. He placed a demand of 2,500 rupees for the sacred fire, in addition to some quantities of grains. The mourners refused to pay this amount and requested him to reduce it. After a brief negotiation, the deal for the sacred fire was finalized at 1,300 rupees without any grains. The mourner attempted to hand over the amount directly to Raju, but he instead asked them to place the cash on the floor. Raju then picked it up and kept it in his diary. The mourners were provided with the fire, after which they left for the cremation ground.

During our conversation on the discriminatory practices of the upper caste, the Dom often use the phrase *everyone has to come here in the end*. The above narrative portrays how the Dom utilized the negotiation situation as an opportunity to convey to the other caste groups the need to acknowledge their status as 'Dom-Raja'.

One of the interesting points is that in the Endavur district of Tamil Nadu, the studied area of Moffatt (1979), King Harishchandra is known as Arichandran, and a stone is placed in his name at the cremation ground, where the vettiyan (the cremation ground attendant of Paraiyan caste), who precedes the funeral bier, pauses and chants out loudly to the upper-caste mourners:

I was the firstborn,
I first wore the sacred thread.
I am Sangu Paraiyan

Samba Kulam is superior to all castes.
Arichandran was our slave
He minds his own business;
I mind my own business[9]

Only after this the process of cremation proceeds. The upper caste of this village mentioned that they recognized the importance of the Harijan (Dalit) work as 'honouring the dead' and hence gave respect to them at this point (Moffatt 1979:196). This illustrates that the myth described above holds recognition across India and is used by cremation ground attendants to mark their superiority by reminding that Raja Harishchandra, a Kshatriya, was their slave.

In the broader context of their attitude towards the caste system, it seems that the Dom in Banaras are in consensus with the wider culture and hence replicate the same within their microcosm, from which they have been excluded by upper castes (Moffatt 1979:98). This becomes evident from the presence of hierarchical divisions among the three subcastes of the Dom in Banaras: Rahadari Dom, Banarasi Dom and Gotakhor Dom. These subcastes are engaged in different occupations. Banarasi/Maghiya Dom sweep, Rahadari Dom are basket weavers and Gotakhor Doms are the custodians of the sacred fire at cremation *ghats* (Kaushik 1979:1:32). Each subcaste maintains a distinctive identity by observing restrictions in marriage and commensality.

The Gotakhor Doms claim themselves to be superior to other subcastes, as they feel others are engaged in menial tasks to earn a livelihood, whereas they consider themselves to be fallen Brahmins 'forced to become *Chandal* through the folly of their ancestors' (Kaushik 1979:33). The Gotakhor Dom treat the Chamar, a subcaste, as inferior to themselves because they are involved in sweeping, cleaning work, and consume pork. The Dom pointed out, 'We *do not even drink water from their hands*.' This case makes it evident that they are in agreement with their caste ranking and, moreover, contest their superior position with respect to another inferior caste.

The reasons provided by them to consider the Chamar inferior do indicate that they agree that a breach of the rule of pollution results in an inferior status. They still legitimatized the position of those who engaged in menial work based on ritual pollution (Deliege 1993:166).

Division of *Pari*

Families of the Dom are located at the cremation *ghats* of Harishchandra Ghat. In 1979, the Gotakhor Dom population was 670 in Banaras (Kaushik 1979:1:36). The population of Dom in 2019 was found to be 357, with 178 males and 179 females at Harishchandra Ghat.

The Dom community of Harishchandra Ghat is divided into four clans. The ancestors of each clan were the original *patidars* (partners) of the cremation *ghats.* There are two distinct types of *pari* systems present at both Harishchandra Ghat and Manikarnika Ghat. For instance, during *pari,* a person has complete ownership of the Manikarnika Ghat. However, at Harishchandra Ghat, their ancestors divided this *pari* (ownership) of a single day into four subparts. The cremation *ghats*' entire earnings are distributed proportionately among its members based on their subparts of ownership. These earlier *patidars* were Kashi Chaudhary, Chedi Chaudhary, Shamu Chaudhary and Mohan Chaudhary. The subparts of the main *pari* are *pari, bheek, tahel* and *sona.* Out of all these distributions, *tahel* is the most profitable one, as it grants the right to receive the entire amount of money earned from burning the dead bodies. During the *pari* turn, the amount charged for the sacred fire from the mourners, along with shrouds, bamboo biers, and items of the corpses, are received. During the turn of *sona,* the person has the right to claim pieces of jewellery from the dead bodies, and during the *bheek* turn, about 10 per cent of the total earnings of that day are provided to the person. In earlier days, the monetary division was based on the *anna system,*[10] which has continued. For a single day, during earnings distribution, 16 *annas* are divided into three subparts: 6 *annas* are given for the *tahel* turn, 6 *annas* are for *pari* and the last 4 are for *bheek*.

There are two exceptions: the first is the corpse of a South Indian Brahmin. Here, the shroud, clothes and gold are divided equally among Dom members having their turns of *pari*, *tahel* and *sona*. The bamboo bier belongs to the person having *pari*. However, in the case of a Bengali Brahmin body, the entire amount goes to the Dom having the turn for *bheek*, except for the shrouds and bamboo biers, which belong to the person having *pari*. It seems this division was made because the majority of dead bodies come from the South India, followed by Bengal,[11] and these families pay more for last rites. This technique of dividing shares has been devised to ensure a livelihood for all Dom families residing at Harishchandra Ghat.

These rights of *pari* can only be transferred among the original Dom descendants. Due to this, richer families often seized the *pari* of poorer families on a mortgage basis, which the latter failed to repay. Kailash Chaudhary's forefathers, who earlier had only one-day's *bheek*, bought the *pari* of other shareholders (Kaushik 1979:1:37).

This facilitated his emergence as the Dom-Raja because of his family's stronger economic hold on the cremation *ghats*. Pieces of literature suggest that 'some of the largest mansions adjoining the Harishchandra Ghat on the riverfront were built in the late eighteenth century by the family of Lakshmi Narayan Dom, reputedly one of the richest families in India' (Bayly 1981:167). Lakshmi Narayan Dom was the father of the late Kailash Chaudhary. Figure 2.1 illustrates the family lineage of the late Kailash Chaudhary, who had two wives. Descendants from his first wife, Saranga Devi, became the next Dom-Raja. He had no direct children with his second wife, Jamuna Devi, who adopted her brother's children. Kailash Chaudhary had divided his *pari* between both wives. His first wife stayed at a large mansion at Manmandir Ghat, whereas his second wife resided at Harishchandra Ghat.

Late Jagdeesh Chaudhary, the Dom-Raja, was selected as one of the proposers of Narendra Modi's candidature in the Lok Sabha

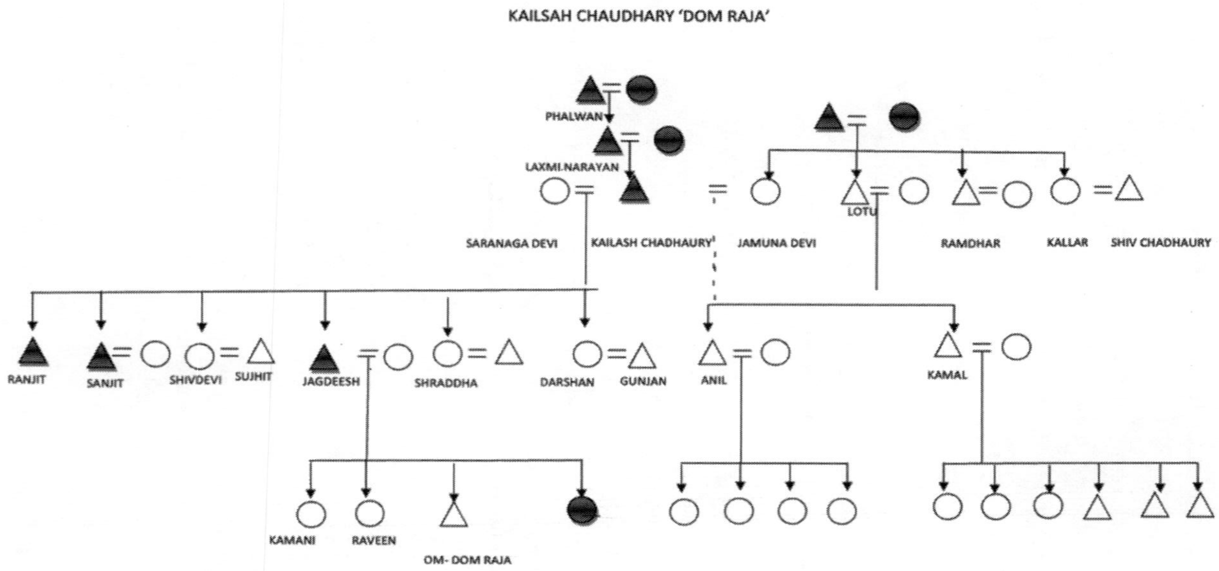

Figure 2.1 Genealogical chart of the Dom-Raja family.

election of 2019 from Banaras. He died during the Covid-19 wave in 2020 and was posthumously awarded the Padma Shri in 2021. His fourteen-year-old son, the current Dom-Raja, received the award on his behalf.

Earlier during my field visit, I met him, a chubby and short boy. He could not read or write as he had dropped out of school at a young age due to family rivalries. In the past, there have been many cases of kidnapping and murdering potential Dom-Rajas, so his family mostly keeps him in the house to protect him.

Even the title of Dom-Raja does not remain uncontested here. This title is not provided based on majority choice among the Dom; instead, it is claimed based on one's economic capital and social capital.

Another important figure is Ishwar Chaudhary, a relative of Kailash Chaudhary. Both of them are *patidars* and are referred to as Dom-Raja due to being economically prosperous and having the maximum number of *pari*.

Kaushik also mentioned that all had accepted their status as 'Chaudhary' of the Dom community, which is evident during the propitiation of 'Saiyer-Mata[12] (Kaushik 1979:1:37). Kailash Chaudhary's and Ishwar Chaudhary's families now propitiate the goddess at their respective homes. Due to their strained relations, the Dom community is divided into two factions. People supporting Kailash Chaudhary do not go to Ishwar Chaudhary's house and vice versa.

Both the affluent families had seized the *pari* of other Doms. There are many such cases among the Dom community. Sonu, a *naukar* at Harishchandra Ghat, reveals that his father, Ram Chaudhary, was an alcoholic. In 2015, after Ram's family refused to give him money for drinking, he borrowed money from a friend. Sonu recalls that 'the person maintained a record of the money he lent to my father. He took half of our pari, worth 45,000 rupees, after we failed to return the cash. Later, we had to mortgage our remaining pari, as my father was admitted to the intensive care unit due to excessive drinking.'

There are three ways through which *pari* ownership could change (i) when *pari* is mortgaged for a specific period called *Ikrari*, (ii) when there is no specific time bound for the mortgaged *pari* called *Rehanama*, (iii) The outright sale of one's *pari* is called *Benama*. As *pari* are subjected to sale, gifting and mortgage, it is difficult to get an exact idea about the original partner and their descendant (Kaushik 1979:1:46).

These *pari* are kept on a lease within the Dom. Raman disclosed that his elder brother Mayur fell severely ill last year, and they were out of money needed for the treatment. So, his mother kept their *tahel* on a mortgage for 40,000 rupees to Piyush's family. Currently, Piyush's family is earning via Raman's *pari* until they repay the debt.

Due to the difficult nature of their work, Dom males rely on the excessive consumption of intoxicants. Family urgencies, such as marriages, illnesses, and their tendency for 'conspicuous consumption'[13] forced them to borrow money. Most descendants of the original *patidars*, after losing their *pari*, had either migrated to the rural areas of Banaras or worked as *naukar*[14] under the Dom-Raja. This was the case for Cheetilal Chaudhary (one of the original *patidars*), who stayed at Meer Ghat. Due to his alcoholism and womanizing, he lost all of his *pari* to the Dom-Raja. Consequently, his son, Chootelal Chaudhary, migrated out of the city, purchased some land in Narayanpur village, and now resides there. Cheetilal Chaudhary's great-grandson currently works as a *naukar* during the *pari* of Kailash Chaudhary at Manikarnika Ghat.

Out of the four original *patidars*, only Kashi Chaudhary's descendants are primarily present at Harishchandra Ghat, along with two grandsons of Shamu Chaudhary. The remaining families have migrated to rural areas.

Dom Families

The residential area of the Dom is located near the cremation *ghats* in Banaras. People working at Harishchandra Ghat stay there, while those working at Manikarnika Ghat stay at Meer Ghat. Both these *ghats* provide better earning opportunities, so Dom men,[15] primarily from rural areas who do not have ownership of cremation *ghats*, often work here. Besides this, the location of these *ghats* in urban spaces also provides options for secondary occupations, such as working as sales assistants at various stores, driving auto rickshaws and taking up other odd jobs as well.

The Dom are an endogamous group with a smaller population; this results in their community being limited to nearby places and forming closer kinship ties. Mostly, grandsons from rural areas migrate and stay at their maternal grandparents' house for years. Men whose in-laws have *pari* prefer to stay with them for a source of income.

Migration is an essential requirement for earning a livelihood. Generally, people migrate from rural areas to Banaras city to work at the cremation *ghats* or in search of better earning opportunities. However, among the Dom, it is a two-way process. Some of the economically better-off families from Harishchandra Ghat and Meer Ghat purchase land in rural areas due to congestion in living spaces in the city. As these areas are close to the Banaras *ghats*, it is convenient for them to travel back and forth for work.

At Harishchandra Ghat, we can find three distinctions among Dom families: (i) Family Type I – Original descendants of Kashi Chaudhary, (ii) Family Type II – Dom-Raja family,[16] (iii) and Family Type III – The Dom residing in the *bageecha* (garden) area. These are migrated Dom from other regions and are not descendants of the original *patidar*. They had constructed their houses on the *bageecha* land owned by Kailash Chaudhary's second wife. Figure 2.2 provides a diagrammatic representation of the residential area of the Dom at Harishchandra Ghat. There are around thirty Dom houses, with around seventy-two households.

Entryways into the Dom neighbourhood are indicated with an arrow pointing towards the Harishchandra cremation site. Most lower-caste residential sections are often situated closer to cremation sites and at the outer edges of villages. Here too, the Dom locality is located nearer the cremation ground, after which the territories of other caste groups begin. It is conceivable that the Dom acts as a mediator between the malevolent ghosts from the cremation grounds and other upper castes, as the role of the lower caste is not limited to removing the impurity of the upper caste but also includes acting as an intermediary between the higher beings and malevolent ghosts (Moffatt 1979; Quigley 1993).

As the descendants of Kashi Chaudhary primarily occupy Harishchandra Ghat, a genealogy chart of the Kashi Chaudhary family is provided in Figure 2.3. The chart highlights his six sons: Kunnur,[17] Shiv, Sitaram, Bamboo, Krishna and Shambu. On tracing the genealogical chart it was found that the families of these sons are currently staying at Harishchandra Ghat. Though these are larger families – in terms of their same ancestor but these families are staying in separate households. For instance, number 8, Mansur Chaudhary, had five sons: Sukdev, Vickey, Pramod, Sahil and Sushil.

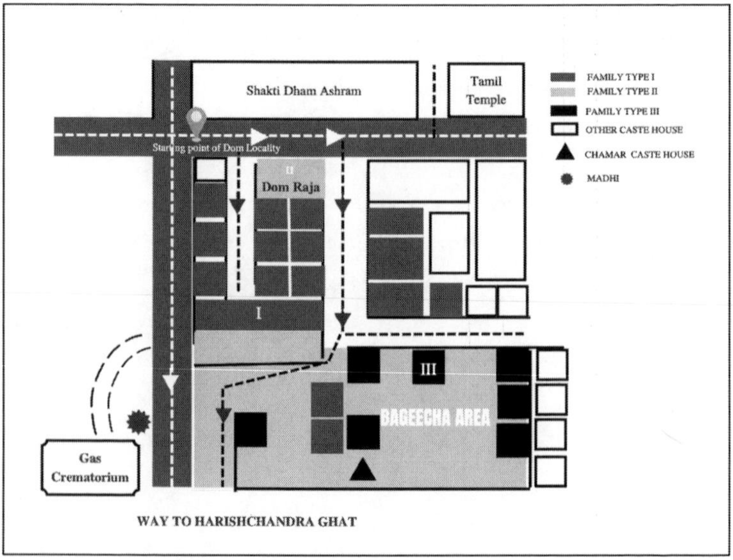

Figure 2.2 Residential area of the Dom at Harishchandra Ghat.

Genealogical Chart of Kashi Chaudhary Family

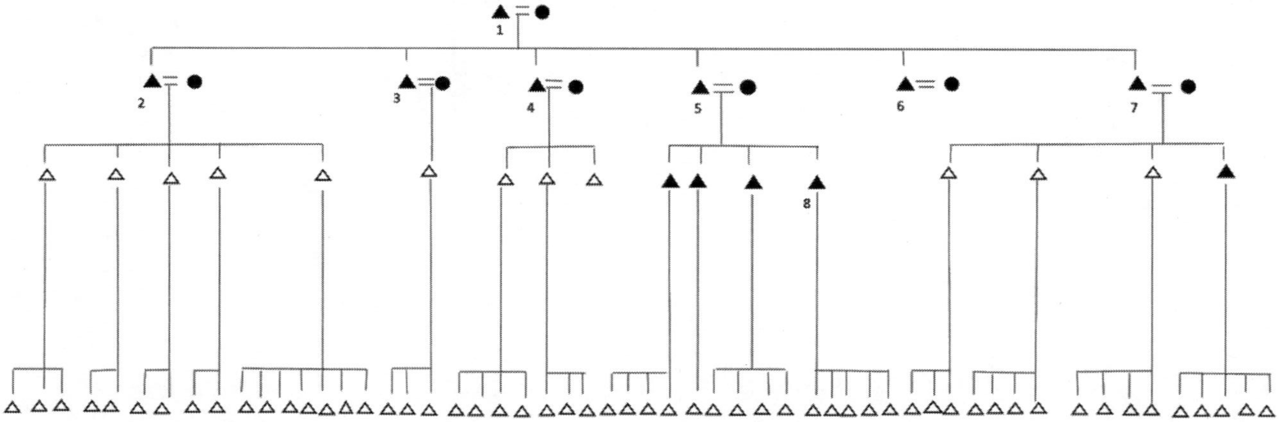

1 Kashi Chaudhary
2 Sitaram Chaudhary
3 Shiv Chaudhary
4 Bamboo Chaudhary
5 Shambhu Chaudhary
6 Kunur Chaudhary
7 Krishna Chaudhary
8 Mansur Chaudhary

Figure 2.3 Genealogical chart of Kashi Chaudhary family.

As Mansur is dead, his married sons stay in the same house with their widowed mother. However, they have separate households, which are differentiated based on separate kitchens and different sources of income. Only during their family *pari,* these brothers work together, and at the end of their shift, their mother divides the earnings equally among them.

Hence, the reason for still residing in the same house[18] but in different households can be explained by the fact that the house and *pari* are shared properties among all the brothers. The house has been divided based on one room being allotted to each of them.

Many years ago, the eldest son, Sukdev Chaudhary, leased his family's *pari* to Kailash Chaudhary. Now, the youngest son, Sushil Chaudhary, wants to reclaim this *pari* after managing to save some money, but there is a possibility of a family dispute, as once the repayment for the *pari* is made, all the brothers will demand an equal share. So, he is waiting for the time being. Thus, here, the *pari* and ancestral houses are shared properties acting as key links in keeping the family together. This particular family can be categorized as one having a better economic condition than many other families. On account of the fact that it has more family members, for better adjustment, three floors were constructed on a smaller area of land. On each floor, two rooms and a shared bathroom were built. The youngest son and the widowed mother stay on the ground floor in separate rooms. Similarly to this, different households occupy separate rooms.

When I first visited this house, I discovered that my respondent's mother was preparing lunch while seated on the floor. Generally, the Dom never make tea at home or prepare breakfast; they rather purchase it from the market. Furthermore, poor families often prepare their meals using charred wood logs taken from the cremation ground. Even in the Dom-Raja's household, food is still cooked on these woods. These days, however, some families are shifting to the use of gas stoves.

Returning to the above household, only seven utensils were set aside beside the gas stove, which was placed next to the front door. A water tap had been installed inside this room to wash their dishes. The rest of the utensils and other items were kept in the space underneath the bed. One single bed was present, and many beddings were piled on top of it. Indeed, they store these beddings and blankets in this manner due to limited space; at night, these beddings were used to sleep on the floor.[19] In this family, only the father and youngest daughter sleep in the bed and the rest of the four members on the floor. In other households, if the number of members is more and space is not enough, then ladies make arrangements to sleep on the floor beneath the bed, and male members go to the cremation *ghat* and sleep in boats, kiosks or *madhi*.

Figure 2.2 demonstrates two other families in addition to the Kashi Chaudhary lineage. The most significant is the family of the late Kailash Chaudhary's second widow, Jamuna Devi. She resides at and owns a sizeable amount of land at Harishchandra Ghat. Both Manikarnika and Harishchandra Ghats are frequent places for the maximum *pari* of Kailash Chaudhary. Since he had two wives, the earnings from the *pari* are divided among them in such a way that one dead body would be burned by the *naukar* of his first wife and the next by his second wife's *naukar*. Hence, the income from the *ghat* is distributed equally.

From family type II, Ram Chaudhary and his brothers migrated from Narayanpur village and settled at Harishchandra Ghat. Families that migrated from rural areas do not have any *pari* at Harishchandra Ghat. Suraj Chaudhary and Neel Chaudhary, sons of Ram and Shyam, married the daughters of Kailash Chaudhary. They now manage *pari-ghat*[20] of the late Kailash Chaudhary, where they compile financial records. Suranganga Devi, Kailash Chaudhary's first wife, divided the management of her *pari* among her sons-in-law so that each receives a livelihood for six months of the year.

Suraj Chaudhary manages this *pari* from the month of July to December. He and his two sons cremate all the bodies during this period. At the end of every *pari* cycle, he gives his mother-in-law the earned money, collectively received from the charges for the sacred fire, *sona*, *bheek* and *tahel*, after deducting the value of his labour. Similarly, Neel manages the *pari* from January to June.

These two do not work as *naukars* under the descendants of Kashi Chaudhary but instead cremate bodies during the *pari* of their mother-in-law. They also have their *pari-ghat* at Narayanpur, through which they earn money. According to my Dom informant, *in six months, after these brothers earn lakhs, they repay their debt for rations, which they had purchased during that period. For the next six months, they do nothing but lounge around and smoke*. This is one of the key illustrations of the dependence of males on their in-laws for livelihood.

During colonial times, Udit Chaudhary, from family type III, migrated here from the Madigini area. He recalled that his father left their previous residence during the Hindu-Muslim riots and moved to Harishchandra Ghat. They stayed in a single room at his grandaunt's place. Even though they do not own any land, they have constructed an opulent home on their grandaunt's property at Harishchandra Ghat.

Since this family does not have any *pari* here, all male members are engaged in other works. Udit Ji secured a permanent job at the gas crematorium, while Siya, his brother, is a tour guide. Shirju, their other brother, has passed away. The family of Shirju resides in a mud hut, as they were unable to reclaim their land from the lease. Shirju's eldest child, Raj, married Suraj Chaudhary's daughter. Raj has moved out of his home with his spouse and child and now lives with his in-laws. He assists Yadav at the woodshop and measures the wood. These migrant families reside in the *bageecha* region owned by Kailash Chaudhary's wife.

The detailed information on the families in the aforementioned section reveals crucial insights. The Dom can be classified into three main categories depending on their work at the cremation *ghat*. During his *pari*, *malik* (Dom-Raja) is the proprietor of the cremation *ghat*. In his absence, the manager oversees the accounts of dead bodies that arrive, alongside dealing with customers, and he is typically one of *malik*'s close relatives.

Most often, the *malik* ensures that someone else manages his *pari* and, in return, provides him with 10 per cent of the entire earnings. The last category is the *naukar*, who burns dead bodies, cleans cremation grounds, and sieves ashes in search of jewellery under *malik*'s authority (Kumari 2018:97).

Figure 2.4 is the visual representation of the class hierarchy within the Dom. Here, *naukars* stand for five to six hours in water to sieve ashes in search of pieces of jewellery during the shift of *sona* (gold) for their *malik,* who attentively observe the work while sitting in the boat.

The two Dom families, *bageecha* Doms and Kashi descendants, vary in a few ways. The former has no right to *pari* at Harishchandra Ghat, are employed in different sectors and are educated. The lack of *pari* seems to be a reason for their focus on education and different employment. The *pari ghat* inadvertently tempts youngsters to work for money and frequently causes them to drop out of school. Younger boys have often been compelled to leave school in hopes of contributing to their family's livelihood during financial difficulties. They are often tempted by the promise of an easy way to make money in a shorter duration, as Pawan, a twelve-year-old boy, did when he approached the cremation ground and received 20 rupees from a mourner as part of the ritual of breaking pots at the end of cremation.

Figure 2.4 *Naukars* sieving ashes in the river under *malik*'s observation.

Pawan came to me and exclaimed, 'See, Sarita didi, I made 20 rupees in just five minutes.' He was delighted and repeatedly asked me, 'It is good, no? Is it not good?', as I remained speechless.

Cremation *Ghats* in Banaras

The cremation *ghats* serve as a focal point for migration among the Dom. This section will elaborate further on this. The population of Dom was discovered to be dispersed in proximity to cremation *ghats* in rural areas. Table 2.3 lists these places, followed by a detailed description of these areas. After completing the genealogical chart, I visited adjacent places during my fieldwork in 2019 and 2020.

An important point to consider here is that these areas are closer to the river's bank. For instance, the Gomti River is more proximate to Sultanpur and Jaunpur districts. At the same time, other areas such as Chunar, Narayanpur and Vindhyachal are part of the Mirzapur district and are situated along the Ganges River. Both these rivers converge in Saidpur, located in the Ghazipur district. The presence of the Dom in these areas could be due to the deeply held beliefs in Hinduism regarding performing cremation rites near the riverbank and immersing ashes into the flowing water. As 'annihilation of the world through fire and flood is a precondition', argued Parry (1994), which is 'similar to the condition of cremating the deceased with fire and then his ashes are immersed in water, so that he may restored to life' (Parry 1994:31). This justifies the importance of performing last rites at the cremation *ghats* located alongside the river and explains the reason for the dispersed Dom population in the above-mentioned areas located near the riverbanks.

Further, there is an interesting practice of capturing isolated *ghats* called '*ghat chekhna*'. For this, the Dom requires permission from the head of the panchayat in that specific region. By obtaining this permission, he can have complete ownership of that cremation *ghat*. Though in the beginning a single family would have full ownership

Table 2.3 Locations of the Gotakhor Dom across Uttar Pradesh.[21]

No.	District	Cremation *Ghat*
1	Banaras	Domri Ghat
2	Banaras	Harishchandra Ghat
3	Banaras	Koniya
4	Banaras	Manikarnika Ghat
5	Banaras	Rameshwar
6	Banaras	Varuna Ghat/ Barna Ghat
7	Chandauli	Chandauli
8	Ghazipur	Saidpur/Jhorganj
9	Jaunpur	Kirkat
10	Mau	Dhori*ghat*
11	Mirzapur	Chunar
12	Mirzapur	Narayanpur
13	Mirzapur	Vindhyachal
14	Sultanpur	Sultanpur

of the *ghat,* at a later stage, that ownership is divided into *pari* among brothers, similar to the Banaras *ghats*. That's why the Dom are scattered across the above-mentioned areas with a limited population.

The working conditions influenced by caste factors represent a significant distinction between the cremation *ghats* of urban and rural areas, and they affect the lives of the Dom residing there. The vast differences in the working domains of these *ghats* result in varying conditions for the Dom of Harishchandra Ghat, Manikarnika Ghat and rural areas. The following section elaborates on this further after providing a brief sketch of the cremation *ghats* in two villages.

Narayanpur Village

Ram Chaudhary's family migrated from here and settled at Harishchandra Ghat. His son earns a livelihood by managing the *pari* of his in-laws, the Dom-Raja. Chaudhary's family has its hereditary *pari* at Narayanpur village, so during the time of their *pari*, they return to the village and stay in a temporary room constructed at the cremation *ghat*.

On 18 November 2019, I left for Narayanpur village at 10:30 a.m. with my key informant. We took a shared auto, and after a journey of one hour, we managed to reach the village's main road. After that, we walked further for twenty minutes to reach the cremation *ghat*, known as Rapunia *Ghat*, located at the end of the village. On our way to the *ghat*, we crossed vast, lush green paddy fields present on both sides of the road. We came across many houses and got different glimpses of village life, where some children were playing under a tree, a woman was fetching water from a handpump, and there was a small private medical store from which villagers were receiving treatment for their ailments. Lastly, we reached the house of a member of the potter's caste, where mud pots were kept in the bright sunlight. Suddenly, my gaze fell on big piles of wood logs arranged at a distance, and I realized we had reached the cremation *ghat*. The *ghat* was in contrast to the infamous cremation *ghats* of Banaras, as it was located in the outer region of the village near the bank of the Ganges. The *ghat* was crowded with men, and then, within a fraction of a few seconds, I transformed from an observer to observed for the locals. I became conscious as all collective gazes

Figure 2.5 Mourners cremating bodies at Narayanpur.

fell on me, and they were shocked to see a woman at the cremation *ghat.* Walking through the uncomfortable gazes, we reached the bank of the Ganges and saw a small room where the sacred fire was kept in one of the corners. Under a huge banyan tree, two funeral kiosks were situated, and people were standing there. Suraj (Dom) was sleeping on a cot under the shade of the tree just outside that room. My key informant woke him up, and Suraj rushed inside the room and woke his father and uncle. They all greeted me and arranged a cot for me to sit outside the room, as it was full of smoke due to the fire.

Here, in the name of *madhi*, a small, carelessly plastered room with no window was available. An opening was left during the construction for the door, which was never installed. As these people (Dom) had come to look at their *pari* here for six days, they brought their utensils in which food is cooked on the sacred fire itself.

The absence of a toilet facility leads to open defecation, and drinking water is fetched from a nearby hand pump. Here, electricity is available for only one hour a day. As the whole family has shares in this *pari,* all three brothers, with their sons, came to work here.

In rural areas, the role of a Dom is limited to providing the sacred fire and arranging three logs of wood for the pyre. After completing his duty, he takes his fees and sits in the *madhi.* Here, the charge for the fire is 200–250 rupees only. Suraj Dom complains that '*no income is here, and we cannot even take a single wood log from the pyre*'.

While Dom's men were seated in *madhi*, mourners were attempting to bury the dead and using shrouds to block the breeze, which was preventing the bodies from burning (see figure 2.5). The Mallah caste of Narayanpur manages the wood business required for cremation. At some distance, a few people in a boat arranged wood logs that needed to be transported to Manikarnika Ghat.

Jhorganj Village

On 24 November 2019, I visited Jhorganj with Ramu (Dom). I met him around 9 a.m. at Godowlia Chowk, and from there, we left for

Chowka Ghat and took a bus to Ghazipur. Our bus started at 9:30 a.m., and after one and a half hours of travelling, we reached Udiyar Market. The bus was crowded, but after some struggle, we managed to get out, and I found myself on a highway road, where only a small restaurant was situated on one side of the road. On the other side, a big banner was hanging with '*Shamshan Ghat*' (cremation ground) written on it. Here, the cremation *ghat* is known as the Saidpur Ghat.

As we moved towards it, I found that it was entirely different from Narayanpur. It was quite spacious and occupied a vast area solely for parking. We moved further and saw that the *madhi* was well-constructed. A round funnel was built above the sacred fire so that plumes of smoke could escape through it. Many wooden cots were placed in the open space under one roof, where mourners could rest while waiting for cremation. As we continued towards the cremation ground, I came across a shop selling wood for funerals, managed by Chaudhary (Dom), which is rare compared to other cremation *ghats*. Then I saw a huge crowd gathering at a small kiosk that was providing death certificates. At this *ghat* too, iron grill structures are constructed, similar to Harishchandra Ghat, to cremate dead bodies. Yet, bodies were cremated using wood near the bank of the Ganges. I was informed that these structures were used only during floods, as the smoke troubled people sitting near the *madhi*. Additionally, for Doms, it is easier to burn bodies near the bank of the river as they can sieve ashes for jewellery. Moreover, mourners are more particular about cremating the body near the bank of the Ganges.

I went to the bank of the Ganges and found the dead body of a pregnant woman placed in a boat for immersion. After purchasing fire from the Dom, the chief mourner performed *mukhagni* by placing it in the mouth of the dead body. Only one boat was available at the *ghat,* and three persons were sitting on it with the dead body (see figure 2.6). One of them was the mourner, performing rituals under the guidance of the others. I considered the others to be Mallahs, as they generally perform immersions elsewhere. Later, I noticed that the boatmen were arguing with the mourners. The former

Figure 2.6 Immersion of body in Jhorganj.

were asking to remove the gold nose pin from the body and hand it over to the Dom, as it was their right to receive items from a dead person. However, the mourner was reluctant and refused to provide the jewellery, suggesting that the Mallahs could take it out after the completion of the immersion.

Only later I realized those boatmen were Dom, and everything on this *ghat* is under their control. Here, they handle the wood business, own funeral kiosks, provide sacred fire, and perform rituals of body immersion with *pinda-dan* too.

I noticed Dom children as young as six years old on the cremation ground, collecting leftover shrouds from the dead bodies. By selling those, they earn one rupee per shroud but have to work hard, as mourners often burn the shrouds with the body. The mourners can be seen shouting at and abusing these children as they attempt to snatch shrouds and run away.

Dom's control over this *ghat* is evident, but their earnings are lower than those in Banaras city. For instance, at Jhorganj, the cost of wood for one *Maund*[22] is 300 rupees, whereas in Banaras, it costs 440 rupees. Furthermore, the amount charged for the sacred fire at the former place is 200 rupees, whereas at Harishchandra Ghat, it begins at 1,300 rupees and largely depends on the mourners' economic conditions. Lastly, at the city cremation ground, Dom cremate dead bodies, unlike in rural areas. Thus, the total costs of cremation in the latter case fall in the range of 3,500 rupees to 5,000 rupees. These variances in income between rural and urban areas elucidate the reasons for migration.

Though at both places sacred fire is taken after paying a fee to the Dom, the status of Dom differs depending on the area. Even though they belong to the same caste, there is a disparity in their conditions. People working at the cremation *ghats* of the city make use of myths glorifying Kashi as the 'city of death', which facilitates their business. Both Harishchandra Ghat and Manikarnika Ghat of Banaras are famous because of their mythological linkage with the notion of salvation. Additionally, at Harishchandra Ghat, Dom have created a monopoly due to their importance in the mythical story and their numerical preponderance. As a result, they have established many rules for their convenience. For instance, Dom at Harishchandra Ghat collect five logs of wood from the pyre, whereas at Manikarnika Ghat they can take only one log. However, in rural areas, they are helpless because villagers of Narayanpur do not allow them to remove even a single log of wood due to their smaller numbers and inferior caste status.

Working Sphere of Cremation *Ghat*

In Banaras, both Harishchandra Ghat and Manikarnika Ghat constitute a social sphere facilitating interactions across different castes and classes. Most people are engaged in their caste-based occupations and earn a livelihood through them, such as Mallah ferrying dead bodies for *pravaha*,[23] barber tonsuring heads of mourners, Dom burning dead bodies, Mahapatra carrying out rites and rituals for the deceased and Yadav caste holding the business of selling wood required for funeral pyres. Besides these, mourners performing the last rites of their relatives also participate in this interaction.

Among the Gotakhor Dom, three different classes earn their livelihoods by being involved in various domains at the cremation *ghat.* As mentioned earlier, *the malik* is the owner of the cremation *ghat* during his *pari.* In his absence, the manager oversees the accounts of the dead bodies cremated and deals with customers. He is typically one of the *malik*'s close relatives. *The naukar* arranges and cremates bodies under his *malik*'s ownership. He stays at the cremation *ghat* for a fixed number of days until his *malik*'s *pari* lasts. People from Harishchandra Ghat also work at Manikarnika Ghat. Kailash Chaudhary and Ishwar Chaudhary, the richest of all the Dom, have around thirty-five to forty Dom *naukar* under them.

The following section provides a glimpse into Dom's life and the variety of ways he depends on the cremation grounds for survival. Satish, twenty-five years old, a casual *naukar*, recalls his childhood with memories of his father as an alcoholic who abused his mother, which ultimately led to her suicide. Satish began picking up shrouds in 2009 because his father would not give him money. His father remarried and had three children, after which his second wife passed away. Meanwhile, Satish's grandmother took care of him until her death in 2011. After marrying for the third time, his father passed away in 2015. Now, Satish takes care of his three younger step-siblings and widowed stepmother. His stepmother works as a domestic helper to earn a living.

Satish does not have any family *pari*, so he works as a *naukar*. First, he began working under one *malik* but left because he was given extra workload. He then went to another *malik* and left that job too. Recalling his experience, he said, 'Generally, 650 rupees is fixed for burning one body, and the mourner pays this amount, but the malik gives us just 300 rupees. We work hard all day, trouble our bodies, and get merely 300 rupees.' He added, 'I had worked enough under another person; now I will daily dig a well and drink water.' This meant that he would go and sieve ashes in the Ganges in search of jewellery (See Figure 2.7). However, this seemed unlikely because the person responsible for the shift of *sona*, that is, sieving ashes, had already collected the pieces of jewellery. To this, Dom often mentions that while eating food, some grains do fall on the floor; similarly, while gold is sieved by one party, some pieces might have fallen into the Ganges. So, he, along with Arun and Suraj, planned to search for it and divide the amount among themselves.

Last time, they found a piece of jewellery worth 2,000 rupees. This work requires more people, as one has to remove dumped ashes from the Ganges, place them on the ground, and then sieve them again. Besides this, Satish started catching customers too. He shared his routine.

> Yesterday, from 7 p.m., I started looking for mourners (at Harishchandra Chowk, where people compete for the verbal claim over dead bodies) and continued till 3 a.m. At that time, all other people were asleep, and the shops were closed. Then I slept from 7 a.m. till 12 p.m. Now I will sieve the ashes and put them on the ground; tomorrow, we will sieve them again, as it will take around one hour.

His life illustrates a variety of means through which the Dom can earn a livelihood from the cremation grounds.

Figure 2.7 Dom searching for jewellery pieces.

Besides working as a *naukar,* another way to earn a livelihood is by keeping funeral kiosks—small wooden shops in which materials essential for cremation, such as shrouds, *ghee*, a few sandalwood pieces, and *havan samgiri*[24] are stored for sale. Generally, it costs around 15,000 rupees to construct a funeral kiosk. In addition, an extra amount is required to store funerary items. These kiosks are placed on the stairs of Harishchandra Ghat. However, even in this, internal dynamics within the Dom community determine the position of each funeral shop.

There are around thirty-one funeral kiosks of the Dom community at Harishchandra Ghat; twenty-eight of these shops belong to the descendants of the Kashi Chaudhary family. Some of the grandsons of Kashi Chaudhary are influential due to their better economic status. Out of all these kiosks, only a few remain mostly open, while the rest stay closed. In the latter case, the Dom take out funerary items from their kiosks after finalizing a deal with mourners. If another person tries to sell funerary items to an already fixed customer, it often results in a fight.

Another way to earn a livelihood is by searching for jewellery in the leftover ashes of dead bodies in the Ganges, as already discussed. Finally, a type of work in which all males from the Dom community are engaged is known as *grahak pakadna* (catching customers through verbal claim). Here, almost all male members of the Dom community stand at the crossroads from where Harishchandra Ghat begins. The moment anyone sees a dead body, they shout *matti* (body) loudly. Whoever shouts first gets the right to deal with the customer instantly, and the other Dom men will not interfere with his customer (mourners). After the dead body reaches the cremation *ghat,* that person goes to the customer and engages in making a deal. The customer is informed about various types of *theka* (services). There are two kinds: the first is cheaper and mainly opted for by poor families. In this case, the customers are provided with partly burnt wood from another pyre, which is rearranged to make a funeral pyre for the dead body. In the second type, fresh wood is provided. There are various kinds of services starting from 2,200 rupees. The range of packages includes 3,000 rupees, 5,000 rupees, 6,100 rupees, 7,000 rupees and 10,000 rupees, with prices continuing to increase. In the contract of 2,200 rupees, the customer gets *agni* (sacred fire), *karna* (reed straw) to receive fire and a *mazdoor*[25] (labourer).

Normally, mixed wood that is already half-burnt is used in a contract costing between 3,000 rupees and 4,500 rupees. The perks in a contract costing 5,000 rupees include a sacred fire, new planks of wood, and one *naukar* for preparing the funeral pyre and cremating the body. In higher-value contracts, the Dom men decorate the *Vishnu Charan Paduka* with flowers and create rangoli designs. The *Vishnu Paduka* is a round, circular structure made of concrete, on top of which small marble footprints are crafted; these footprints are claimed to be that of Lord Vishnu. However, the original Vishnu *Charan Paduka* is believed to be located at Manikarnika Ghat, where, according to mythology, Lord Vishnu observed austerity for years. At the cremation *ghat*, there are different spaces available for burning bodies, such as areas closer to the riverbank, slightly elevated spaces where iron grill structures are fixed and the place known as *Vishnu Charan Paduka*.

Lastly, major work in which Dom males are engaged, besides cremating dead bodies, includes working in the gas crematorium, serving as labourers measuring wood for the Yadavs, acting as tour guides or owning funeral kiosks.

Interactions at Cremation Grounds

This section provides descriptions of the different working conditions at the infamous cremation grounds of Banaras. At Manikarnika Ghat, around 200 to 250 bodies are cremated in one day. Although the Gotakhor Doms are connected through kinship ties and everyone does become *malik* of the cremation *ghat* during their *pari*, Dom workers are referred to as *naukar*. Due to their lesser frequency of *pari*, they work for others. They are referred to using derogatory language instead of their actual names, and the use of physical force against them is not uncommon. At Manikarnika Ghat, mourners pay 300 rupees as labour charge to cremate the dead body, yet *naukars* receive only 250 rupees per body. Furthermore, this amount includes charges for additional work such as sieving the ashes in search of jewellery and sweeping the cremation ground. The remaining amount, 50 rupees per body, is handed over to the Yadav from whom the wood is purchased.

In case of the occurrence of any accidents at the workspace, such as burn injuries, the *naukar* has to pay from their own pocket. Here, the government has fixed the rate for the sacred fire, which is 500 rupees. Of this amount, 450 rupees are kept by the *malik*, and 50 rupees per body are given to the Dom manager for managing the *pari*.

In contrast, at Harishchandra Ghat, around 30 bodies are cremated daily. There is no fixed price for the sacred fire; *the malik* demands anything starting from 1,300 rupees. Like at Manikarnika Ghat, mourners pay 650 rupees as a labour charge, but the *naukars* receive only 350 rupees per body. Secondly, there is a rotation of shifts among the *naukars,* based on which they are assigned duties to burn bodies. In these rotations, the *malik* includes himself too, but instead of him, the *naukars* cremate the body. For this, the *malik* keeps 400 rupees, as it was his shift, and provides 250 rupees to the *naukar* as a labour charge.

The distinction between *malik* and *naukar* is more evident at Manikarnika Ghat than at Harishchandra Ghat. The possible reasons are that the original *patidar* maintained a monopoly at Harishchandra Ghat and made certain rules, such as the division of *pari* into its subparts. Furthermore, there is a sense of unity and community feeling, as a majority of families residing here are descendants of Kashi Chaudhary. This is revealed by the use of the terms '*ghar ki pari*' (ownership of the family) and '*ghar ki baithaki*' (sitting period of the family). As mentioned above, at Harishchandra Ghat, the *pari* of outsiders, besides those of Kailash and Ishwar Chaudhary, are not present.

At Manikarnika Ghat, most of the earlier *patidars* had migrated to rural areas after losing their *pari*. Secondly, the Gotakhor Dom from various places do have their *pari* here, but its frequency is quite low; for instance, a *pari* for a single day comes only once every three years. Thirdly, *naukars* from different rural areas come to work during their *malik*'s *pari*, where they are already subjected to caste discrimination. At the workplace, they attempt to avoid getting involved in any conflict. As a result, a sense of unity is absent among them. Lastly, Dom families from Meer Ghat, after losing their *pari*, are engaged in different occupations as well, besides working as labourers. *Naukars* often look out for better opportunities and frequently shift to work for another *malik*. Thus, a sense of solidarity is lacking among these Doms at Manikarnika Ghat.

Moreover, the presence and regular interactions with different upper-caste groups at the cremation ground complicate the situation. Brahmins, Thakurs and Yadavs earn a livelihood from the death industry by engaging in the business of selling wood and funerary materials. This section belongs to the dominant caste at Manikarnika Ghat. Further caste hierarchy and the polluting nature of the Dom's work of dealing with corpses result in their subjugation. The better social and economic capital of the upper castes enables their hold on the death economy (Kumari 2018:106). Whereas Dom's work remains limited to providing sacred fire for a fixed amount and handling the corpse.

In contrast, at Harishchandra Ghat, the Doms are trying to assert their authority at the cremation ground but have not succeeded completely. For instance, in past years, Yadav had encroached on the profitable business of selling funeral wood, which was earlier owned by Kashi Chaudhary. However, the Doms here have been able to maintain a monopoly on having funeral kiosks, unlike at Manikarnika Ghat.

The following instance that occurred in 2021 provides crucial insights into the caste dynamics of Harishchandra Ghat. A middle-aged Dom made a deal with customers at around 10:30 p.m. To complete the cremation procedure, there was a requirement for wood. When he asked workers (Bengali) employed under Yadav to provide the wood, they declined to give it after 10 p.m. The Dom man verbally abused the worker, helped himself and took the logs. The next day, when Yadav came to know about this incident, he thrashed the Dom man. Learning about this violence, the other Dom of Harishchandra Ghat quickly gathered, armed with sticks. This conflict soon reached the police station, where it was settled verbally. This incident highlights the fact that at this *ghat,* too, there has been a tendency to make Dom submissive, but their unity and numerical preponderance have created a space of resistance against upper-caste dominance.

Another incident occurred in 2020; a procession of *Shiv baraat*[26] was carried out through the main road of Sonarpura before the *Shivratri*[27] festival. Performers dressed up as gods and goddesses were dancing, accompanied by musicians. There was a huge crowd enjoying the parade. I also went with female members of the Dom community. The atmosphere abruptly shifted from celebration to one of tension as the males of the Dom community started running in one direction.

News spread that a brawl had broken out between the two groups. My key informant's mother took me to her house as it was past 9 p.m., assuring me that some male members would safely escort me to my room. Without knowing what had truly transpired, we were all terrified and frantically headed to their homes. As soon as we arrived at the Harishchandra Ghat crossroads, I was shocked to discover that all the shops were closed, and not a single male was in sight. After reaching their homes, the females began dialling their male family members. We later learned that male members of the Dom and *Khatik*[28] castes had engaged in combat, and two men from the Dom caste were mercilessly attacked due to their involvement in talking with a Khatik woman.

The police arrested a few suspects. Since Dom's voices were being ignored, they decided to temporarily halt the functioning of the cremation *ghat*. My female respondent informed me that 'whenever the police do not listen to us, we halt cremation. Because of this, mourners face trouble and eventually reach out to the police for help, and then, unwillingly, they have to listen to our side too.'

This incident highlights one of the strategies adopted by the Dom to make themselves heard and the pivotal role of mourners in everyday interactions at the *ghat*. There have been ample incidents when mourners engaged in verbal combat with the Dom over the higher costs demanded for cremation. In a few cases, they seek support from the police, and in other cases, they leave Harishchandra Ghat with the bier on their shoulders and move to Manikarnika Ghat.

While sitting on the stairs of the *ghat*, I overheard a conversation between Dom *naukars* and a man from the Mallah caste. One of the Dom *naukars* shared an incident about a verbal argument between mourners and a Dom, saying that 'one should not demand too much out of greed.' Another Dom pointed out that 'if the cost of the fire is 1,350 rupees and the cost of wood is 4,000 rupees, then accordingly, the bill should be in the range of 6,000 rupees. However, instead, a bill of 15,000 rupees is handed over, which would obviously leave the mourners shocked and anguished.'

Consciousness Formation

The workplace dynamics at the cremation *ghat* contribute to the Dom's consciousness formation. In rural areas, the role of the Dom is limited to handling the sacred fire, as upper castes in villages rigidly follow caste practices. Dom's children are brought up in an environment where they witness discrimination and are derogatorily referred to as '*achhuth*' and '*chandala*', which shapes their identity. Fourteen-year-old Marshal, from a rural area, made an interesting point during our conversation: 'We become Raja (king) for merely five minutes (during the negotiation of the fee), but after reaching the cremation ground, you are the Raja.'

The Dom from poor economic backgrounds believe that the traditional ascribed occupation of cremating bodies is their destiny given by God. One *naukar* from Manikarnika Ghat, during our conversation on the challenges encountered in cremating dead bodies, sadly said, 'We do not know for which evil deed God has punished us, as a result of which we were born in this caste' (Kumari 2018:101). Similarly, at Harishchandra Ghat, another Dom *naukar* added that 'this work is given to us by God; if we will not do it, then who will?'

This similar attitude was observed among the Chamar caste of Senapur, who pointed out that, due to their fate, they had been assigned this low position; however, they do not rationalize it based on *karma* and *dharma* (Cohn 1958:413). Though lower castes can accept the rationalization of the caste system based on *karma* and *dharma* notions to some extent, it is crucial to distinguish between their covert and overt acceptance (Mencher 1974:476). This admission of acknowledging one's status as lower because of evil deeds in the past creates 'religious anxiety' (Kolenda 1964). From the narratives above, it could be said:

> The consciousness of the [Dom] is basically in consciousness with the system that has placed them lowermost. Given their position at the bottom of the system, and given the small stage on which they operate territorially, their arena in the 'game' of caste interaction is doubly squeezed.
>
> (Moffatt 1979:58)

Quite interestingly, the males of Harishchandra Ghat assert themselves as the 'Chaudhary' to reaffirm their identity as the owners of the cremation *ghat* rather than being recognized as merely Dom. They assert that 'we are Dom-Raja, and it is through us that people attain liberation'. This change in the consciousness among the Dom was observed primarily among the upper-class males of Harishchandra Ghat.

At Manikarnika Ghat, even though the numerical strength of Dom *naukars* is greater, they are continuously reminded of their lower status by other caste groups. The discriminatory practices against them are brazen. After the tiresome work of handling dead bodies surrounded by pyres, they are not allowed to drink water from any shop or touch any utensils.

The late Dom-Raja Kailash Chaudhary is often described as a womanizer and alcoholic, yet he is still respected among the Dom, as he always stood for his community. In 2017, when I went to Manikarnika Ghat for fieldwork, a Dom *naukar* pointed out that 'if a fight breaks out with other castes, the Doms will not form a unity. Even though we might be beaten up by them, still our *malik* will not interfere. It was only Kailash Chaudhary, of whom even the Yadavs were scared. During his time, no one dared to raise a hand against us.'

But after his demise, the situation has worsened. My respondent, a descendant of Kashi Chaudhary, who stays at Harishchandra Ghat and was working under the *pari* of Ishwar Chaudhary at Manikarnika Ghat, said:

> At Ishwar Chaudhary's house, naukars have to arrive one night before the *pari* starts. We have to do his household chores, such as sweeping, cleaning, and fetching vegetables. No one is allowed to go upstairs; *naukars* are restricted to the ground floor. If there are 20 people working under his *pari*, then we cook food for ourselves. When Ishwar Chaudhary's sons or even younger children come, we have to stand up with folded hands, bow our heads with serious looks on our faces, and greet them. Once they go upstairs, we can relax and talk to one another. This is the condition despite the fact that we are from the same caste.

Now, an important question is why this assertion of being 'Dom-Raja' and 'Chaudhary' is seen only among Dom residing at Harishchandra Ghat. One of the reasons is the location of these workplace dynamics, which is in an urban setting. While Dom families of Harishchandra Ghat stay in an urban setting, those working at Manikarnika Ghat mostly come from rural areas. In an urban setting, the 'caste system uses an adaptive structure that retains its hierarchical structure through endogamy and preservation of the structure of religious sanctity' (Gould 1963:437). It provides space to disregard some restrictions, such as engaging only in ascribed occupations. Furthermore, the urban area provides a chance to hide one's caste identity, as numerous unfamiliar people from different backgrounds work together in a shared space. This is especially true in a tourist city like Banaras, which provides a wider range of occupational choices for people seeking livelihoods.

The younger generation of Doms is engaged in different occupations, such as working as tour guides, sales assistants at saree shops, or technicians at mobile repair shops. They have opportunities to interact with people from other castes on equal footing, often by either hiding their caste identity or denying that they work at cremation grounds. Many of them work at the cremation *ghat* at night to conceal the fact that they cremate bodies from their friends.

There is a difference in consciousness formation based on one's economic class. Dom from poor families have to burn bodies for a living on a hand-to-mouth basis and are thus engaged in it, while others who are relatively well-off try to conceal their identity from their friends belonging to other castes.

In addition to the above-mentioned aspects, urban spaces also provide a platform for the lower castes to participate in and relate to Hindu rituals, practices and beliefs (Cohn 1958:416). Contemporary studies show that lower castes do not practice Hinduism. Deliege (1993) criticized Weber's idea that 'the lower caste perfectly internalises the Brahmanical concept of *samsara, karma,* and *dharma,* because of which they do not revolt against their state of servitude' (Weber 1958:130). However, in the context of the Dom of Banaras, Weber's view becomes valid, not only because the Dom seem to be 'tamed by Brahmanical theory' as Banaras city is the religious centre of Hinduism, but also because the economic aspects of their livelihood are directly linked with the religious domain of death rites. The myth associated with the religious domain of salvation facilitates them in acquiring, even if not a respectable position, yet a position to demand payment for the sacred fire.

Though the Dom have their own religious practices and festivals, as elaborated by Kaushik (1979), in contemporary times it seems that the Dom are embracing the customs of Hinduism. Crucial shifts are happening, such as the arrangement of a temporary pavilion for the Goddess Saraswati idol in their locality, a recent trend over the past few years. Younger Dom males perform *havan* (offerings to fire) in the presence of a priest, followed by the distribution of *prasad*. Elderly men, along with females of all age groups, remain absent from this religious gathering until the last day, when the religious procession of the idol is taken out for immersion. At that point, all members of the community gather to bid farewell to the deity.

Another example is the formation of *Massan Nath*[29] *Damru Dal*, a group formed by male members of the Dom community to play the *damru* (pellet drum) at religious gatherings, especially at temples. There is *Shani*[30] *Dev Damru Dal,* which includes members from different caste groups, including two Dom males from affluent families. When the *Shani Dev* group refused to accept more Dom men, the excluded members formed their own group, consisting solely of individuals from their caste, and named it after *Massan Nath* (Lord of the cremation ground). Since there are many other *Damru Dals* that include members from various caste groups, the Dom caste identity becomes less distinct. This provides them with an opportunity to access religious domains, such as playing the pellet drum at the Lord Vishwanath temple during worship, a privilege that was denied to them in the past.

But quite strangely, the Dom do not engage in conducting *puja* at the *Massan Nath* temple or Raja Harishchandra temple. I enquired about it: when it is the temple of *Massan Nath*, then why do the Dom not perform *puja* and needs a priest for it? Currently, a Mahapatra is working as a priest here. Babu Chaudhary, in his late seventies, answered:

> Babu: *Masaan Nath* is for all. Anyone can offer their prayers to him. But it is not our *dharma* to perform *puja,* as we are not Pandits. At most, we can give money, flowers, and garlands to

the Pandit so that he can offer prayers on our behalf and give us *prasad;* this is *bhakti.* These days, anyone can enter temples; who knows what the caste of that person is. Earlier, this did not use to happen. People used to give their offerings to the Pandit and receive *prasad.* Now, anyone can enter the temple.

Question: So, do you think it is right or wrong?

Babu: Do the *darshan* from the temple gate. We are getting *prasad*; take it and come back home.

The older generations seem to hold on to earlier caste practices, but the younger generation is embracing the changes. Besides this, in the past few years, some dramatic shifts have been occurring at the Harishchandra cremation ground, such as arranging grand celebrations for playing *Massan Holi*[31] and the festival of *Dev Deepawali.* Here, stage artists are invited to perform religious dances. Hundreds of people gather on the cremation ground to enjoy the performances, and the burning of pyres is halted for a few hours. During *Massan Holi,* people play Holi with the ashes of dead bodies, accompanied by aghoris and artists. Performers dressed in the attire of Lord Shiva and Goddess Parvati take circumambulations around the actual burning pyre. As Shiva is known as the Lord of Cremation, this performance provides a visual representation of Shiva dancing around the pyre and playing Holi with the ashes of the dead, thus mesmerizing people. It helps reinforce their belief in the myths of Lord Shiva as the God of the cremation ground.

Both these times, the area of the cremation ground becomes crowded with people, and no one seems concerned about the dead bodies being cremated there daily. Surprisingly, the everyday space of the cremation *ghat,* where death dances furiously, suddenly shifts or is 'side-shadowed' into a temporary space of entertainment. Morson argues that 'in side shadowing, two or more alternatives present, the actual and the possible, are made simultaneously visible. This is not a simultaneity in time but of times; we do not see contradictory actualities, but one possibility that was actualized and another that could have been, but was not' (Morson 1998:602).

The same space of a cremation ground undergoes dynamic shifts and displays different aspects, where one side shadows the others. Thus, from the space of burning bodies, it shifts into a space of performing ascetics by aghori, and to a space of entrainment involving masses. Here, the last one differs from the above two, as it excludes the aspect of death pollution.

Generally, cremation *ghats* in India are located outside the city or village, but Kashi is the exception. Here, the cremation *ghats* are the focal point of everyday activities, and death is celebrated instead of feared. Kashi has been glorified as a city of *moksha* (salvation), due to which the death industry has prospered. The role of sacred myths, along with sacred complexes, is crucial, due to which ritual specialists assert their importance and earn a livelihood. The Dom of Harishchandra Ghat use this sacred space and these myths to assert their importance.

3

Salvation in the Death Industry

Corpse as a Sacred Object

During the dusky hours, as the sun was setting on the other side of the riverbank, pyres on this side were blazing with high flames, emanating plumes of smoke that ascended into the sky. I was suddenly drawn to the voice of a middle-aged man dressed in a white *kurta*[1] and saffron-coloured *dhoti*, conversing with another person. He was waiting for his relative's remains to be burned while sitting on the stairs of Harishchandra Ghat. His attire made his Brahmanical status quite evident. I approached him to gain insight into the significance of conducting cremation in Kashi. During our conversation, he said that 'Brahmins would not let Dom touch their dead bodies because of concerns about pollution, but they would pay their fee for the sacred fire.'

After talking to him, I recalled instances from *Samskara*, a novel by Anantha Murthy (1978) about a decaying Brahmin *Agraharam*[2] of Karnataka due to the plague. The story revolves around orthodox Brahmins facing anxiety and agony as they decide who should be held responsible for conducting the last rites of their neighbour who had died without any heir. The deceased Brahmin had indulged in activities forbidden by their *dharma* (code of conduct), such as alcoholism, flesh-eating and keeping a low-born caste woman as a mistress.

The dilemma was whether Brahmins should perform his last rites after he had condemned his religion. Could he be called a Brahmin, or should they ask lower-caste people to perform his death rites? But lower castes were forbidden to touch a Brahmin's corpse. In this conundrum, they sought answers from various religious texts, and meanwhile, the body rotted in the *agraharam* for three nights. This led to the spread of plague and the decay of their colony. This novel explicitly stresses the contradiction between caste purity and death pollution.

In Hinduism, after death, relatives must observe mandatory rituals for a certain period of time to free themselves from death pollution. Yet Brahmins cannot allow certain caste groups, which are considered lower due to prescribed caste rankings, to touch a Brahmin corpse, as their touch is believed to pollute the dead body. How could a touch from lower castes defile a corpse?

Furthermore, the Dom view touching a corpse as dishonourable work. Though they have to burn it with the help of a bamboo shaft, they make sure not to touch it. During the coronavirus pandemic, they called men from another caste to become pallbearers and arrange the body on the pyre, in the absence of deceased relatives, in exchange for money.[3]

This alludes to an intriguing issue as, on the one hand, it emphasizes the issue of purity and pollution in the caste system and death pollution, on the other. This chapter tries to deal with this conundrum and to understand the role of this caste (Dom) as the custodians of salvation in Kashi.[4]

Kashi the *Mokshadayini*[5]

Over the years, several foreigners who came to India to learn about Indian culture have recorded intriguing information about Kashi in their travel journals. Kashi, the city of salvation, has been a glorified city in Hinduism since ancient times. For ages, it has been a representative sample of Hindu ways of life in all their significant complexities and contradictions (Kane 1973:620).

The popular belief depicting Kashi as the bestower of salvation during colonial times led to many cases of religious suicides at

Prayag and Kashi. Earlier records reveal that since 1600, Kashi has been regarded as an important *tirtha* (crossing ford). The marked improvement in transportation and communication facilities, along with the levying of taxes on pilgrimage during the Mughal and British eras, led to a surge in pilgrimage (Bayley 1981:169). The number of pilgrims to Prayagraj, Gaya and Kashi between 1780 and 1820 trebled each year (Bayley 1981:170). People wish to get cremated here, as described by Louis Rousselet (1876) in his writing:

> We are now in the centre of the line of wharves fronting the Munikurnka *ghat* (Manikarnika Ghat), the holiest of holies, the place where funeral piles are incessantly burning, destined to consume the bodies of all those to whom fate has granted the happiness of ending their days in the sacred city. Happy, indeed, thrice happy are those whose mortal envelope here becomes prey to the flames, for the soul will depart directly from the spot towards paradise, where, if they have not been great sinners, it will animate the body of some future Brahmins. This felicity is, therefore, eagerly desired by every orthodox Hindoo. Rich people, on the approach of a serious malady, hasten to Benares in the hope of ending their existence at the gates of paradise, and those surprised by deaths give orders for their bodies to be conveyed thither, sometimes from a distance of hundreds of miles, to be burned on the Munikurnika (Manikarnika Ghat). On landing at this wharf, one is half suffocated by the dense foetid smoke that hangs over it like a bluish dome. On all sides, the funeral piles send up their long flames, and their cracklings are accompanied by sinister sounds. The men of this dismal place, with their bodies naked and blackened by the soot, stir the fires by means of long bars of iron or throw jars of oil upon them. At each step, we stumble over bones, and our feet sink deep into the still-warm human dust, which, heaped in this spot as it has been for centuries, forms a layer of considerable depth (Louis Rousselet: *India and its Native Princes* [1876]).[6]

The rapidly increased glorification of religious places as the providers of salvation led to a rise in the number of suicides, such as the leper suicides observed at Prayagraj (Allahabad) until they were forbidden by the British in 1810. Similarly, there were incidents of suicide at the Kashi Karvat Temple (Justice 1997; Parry 1994). After the British outlawed these suicides and Sati practice, this led to another method where people preferred to die a natural death in Kashi to bear the fruit of salvation through *Kashi-vaas* or *Kashi-labh*. The term *Kashi-vaas* refers to a practice by individuals who come to Kashi in their declining years to live a religious life and await their death, while *Kashi-labh* refers to those who come to Kashi 'at the eleventh hour', just at the time of death (Eck 1983:329).

Thus, from the colonial era, the trend of bringing dying people in their last days to the banks of the River Ganges has been observed. As these people came from distant areas and had no place to stay, they died while camping out in any available spot on the edges of the river. Relatives accompanying the dying person stay there until the person dies, which can range from a period of one day to one week. Travellers describe this practice as follows:

> Most of the *Gentiles* burn their dead, but some partially broil the bodies with stubble near the side of a river and then precipitate them into the water from a high and steep bank. I have attended these funeral rites on the Ganges several times and observed flights of crows fluttering about the carcass, which become as much the prey of those birds as of fish and crocodiles. Some again carry a sick person, when at the point of death, to the river-side; place his feet in the water, let him sink gradually to the neck; and when it is supposed that he is about to expire, they immerse his whole body into the river, where they leave him, after violently clapping their hands, and crying out with great vehemence. The object of this ceremony is that the soul may be washed, on taking its flight, from all impurities which it may have contracted during its abode in the body. (François Bernier: *Travels in the Mogul Empire*, A.D.1656–1668 [1891])[7]

By 1820, the Baptist missionaries of Bengal were against this practice and termed it '*ghat* murder' in an attempt to stop it. Missionaries argued that many family members were leaving their terminally ill relatives at the *ghat*, who were then dying due to a lack of food, water and care. Thus, missionaries explained it as a practice of manslaughter by greedy relatives seeking to get their hands on the deceased's property. Consequently, a legislation was passed that led to formal policing at the *ghat* and forbade the exposure of persons considered to be living, according to Western perspectives (Bayley 1981:172). However, Bayley (1981) elucidates this by taking into consideration Hindu beliefs and mentions:

> *Ghat*-murder was not the result of some peculiar viciousness of the Hindu character. Dying people were a desperate liability to a Hindu household, since a death inside the house would require expensive and lengthy rites of purification and death on a bed might expose the family to malignant spiritual visitation.
>
> (Bayley 1981:172)

Still at Tulsi Ghat in Banaras, there is a remnant of a stone structure with a roof and three walls where, earlier, dying people were kept, and after death, they were cremated at Harishchandra Ghat (Justice 1997:48). Mahantji, who owns this area for the dying, pointed out, 'If in 1990, one hundred people are coming to die, then in 1955, perhaps one thousand people were coming to die' (Justice 1997:51). This practice has been considered part of a tradition, which has slowly faded away due to non-availability of space at the *ghat*, as more buildings have been constructed (Justice 1997). A few families constructed charitable places to help these people in keeping this tradition alive by providing space to the dying person, who wishes to die in Kashi, as most of the people coming here do not have any place.

One such charitable place is 'Kashi Ganga Labh Bhavan' at Manikarnika Ghat, which was opened in 1958. During the 1970s, it was the preferred place for most people. However, this place remained empty in the 1990s due to the growing popularity of another place known as 'Kashi Labh Mukti Bhawan' at Godwalia Chowk (Justice 1997:65). Recently, during the construction of Lord Vishwanath's corridor 2021, the shelter of Manikarnika Ghat was renovated and renamed as '*Mumukshu Bhavan*'. It is now a two-floor building with twenty-five beds on each floor. The third *Mumukshu Bhavan* is at Asi Ghat, constructed in 1920. It has 116 beds, of which 40 are reserved for those who wish to die in Kashi. These places have specific rules according to which only those above the age of sixty are provided room for fifteen days. In case, the person does not die within the allotted time, she or he is sent back to their home. The shelter of Godwalia Chowk was made for the twice-born caste, so lower castes were referred to the shelter of Manikarnika Ghat (Justice 1997:60).

The number of people who have come to Kashi Labh Mukti Bhawan from 1960 to 1990 was 8,500, and in Kashi Ganga Labh Bhavan, which dates back to the mid-1930s, until 1990, 20,000 people were registered (Justice 1997:26). In one year, around 356 people registered for *Kashi-labh* at Mukti Bhawan, and out of these, around 90 per cent died (Justice 1997:89). Those people who are aware of these shelters tended to go there. But there is a possibility that many people across India who choose to die or at least get cremated in Kashi are unaware of such shelters.

According to the data collected for this study, people are arriving from Nepal, Maharashtra and Tamil Nadu,[8] which is in agreement with Parry (1994). Furthermore, many people stay in a hotel or rented apartment. A similar case is mentioned below.

An aged man, in his late sixties, a native of Tamil Nadu, was staying on the ground floor of the building where I stayed for my fieldwork. He had a good physique, appeared healthy and was fluent in English. After retiring from his bank position and after his two daughters relocated to the United States, he decided to spend his remaining days in Kashi for *Kashi-vaas*. His possessions included a wooden cot and a few pieces of clothing. His daily routine was fixed, such as waking up early at approximately 5 a.m., completing his morning ablutions, and leaving for the Kedar temple to offer his prayers. By then, his breakfast was delivered by a South Indian restaurant. After this, he spent his entire day in the company of people from the monastery who frequently visited his room and read religious texts to him. One fine morning, at around seven o'clock, I overheard several people yelling at his door to open it. After several failed attempts to receive any response from the elderly man, they knocked on my door to enquire about him. I was as equally clueless as any other person gathered there.

His door was finally broken after a struggle of two to three hours in the presence of the house owner. Meanwhile, people from the monastery also arrived. It was found that the elderly man had passed away in his sleep. Local people informed the Dom community about the death. A coffin was arranged, and after placing the body inside, people carried it to the open area of the Dharamshala at Harishchandra Ghat. His family was informed of the demise, and people waited for their arrival. Meanwhile, four Dom men placed larger ice blocks around the body. They guarded the body against dog attacks for three consecutive days until his family members arrived and completed his cremation. People at the cremation *ghat* and even in my neighbourhood said that 'the deceased man had attained salvation, and his desire for *Kashi-vaas* had been fulfilled'.

Many factors affect one's decision to die or be cremated at Kashi, such as gender, class and caste, which are briefly discussed here. People visiting Kashi for *Kashi-labh* either hail from affluent families or are aware of shelter facilities such as Mukti Bhawan. The journey of a person accompanying a dying individual to Kashi is arduous. Most people carry the dying on their shoulders for many kilometres until they reach railway stations, where the trains are often crowded. The very rich, on the other hand, bring the dying in jeeps or cars (Justice 1997:119). Another significant point is that more men are brought to die in Kashi. Death records of the bodies cremated in the gas crematoriums in 2020 show the dominance of men. Secondly, one's caste status is also a contributing factor. In Mukti Bhawan, Justice (1997) noted a predominance of Brahmins, followed by Rajputs, with only a few individuals from the lower castes recorded at Ganga Labh Bhawan (Justice 1997:114–15).

Parry (1994) also noted that in 1976–7, the majority of bodies were from Uttar Pradesh districts: 83.3 per cent were from Banaras, Jaunpur and Mirzapur. The rest, 16.4 per cent, were from Bihar districts – Rohtas and Bhojpur (Parry 1994:57). There has been a seasonal trend, too, as a maximum number of people came to Mukti Bhawan during August, September and October (Justice 1997:91). It is connected with the timing of planting and harvesting seasons of crops. During above-mentioned months, family members can stay away from their fields (Justice 1997).

The family or village tradition of coming to Kashi for *Kashi-labh* or *Kashi-vaas* has been followed for generations. Justice's (1997) work provides two different incidents. In the first instance, an ill woman in her late fifties was brought to the hospital in Banaras for treatment. However, due to the unaffordability of the expenses required for her treatment, her son took her to Mukti Bhawan. Despite her continuous requests to return to her village, he did not take her back, aiming to avoid the further expense of bringing her back again. Ultimately, she died due to a lack of treatment (Justice 1997:129). The second instance was of another ill woman, whose husband forcefully brought her to Ganga Labh Bhawan. He was under pressure to follow the tradition of his village and was fully convinced that her dying day was nearer. Despite continuous protests by the woman that she would not die any sooner, he did not listen to her. When the woman survived after waiting in Kashi for many days, they finally returned to their village (Justice 1997:130).

My informant, who accompanied his relative's dead body for cremation at Harishchandra Ghat, stated the same reason. He revealed that they had accompanied him for treatment at a hospital in Singrauli district, Madhya Pradesh. However, the person died on the way, so everyone decided to cremate the body in Kashi. The mourner mentioned that 'the deceased would achieve salvation by being cremated in Kashi, and, meanwhile, the cost of transporting the dead body back was also reduced'. These instances provide a brief idea regarding the firm beliefs of people in attaining salvation and their desire to spend their last days in Kashi. Thus, it becomes important to understand the whole concept of salvation. This chapter attempts to show that the sacred geography of a place and its sacred specialists constitute significant elements of the sacred complex and are sustained by traditions of sacred myths. In other words, myths have led to the glorification of Kashi, which facilitated its important position as a sacred complex. Its sacred geography finds reference in myths, along with the role of ritual specialists such as priests, the Dom, the Mahapatra and the Mallah, who constitute important elements of this sacred complex and contribute to glorifying Kashi's existence.

Salvation in Hinduism

Myths and beliefs play crucial roles in continuing certain rites and rituals, for instance, the continuous flow of pilgrimages and performing religious practices to please Lord Vishwanath in Kashi. Analyses of different pieces of literature show the presence of myths in every context of Kashi, from the name of the city to its importance in Hinduism and even the presence of certain sacred places such as temples or *kunds.*[9]

There are many stories regarding the name of the city, Kashi. One such story mentions that Kashi got its name from its ancient king, Kasha, who was of the lineage of King Divodasa. Another famous *Mahatmya*[10] in *Kashi Khanda* explains, 'As the light, the unspeakable Shiva, shines here, let its other name be Kashi.' It is called the 'city of light' that illuminates liberation, '*Moksha Prakashika Kashi*' (Eck 1983:26).

Another popular name for the city, Varanasi, also has its glorification in myths. The myth in the *Jabala Upanishad* states that God created two rivers and positioned them to guard the entry of evils into the city. The one in the south was named the sword (Asi/Nasi) as it destroys all the sins of the senses, and the other in the north was named the averter (Varuna) as it obstructs all sins of the senses. These interior rivers are described as mystical veins of the subtle body's physiology (Eck 1983:27). This also highlights the use of the concept of space in Hinduism, as mentioned by Beck (1976), is 'intimately linked with the conceptualisation of cosmic forces and the basic structure of the human body' (Das 1977:10).

In Hinduism, sacred places are referred to as *tirtha*, which means 'to cross over,' 'crossing place' or 'spiritual ford'. Here, one crosses the river of *samsara* (the cycle of birth and rebirth) and reaches the far shore of salvation (Eck 1983:35). There are seven prime *tirthas* as described in the *Garuda Purana,* a religious text in Hinduism that consists of teachings related to death rites and prescribed rituals.

> At the time of old age, he who becomes detached and leaves all feelings and he who remembers me, that happy soul, will definitely get *mukti*. Those people who, want to die, leave their homes to live(*vaas*) in Prayag or some other *tirtha*, or die in Kashi, etc., will definitely get *moksha*. Ayodhya, Mathura, Maya(Haridwar), Kashi, Avantika(Ujjain), Kanchipuram and Dwarka: these are the seven *moksha* giving *puris.*
>
> (GP 16:112–14 cited in Justice 1997:167)

In India, these seven cities are referred to as *mokshadwar* (door to salvation). Furthermore, different pilgrimage places have peculiar roles and positions assigned; for instance, Prayagraj is glorified for the tonsuring of one's head, whereas Gaya has been recognized for *pinda-dan* (offerings for ancestors), but Kashi has been allotted the top position (Kane 1973:602). It is believed that those who die in these six cities are reborn in Kashi, and after dying there, they can attain salvation (Eck 1983:38; Parry 1994:21). It is also believed that Lord Shiva whispers the *tarak mantra*[11] in the ear of the deceased to help the soul attain salvation (Sherring 1868:51). The famous Sanskrit quote, '*Kashyan maranaan mukti*', is often quoted by natives, to lay more emphasis on their argument that those who die in Kashi attain salvation.

Hinduism's highest and most valued goal is salvation (Rambachan 2003:640). Human suffering is the result of one's unawareness of the true nature of *atman* (self) and *Brahman* (God) (Rambachan 2003). This concept of self has been understood differently among the three great traditions within Hinduism – Advaita by Shankara, Visishtadvaita by Ramanuja and Dvaita by Madhva. According to Shankara, 'self is ultimately identical to *Brahman*; for Ramanuja, it is inseparably related to *Brahman*; and for Madhva, it is entirely different but completely dependent on *Brahman*' (Rambachan 2003: 641).

Though different traditions have different understandings of the self, the idea of salvation in these traditions 'implies the recognition of the self as different from the psychophysical apparatus and as immortal', and this understanding means an end to the cycle of birth, death and rebirth (Rambachan 2003). The primary role of *dharma* is to uphold the established order of the world intact, and *adharma* threatens this order, but salvation is 'the abandonment of this established order in favour of self-realisation' (Buitenen 1957:37). It could be understood as freedom or release from suffering and frustration of desire (Ingalls 1957:45).

For different Indian religions, such as Hinduism, Buddhism and Jainism, the definition of salvation is different, but one thing remains the same: it must be sought outside of *samsara*.[12] As salvation is the elimination of suffering, 'one must abolish rebirth in order to achieve salvation' (Obeyesekere 1980:150).

Davis (1988), in his work *Cremation and Liberation: The Revision of a Hindu Ritual*, examined the conception of salvation that differs in both the Saiva Siddhanta and the Vedic tradition. The latter has been described above. Within the Saiva tradition, there are two branches based on their life goals: First are the *bubhukshus*, the seekers of worldly benefits; they aim to have a better life and secure a rebirth. Second are the *mumukshus*, the seekers of salvation, for whom death is a long passage through which their soul, trapped in worldly illusions through fetters, is freed and attains liberation (Davis 1988:42).

A double movement is involved in attaining salvation: the soul must remove its fetters and allow the emergence of its inherent power. Not everyone can attain salvation; one must go through the 'initiation into liberation' process, in which the guru helps remove these fetters through rituals known as '*kalasuddhi*' and '*gunapadana*'. The soul is freed from its fetters through these rites, and its powers manifest. However, one element of fetter remains unaffected by these rites, which is '*prarabdhakarman*'. It is *karma*[13] that has been activated at birth to condition this life. An individual's daily activities eliminate these *karmas*, and at the time of death, their soul is assimilated into Shiva (Davis 1988:42–4).

Thus, after death, the soul either gets rebirth on earth in a temporary life or in paradise. Hence, the soul could be born either in the world of God (*salokya*), near God (*samipya*), or as an apotheosized God (*sarupa*). Rebirth in paradise occurs under the same provisions as on earth, that is, for a limited time, after which another rebirth happens (Weber 1958:22). Another possibility is the cessation of the cycle of rebirths, where the soul merges 'with the all-one (*sayujya*) or submergence in nirvana' (Weber 1958).

In everyday language, people often use *moksha* (salvation) and *mukti* (liberation) interchangeably to signify the ultimate spiritual goal in Hinduism. There are crucial terminologies often used at the cremation *ghat*, such as *mati*, which generally symbolizes clay, but in this context, it refers to a dead body. One of the five elements constituting the human body is earth, and after death, the body is assimilated back into the earth. Another term is *pravaha,*[14] which denotes the immersion of dead bodies in a flowing river as these bodies are not considered fit for cremation. Significant terms important in this context are '*tar jana*', '*paar ho jana*' or '*pare ho jana*'. These terms are often used interchangeably to refer to the liberation of the soul. During conversations with mourners, it was observed that these terms were often used without knowing the exact meaning of what people were referring to cross over. On probing further, they stress that '*tar jana*' means to cross over, to get liberation from this world or to attain salvation.

The words '*paar ho jana*' or '*tar jana*' mean to swim or cross over. Eck (1981) argues that the word *tirtha* has been derived from the Sanskrit verb '*tr/tarata*', which means to cross over. In the Upanishads, this act of crossing is a spiritual transition from this world to the other world (Eck 1981:331). The whispering of the *tarak mantra* (ferryboat mantra) by Lord Shiva, as a guru, into the dying person's ear assists the soul in crossing the Ford.

In Hindu mythology, there is a description of a frightful river named the Vaitarani River, which is composed of blood and floating corpses that the soul must cross. Even now, chief mourners perform many rituals during *pinda-dan* so that the deceased soul can easily cross this river. Hence, these words refer to 'swim across' this river, as people believe that dying, getting cremated in Kashi or immersing ashes in the Ganges will facilitate the attainment of salvation through the spirituality embedded in Kashi.

The understanding of salvation, as described in classical texts, is the release from the cycle of birth and rebirth. During conversations with mourners, it was realized that people developed an understanding of salvation after reading or listening to stories from religious texts such as the Ramayana, Mahabharata and Garuda Purana. This culture of verbal transmission of knowledge has been passed down for generations. Many people recalled at least hearing the significant sections of these stories, even if they were unable to recall the exact details, and through that, they developed an understanding. That's why discrepancies are often observed between the way prescribed in the classical texts and the actual practices performed by people during rites and rituals.

It was noted that some people follow prescribed rituals as informed by their ancestors and continue them as a form of tradition, while others perform them under societal pressure, as their inability to adhere to the prescribed ways can affect their family's status. The idea of salvation among those who wish to die in Kashi is, for some, the avoidance of painful rebirths rather than dwelling in heaven; for others, it is a good rebirth; and for yet others, it is the escape from this world and entry into the realm of God (Justice 1997; Parry 1994).

As people who wish to die in Kashi become important, similarly, people accompanying them are equally relevant here. A person who accompanied his mother to die in Kashi described his understanding of salvation.

> To come on earth, to die, and to again take birth. Again and again. This is the result of man's work – his *karma.* The Hindus want to become free from taking birth and dying again and again. That is called *moksha.* In our holy book, the Gita, Krishna explains this matter. If a man takes *moksha,* he will not be born again. That is the meaning of *moksha.* In our religious faith, if anyone dies in this area of the Kashi, they will go to heaven. For this reason, my mother wants to die in the Kashi.
>
> (Justice 1997:142)

In Hinduism, there is a belief that human beings are reborn in their human form after passing through 8,400,000 different life forms. Thus, performing suitable *karmas* to attain salvation in human life becomes crucial. One of the mourners who came to cremate his relative mentioned:

> *Moksha* means that people who take birth again and again can get rid of this cycle of birth and rebirth. In this way, they do not have to come back to earth again. What I know is that humans are born in different forms, such as animals and other forms (*yoni*). Thus, we attain *mukti* from this cycle. It is not about going to heaven or hell, but about stopping this cycle of birth and rebirth.

Another mourner stresses that liberation is a satisfaction from within; this is our tradition, which has been followed for centuries and it is our responsibility to continue it. Hence, for some, salvation is a way to get rid of human suffering in this world, while for others the practice of cremating bodies in Kashi is a part of family tradition.

A temple priest, well-versed in religious texts, mentioned that by taking the sacred fire for cremation from the hand of the Dom-Raja, people attain liberation, not salvation. He stressed that by 'liberation, the soul would not wander in limbo but attain peace'. I am quoting a few instances from the conversation.

> Question: What is salvation?
>
> Priest: When a man was alive, he was connected to every person in the living state. Even after death, many souls cannot free themselves from these relationships, so people refer to them by various names, such as ghosts or spirits. There is *pitar-dosh,*[15] because of which he cannot attain liberation. So here, salvation means to get beyond all these things. The soul gets absorbed into God and does not fall into the trap of living relationships and illusions. Whoever does not fall into it will only go towards God. And the one trapped in these worldly illusions will not attain salvation.
>
> Question: So, do both salvation and liberation signify the same idea?
>
> Priest: From my point of view, I would say that salvation and liberation are two sides of the same coin. Liberation means getting rid of the bondage of birth and death, and salvation means that the soul becomes absorbed in God and escapes worldly illusion.

Hence, the meaning of liberation and salvation in layman's language is to get rid of the cycles of birth and rebirth and the assimilation of one's soul with God, respectively.

There are some prerequisites that should be fulfilled to attain salvation, such as dying in Kashi or, if not, being cremated there. Before leaving for Kashi, a person gifts a cow to a Brahmin. Immediately at the time of death, Ganges water with basil leaves is poured into the mouth of the dying person. Then, sacred fire from the Dom is taken, followed by the rites of *kapal-kriya*. Finally, the cremated remains and ashes are immersed in the Ganges.

The role of the Ganges becomes important here, as, according to beliefs, the Ganges came to Earth through the austerity of Bhagiratha so that his ancestors' souls could stay in heaven. That is why Hindus give importance to the Ganges River in their everyday practices, believing it helps them rid themselves of their sins.

Furthermore, the nature of one's death, whether timely or untimely, also contributes to the attainment of salvation. I often hear people pointing out that those who commit sins usually die untimely, experiencing a sudden and painful death due to sickness or accident, and are unable to attain salvation.

The above section discussed the concept of salvation among people who come to die in Kashi. It is important to understand the reasons behind choosing Kashi as a suitable place to die and attain salvation. The following section elaborates on this.

Supremacy of Kashi

The cremation *ghats* in Kashi have witnessed many bodies being cremated here from across India. In 1980, over 24,000 bodies were brought in from outside the city to be cremated (Justice 1997:21).

> In Benares, between 1880 and 1908, there was an annual surplus of deaths over births of about 24 per cent, or about 3,000 out of a population of about 180,000, and qualitative evidence suggests that this had been a long case.
>
> (Bayley 1981:161)

The number of corpses in Kashi at both Harishchandra Ghat and Manikarnika Ghat '(from 1917–18 to 1989 shows a pattern of steady growth, from an annual total of nearly 12,000 and a daily average of thirty-two in 1917–18 to an annual total of nearly 33,000 and a daily average of over ninety in 1985' (Parry 1994:53–7)). There was also an increase in the number of corpses belonging to areas outside Banaras as 'in 1917–18, 1,104 outside corpses arrived at Harishchandra and Manikarnika Ghat; in 1989, the number was 12,544' (Parry 1994:57).

In 2020, the number of bodies cremated in the gas crematorium accounted for 1,710 in one year at Harishchandra Ghat.[16] Though this figure would not be suffice as, during this time coronavirus outbreak had struck the world, and the World Health Organization (WHO) mentioned about the presence of discrepancy in the data on the number of deaths reported.

Now the question arises: despite the presence of many holy sites across India, why has Kashi been bestowed with the important position of providing salvation? The possible explanations could be found by linking its topography to the cosmos, which makes it unparalleled among all other cities (Rana Singh 2004:195), thus turning it into a 'spiritualised landscape' (Eck 1983:38). Through this linkage, the city is attributed with the notion of being the bestower of salvation. The sacred geography of Kashi, glorified by myths, plays an important role in attracting worshippers worldwide.

The *tirtha* of Kashi and the river Ganges hold an apex place in Hinduism. Eck (1983) pointed out that both of these symbols – Kashi and Ganges – are shaped by geography, and as geography takes more time to change, these symbols have had a tenacious hold upon the religious imagination (Eck 1983:36). The best example to illustrate this point is the well-known *Panchkroshi* pilgrimage. Kashi's circumference is marked by the route of *Panchkroshi*, a pilgrimage carried out by devotees annually. Earlier, this pilgrimage was completed in five days, but these days, devotees start it in the evening and return by the following afternoon. It is believed that those who die within this range of *Panchkroshi* attained salvation, which is on the west bank of the Ganges. The eastern bank of the Ganges is a deserted area.[17] As per the myth, Lord Ganesha tricked Sage Veda Vyas into writing in the scripture that 'those who die in Maghar will be reborn as asses' (Sherring 1868:173).

The presence of the Ganges River in Kashi further increases its auspiciousness, as the Ganges has been referred to as the 'Mother Ganga,' who purifies all sins. Moreover, the Ganges becomes *Uttarvahini* here, as it flows from the south to the north, making Kashi the holiest place. The direction plays a crucial role here, as the south direction is often linked with ancestors, while the north is associated with God.

Further, it is believed that as long as some part of the body, such as ashes or bones, remains in the flowing Ganges, the deceased's soul resides in heaven. The water of the Ganges is termed the 'nectar of immortality', and just as it gave life to the ancestors of Bhagiratha, so it is believed that it will bring life to all the dead (Eck 1983:215). Another myth in *Kashi Khanda* explains the reason for the immersion of ashes in the flowing river.

Myth 5

> This is the story of Vahika, who was addicted to gambling and had killed a cow. One day, in a forest, he was killed by a tiger. His soul was taken to the Lord of Death for judgment, while he was condemned to hell for his sins. At the same time, his body was being torn apart by vultures. A vulture flew over the Ganga carrying the footbone of his body. When another vulture attacked him, a piece of the dead body fell by chance into the Ganga as Vahika's soul was taken towards hell. At the same time, a chariot came to take him to heaven.
>
> (Eck 1983:216)

Due to these beliefs, people across the world, unable to take benefit of *Kashi-vaas* often bring the cremated remains of their loved ones to immerse in the Ganges.

Returning to the *Panchkroshi* route, it is a clockwise circumambulation of the Lord Vishwanath temple, the focal point. The essence of this pilgrimage is that during the circumambulation of the city, the sacred area is always kept on the right-hand side (Parry 1994:15). It is believed that completing the *Panchkroshi* route is equivalent to circumambulating the whole world (Eck 1983:42). Quoting from *Kashi Khanda,* this myth mentions the origin of the world, and Kashi is claimed to be the centre of the world.

Myth 6

> During the time of great dissolution, there was nothing except darkness. There was no sun, no moon, no stars, no day, and no night. There was only pure reality, Brahman, not graspable by mind or sense, without any form. Then that one desired to create a second,

> and so it took the form of Lord Shiva, the form of formless and with him was the goddess Shakti called Prakriti (matter). Together, Shiva and Shakti created this place. Shakti is matter, and Shiva is the spirit. Both of them are bliss incarnate, delight in this place, this place is measuring five *kroshas*, created to be the very ground under their feet. O Agastya, they do not leave this place even in time of dissolution. Therefore it is called Avimukta 'Never Forsaken'.
>
> (Eck 1983:242)

A *kosa* is a unit of measurement of about two miles; a panch *krosha* is equal to five *kroshas*, which refers to the radius of the sacred circle of Kashi (Eck 1983:350). Kashi measurement, as mentioned in the *Padma Purana,* is as follows:

> Beginning from Madhyameshvara, stretching a string as far as Dehali Vinayaka, move that string in all directions to form a circle. The supreme sacred land (*kshetra*) is what is inside the arc. The Vedas know it as Kashi. That place is famous for liberation.
>
> (Eck 1983:351)

The geographical landmarks that fall within this *Panchkroshi* route are the region of Kashi, within the premises of which salvation is granted.

Kashi Cosmology

Kashi is the sacred zone extending beyond the city to the countryside, whereas Banaras is roughly today's urban city, stretching from the Varuna River to the Asi River (Eck 1983:25).

The territory of Kashi is understood as a mesocosmos between the macrocosmos (cosmos/heaven) and the microcosmos (temple/ the human body). These cosmic layers merged with the city's five pilgrimage circuits and formed a *mandala* (Rana Singh 2008:39). The five pilgrimage circuits of Kashi comprise: (i) the 84-*Krosha* sacred territory (*Caurashikroshi*), the outermost pilgrimage route; (ii) the 25-*Krosha* sacred territory (*Panchkroshi*); (iii) the city circuit (*Nagar*

Pradakshina); (iv) the never-forsaken territory (*Avimukta*); and (v) the inner sanctum (*Antargriha*) (Rana Singh 1993:243–4). The Vishwanath temple is considered the pillar of the centre of the world or the axis mundi of the *mandala* (Rana Singh 1993:242). Quoting Rana here,

> The five pilgrimage circuits of Kashi symbolise the parallelism of the five gross heavenly elements (sky, earth, air, water, and fire) with the five basic parts of the human body (head, legs, face, blood, and heart), transcendental power and its associated sheath, and the corresponding sacred numbers of shrines and images on the route.
>
> (Rana Singh 2008:39)

The Vishwanath temple is the focal point of the concentric circles of *Panchkroshi*, *Avimukta* and *Antargriha*. Their power and sanctity increase as these circles get closer to the temple. Hence, *Antargriha*, the innermost pilgrimage route, has the greatest sanctity. These circles are also interlocked with a hierarchy consisting of different forms of salvation. The circle with greater sanctity, that is, dying in the proximity of the Vishwanath temple, will attain a higher form of liberation termed *Sayuja*, whereas a person dying in the outermost ring of the *Panchkroshi* route will attain the lowest form of liberation, termed *Salokya* (Sukul 1977:39).

Within the *Antargriha*, the pilgrimage passes through seven spiral circles to reach the sacred core of the city, i.e., the temple of Lord Vishwanath. These seven circles are equated with the seven layers of the atmosphere. Here, too, there is a link with the cosmos (Rana Singh 2016:11). Lord Ganesha is the protector of the sacred space of Kashi. Thus, while crossing seven concentric circles, each described by a set of eight shrines dedicated to him, there are fifty-six shrines in the city dedicated to Ganesha (Eck 1983:182). Parry (1994) argues that this suggests the yogic idea that, to attain union with God, an adept's life force should cross through seven circles ranging along his spine (Parry 1994:16). Thus, it can be seen that the geography and architecture of Kashi have been linked with cosmology to justify its supreme position and provide it with a form of spiritualized and sacred geography. Even though the whole of Kashi was defaced by invaders around six times, there are no remains before the seventeenth century, which was during the time of Aurangzeb's reign (Eck 1983:32).

Kashi *Khands*

Generally, cremation grounds in India are considered the most polluted and inauspicious places that should be avoided. Hence, these are often located on the periphery of villages. Even the people dealing with dead bodies are termed inferior due to their contact with the corpses. However, death is celebrated in Kashi, and its cremation *ghats* are considered auspicious places. Kashi is known as the great cremation *ghat*, as here, the five significant elements (air, water, earth, fire and ether) that compose the world come together in the form of corpses (Kane 1973:4:627). Here, not only does the 'genesis of the universe occur at the beginning of time, but the corpses of creation will also burn at the end of time' (Parry 1994:14). *Kashi Khanda* explains the 'etymology' of the word *shmashana*.

> *Shma* means shava, a corpse. *Shana* means *Shayana*, a 'bed'. Thus, do those who are skilled in the meaning of words say about the meaning of *shmashana*. When the general discourse comes, even great beings sleep here, having become corpses. Thus, the *shmashana* is called 'great'.
>
> (KKh 30:103–4 cited in Eck 1983:33)

Manikarnika Ghat is the most famous of all the cremation *ghats* and is referred to as *Mahashamshana* (great cremation ground), as here pyres burn round the clock without extinguishing.

Thus, the process of creation and destruction is continuously performed. Myths facilitate elevating a superior position for Manikarnika Ghat and Harishchandra Ghat above the other cremation *ghats*. Additionally, physical locations like *Manikarnika*

Kund,[18] *Charan Paduka* and continuous confirmations from ritual specialists facilitate these mythologies.

Kashi has been divided into three major *Khands* (divisions), and each of the three *Khands* holds a supreme position in mythology. The famous cremation *ghats*, Harishchandra Ghat and Manikarnika Ghat, fall within these *Khands*. Myths describe an important relationship between Lord Shiva and Kashi. It is believed that Shiva loves Kashi and has never forsaken it. Due to this, it is also known as *Avimukta*. It is also called Anandakanana/Anandavana (Forest of Bliss) because it was a blissful forest when Shiva decided to stay in Kashi.

According to *Kashi Khanda*, Kashi is believed to stand on the trident of Lord Shiva and is not attached to the earth but suspended in the sky. During the time of cosmic dissolution, Shiva lifts it from the rest of the world. Hence, it exists beyond time and space (Eck 1983:24). The two outer prongs of Shiva trident hold two important temples: the Kedar temple in the southern extreme and the Omkareshwar Mahadev temple in the northern extreme. The shaft of the trident is implanted below the Vishwanath temple, which stands on the middle prong of the trident (Parry 1994:17). Thus, Kashi is divided into these three *Khands*: Kedar *Khand*, Vishveshvara *Khand* and Omkara *Khand* (Eck 1983:357). Here, Kashi is again linked with the cosmos, as the three prongs of the trident are said to represent the three qualities of which all substances are composed, along with the three worlds: heaven, earth and the netherworld (Parry 1994:17).

Here, the distinctions between these *Khands* become important, as, out of these *Khands*, it is believed that those who die in Kedar *Khand* are granted immediate and unconditional salvation, as mentioned by Parry (1994:18). The Harishchandra Ghat, the focal cremation *ghat* of this study, falls in the Kedar *Khand.* According to *Kashi Kedara Mahatmya:*

Myth 7

> Kedarnath temple in the Himalayas provided liberation to devotees who visited it, but as it was too far, it was visited by fewer devotees. On the other hand, the Kedar temple in Kashi was visited by many

> pilgrimages. At the request of one of his devotees, Shiva provides the boon that those who visit the Kedar temple of Kashi will receive equal fruit from visiting the Kedarnath temple in the Himalayas. Other Gods protested to Shiva that if liberation is granted to all who just see the Kedar temple, then heaven will be overcrowded. Shiva agreed to it and said that only those who die in the Kedar sector of the city will attain liberation unconditionally. And these people would not have to reap the results of their past *karmas* through the hand of Bhairava before attaining *moksha*.
>
> (Eck 1983:143)

Therefore, those staying in this section of the city and aware of this *Mahatmya* consider it to be the best part of the city for dying (Eck 1983). If Kashi is treated as a sacred microcosm of India, Kedar is a microcosm of Kashi (Eck 1983). Moreover, there has been contestation over the supremacy of Harishchandra Ghat and Manikarnika Ghat as the original and oldest cremation *ghats*. *Kedar Mahatmya* fixed the site of the original Manikarnika Ghat at Kedara temple on the steps of Gauri *Kund*, and it is referred to as Adi Manikarnika, the first Manikarnika Ghat, thus claimed to be the greatest bathing *tirthas* (Eck 1983:144). There has been also an argument that the linga of the Kedara temple is older than the Vishwanath temple, which is confirmed by the *Puranas* (Eck 1983:143).

People residing in Kedar *Khand* of the city believe Harishchandra Ghat to be the oldest cremation *ghat*, surpassing even Manikarnika Ghat. Eck argues that the 'Pandit of Assi *Ghat* and Brahmins residing at Tulsi Ghat will definitely choose Harishchandra Ghat for cremation' (Eck 1983:225). One of the respondents, a temple priest, describes the importance of Harishchandra Ghat and Manikarnika Ghat as follows:

> The important point is the presence of the Tarakeshwar temple at Manikarnika Ghat. Here, the linga is worshipped daily with the ashes of the first cremated body. The second point is the presence of Manikarnika Kund just beside the Manikarnika Ghat. There are some stories about it, but I have not read anything that certifies their

> authenticity. Some people say that one earring of Goddess Parvati fell in that Kund, and because of this, the importance of Manikarnika increased. You can also notice at Manikarnika Ghat that the Ganges stream turns eastward from the north at that specific point, which is Manikarnika Ghat. Kashi is considered holy as the Ganges flows from the north direction to the east here, but the specific location where it turns is considered to be more sacred. If we talk about Harishchandra Ghat, Raja Harishchandra himself cremated bodies here. All the Gods, including Dharmaraj, appeared here to give their blessings. That is why this *ghat* is also essential.

A funeral priest who worked at both cremation *ghats* explains it this way:

> Raja Harishchandra Ghat is more widely recognized for salvation; the *Massan Nath* temple is also located here. Although more people visit Manikarnika Ghat, they often come from rural areas because, according to tradition, a dead body should not cross over a cremation ground. It is also evident why more people choose Manikarnika Ghat—because it is cheaper. There, for 3,200 rupees, a complete cremation can be performed, whereas here (Harishchandra Ghat), it costs over 6,000 rupees. Although I was not born at that time, I have heard that the original Manikarnika Ghat was earlier located in the Maidagin area and was later shifted to its current location. However, Raja Harishchandra Ghat has been at its present site since the beginning.

Both these *ghats* become important as many landmarks described in myths are located here. In myth, Manikarnika *Kund* has been described as a place where Vishnu performed austerities for ages. There is a small representation of his feet is inscribed on the marble which is referred as Charan paduka. It is believed that the original site is at the Manikarnika Ghat, but some people believe that the original cremation site was located elsewhere and then shifted later, as mentioned above in the narrative of a funeral priest. Additionally, as *Kedar Mahatmya* fixes the original site of Manikarnika Ghat at the Kedara temple, the authenticity of the exact location becomes questionable. At Harishchandra Ghat, a similar *charan paduka* has been constructed, and the charges for cremation at this spot are high. One wealthy customer paid a total cost of 20,000 rupees for performing cremation there. The area was decorated with rangoli designs over which the pyre was arranged.

Another important landmark is the *Massan Nath* temple. Dom pointed out that it was established by Raja Harishchandra when he was denied entry into the Vishwanath temple because he was serving Kalu Dom. As these landmarks hold mythical beliefs, their physical presence in these spaces at the cremation *ghat* attracts more devotees. Hence, this results in profitable business for the people earning their livelihood at these *ghats*.

Further, there has been a clear demarcation of areas within Banaras city, and accordingly, people prefer one of the cremation *ghats* closer to their locality. People residing in the areas near Kedar *Khand* or in the southern direction of the Kashi Vishwanath temple prefer Harishchandra Ghat, while people staying on the other side of the temple, including those residing in the rural areas of Banaras, prefer Manikarnika Ghat as it is the closest.

Thus, the cosmology of the city, linked with mythologies, attributes Kashi's position as a provider of salvation. These instances help us understand how myths promote and preserve these traditions. As a result, people come here to reap the benefits of salvation through *Kashi-vaas* or *Kashi-labh*.

On the question of whether death in Kashi guarantees liberation or can be attained through *Kashi-vaas*, Parry (1994) argued that the vital breath leaves one's body during the ritual of *kapal-kriya* (breaking of the skull). Hence, death does not occur after the cessation of the physiological functioning of the body but after the release of the vital breath. Thus, according to this theory, all those cremated in Kashi can attain liberation (Parry 1994:181).

Parry raised fundamental questions in the context of attaining salvation merely by dying in Kashi, as it implies that one's *karma* does not play any role in the process. Secondly, the role of the ritual specialist in conducting death rites becomes irrelevant. Even the position of God is subverted, as if all people dying in Kashi attain salvation or liberation, then who will make offerings? (Parry 1994:27–8). This problem is solved for those who believe Kashi is present within one's heart and that 'it is by reaching internal *tirtha* that *mukti* is attained'. For *Karma*, it is argued that one soul must suffer immediately after death before attaining liberation. But the underlying contradiction cannot be quickly resolved (Parry 1994:30).

Thus, myth plays a crucial part in strengthening beliefs and leads to the glorification of Kashi as the city of salvation. The sacred geography and specialists constitute major elements of the sacred complex, which are sustained by traditions of sacred myths. The following section will link the roles of ritual specialists as facilitators in helping souls attain salvation further, and how these different ritual specialists use these myths to earn a livelihood. They are engaged in power dynamics at the cremation *ghat*, along with their claims of superiority compared to others.

Death Industry

The popularity of Kashi as a pilgrimage destination facilitates a majority of people in earning a livelihood. The pilgrimage industry of Kashi engages around three-quarters of the residents of Kashi (Saraswati 1975:45). While using the term 'death industry' to describe the expanding death business in Banaras, it is understood that the meaning of death and salvation cannot be solely reduced to the economic aspect, as it also involves a spiritualized landscape (Kashi), specific ritual specialists and religious beliefs. This necessitates an extensive investigation of the synergy between both the ritual and economic domains in the death industry in modern times, as will be discussed.

In Western countries, the death industry is a recognized service industry, but this is not the case in India. Here, death is a collective representation of relatives, family and friends. Everyone participates in the execution of death rites whereas it remains a personal affair in Britain, as expressed by Laungani, 'it appears that crematoria in Britain are designed to conceal funerals rather than express them' (Laungani 1997:69).

In India, after death, the body is immediately removed from the bed and placed on the ground. This practice is not allowed in hospitals in Britain or Canada. After death, funeral directors keep the body in the mortuary until the day of cremation. The time and day of cremation are arranged by the funeral authorities rather than by the priest or family members. Family members have no role in the last rites of bathing, anointing and dressing the body (Laungani 1997:68). There the appearance of Hindu funerals resembles the funeral of Christians, where undertakers are dressed in black and bring the body in a coffin to the crematorium, and bereaved family members cannot be the pallbearers (Laungani 1997).

In Canada, too, funeral facilities do not allow indoor fires with hymns and *agni* offerings. The physical contact with the offerings and funeral pyres is expressed there through a mere token gesture. *Ghee* is placed over the body, a drop of water is put in the mouth and the body is placed in a casket. Instead of a dead body, the coffin becomes visible in the furnace (Coward 2000:156).

In both Canada and Britain, it is the funeral directors who have sole responsibility for the cremation. The experience there is more abstract and distant for mourners, as they can 'see nothing, hear nothing, and feel nothing; there is just the dull realisation that their loved one is cremated by an anonymous, faceless bureaucratic fiat' (Laungani 1997:198–9).

Only if some orthodox Hindu families are wealthy can they afford to fly back to India or send cremated remains to be immersed in the holy waters of the Ganges River (Laungani 1997; Parry 1994).

Unlike these countries, in India, relatives prepare the dead body for cremation by washing and anointing it with oil, dressing it, providing a shoulder to the bier, and carrying it to the cremation ground. A funeral pyre is arranged in an open space near the bank of a river, followed by the cremation and the immersion of the ashes into the flowing water.

In recent years, there has been an advent of funeral services in India. The Covid-19 pandemic has accelerated their growth. Here, similar to Western countries, funeral services are making all the necessary arrangements required for cremation, including ingredients for the last rites, a funeral priest, an obituary, funeral memorial decor that includes hearse van decor, coffin/freezer box decor, cremation ground decor, prayer hall decor and catering services. There are different costs per service; for instance, silver service costs 15,000 rupees, gold costs 25,000 rupees and platinum costs 35,000 rupees.[19]

The service details are mentioned on their online websites, along with contact information. Some of these funeral services are: (a) Anthyesti Funeral Service, founded by Shruthi Reddy, has a main branch in Bangalore and has been operating for the past seven years. It has covered six major cities: Banaras, Bangalore, Delhi, Hyderabad, Kolkata and Pune. After the pandemic, it had thirty-five competitors.[20] It provided funeral services to over 5,000 customers in the last seven years, (b) Kashi Moksha Incorporation,[21] with its website named Kashimoksha.com, provides devotees with the facility to send their deceaseds' ashes through the post to Banaras. One of the pandits performs the *asthi-visarjan* (immersion of ashes in the river) and shares a video of the ceremony with the family, (c) other digital death care includes Last Journey, Mokshashil and Shardhanjali.com.

Taking this into consideration, along with the working dynamics of the cremation *ghats* of Banaras, the death industry can be understood as a form of service industry. Stanton (1984) defines the service industry as:

> Services are those separate, identifiable, essentially intangible activities that provide want satisfaction and are not necessarily tied to the sale of a product or another service to produce a service, that may or may not require the use of tangible goods. However, when

> such use is required, there is no transfer of title of these tangible goods.
>
> (Stanton 1984:568)

Parry (1981), in *Death and Cosmogony in Kashi*, argues that 'the transcendental identity of Kashi is both seen and promoted by the sacred specialists who earn their livelihood on or around the burning *ghats* of the city' (Parry 1981:337). Different castes are involved in earning their livelihood through direct or indirect means from the death business. Moreover, the presence of technology at the *ghat* marks a shift from traditional practices towards modernity.

In present times, people are investing in the business of death to earn profit through funeral services, such as Yadav, Thakur or the founder of Anthyesti Funeral Service mentioned above. The cost of cremation services and the profit earned through them are higher in comparison to those earned by the Dom, yet it is the latter who are criticized as the *one profiting from the dead*. Moreover, although a shift can be seen in the involvement of different castes in the business of death and the emergence of crematoriums as part of modernity, it is still the lower caste that cremates dead bodies and deals with polluted substances.

In India, this work has been ascribed to a particular caste group due to its stigmatized nature. Handling corpses is associated with the notion of contamination and is viewed as 'dirty work' (Ashforth and Kreiner 2013; Turner and Caswell 2020). This dirty work removes the filth (corpses) and hence becomes a necessity for the proper functioning of society (Douglas 1966:199). When a funeral worker disposes of a dead body, he comes into contact with four forms of impurity (physical, social, emotional and moral), resulting in stigmatization (Ashforth and Kreiner 1999; Jordan, McMurray and Ward 2019; Thompson 1991).

As funeral workers serve another person, the dead body becomes a means of monetary gain, making it socially and morally objectionable (Bailey 2016:164). The work of handling dead bodies and profiting from death – that is, the misfortune of others – further contributes to stigmatization (Thompson 1991:411).

The death industry in India stands at $3.5 billion.[22] People working here treat it as a workspace rather than merely viewing it as a sacred place. Saraswati (1975) put it:

> What is more revealing about the sacred complex is that those who are professionally involved in it consider sacred as a mere means of livelihood and not something to be treated in a special manner. This attitude towards the sacred is discerned by any conscious observer visiting the temple or observing priests conducting rituals Saraswati (1975:45).

It becomes evident from one of my conversations with a Dom, who admitted that 'we pray to God for more people to die so that our stove keeps burning'. This statement points to the constrained situation where they are forced to have a meal from the misfortunes of others. But it also highlights the economic aspect and their attitude towards their work.

The death industry of Banaras has characteristics of a service industry, such as intangibility, inseparability, heterogeneity, perishability and ownership (Stanton 1984:569). But, it differs from the market economy as it is regulated by traditional values and beliefs, thus providing it with a distinct position.

Further, the 'social organisation of death reflects the way in which death is symbolically constructed' (Parry 1994:3). The economic activities of the death business function based on the rotation system rather than Jajmani, as people prefer short-term ties with workers dealing with death (Parry 1994:75). The rotation system and functioning of the death economy are different from those of the modern market, as 'the business of death is clearly not running on the principles of business economics' (Parry 1994:113). Moreover, the idea of reinvestment seems missing.

In addition, there has been an effort to stop technological intervention, as it affects the livelihood of workers who are engaged in manual labour. People involved in the death industry view technology as a potential competitor that offers numerous benefits to consumers (mourners), as the work performed by machines is cost-effective, efficient, consumes less time and minimizes environmental pollution.

The death economy of Banaras is an unorganized sector that requires unskilled and casual labourers. This industry is organized based on social institutions of caste and gender. The majority of the workers engaged in manual labour here live in poverty (Gooptu and White 2001:90). In the death industry, 'capitalism is not dissolving the matrix of social institutions but reconfiguring them slowly, unevenly, and in a great diversity of ways' (Gooptu and White 2001). Due to this, in an urban space, it is acting as a lever of traditional status and sentiments, often emphasizing caste differences as the remaining centre of communication and socialization for the next generations (Lynch 1969:44).

Lastly, the profit-making notion within this industry became evident during the Covid-19 waves, as families were unable to afford the exponential price rise. Due to the higher cost of cremation and the shortage of wood, some bodies were half-cremated and then dumped in rivers (Kumari 2023:1444).

Taking into consideration both the ritual and economic aspects, it can be understood to be a service industry that retains some features of traditional caste society. Due to the belief in salvation, the death industry has continuously evolved. The increase in the glorification of Kashi has been facilitated by ritual specialists and religious texts such as the *Puranas* (Bayly 1981:156). The next section elaborates on the working aspects of this industry.

Social Sphere of Cremation *Ghat*

To understand how the sacred cremation *ghat*s of Kashi serve as a working space for the death industry and act as a prosperous means of earning a livelihood, it is important to have general information about the workings of the cremation *ghat* at Harishchandra Ghat (see Figure 3.1).

As mourners carrying a dead body on a bamboo bier reach the cremation *ghat*, chanting *Ram Naam Satya Hai* (the name of God is the ultimate truth), they pass by many saree shops, restaurants and hotel rooms. The road is quite crowded due to the presence of rickshaws, automobiles, cows and dogs. Many men can be seen walking in groups to take a break and have a cup of tea or chew betel nuts. While walking, one needs to be careful, as one's foot might accidentally step on a heap of cow dung in the middle of the road.

The moment they reach the crossroads, groups of males from the Dom will be standing there. They can be of any age, from twelve to forty-five years old. There is a *boli* system (verbal claim) in which the person who first shouts *matti* when he sets his eyes on the bier accompanied by mourners will get the right to deal with the customer. Often, three to four boys will join this person in dealing with customers so that they can get a share.

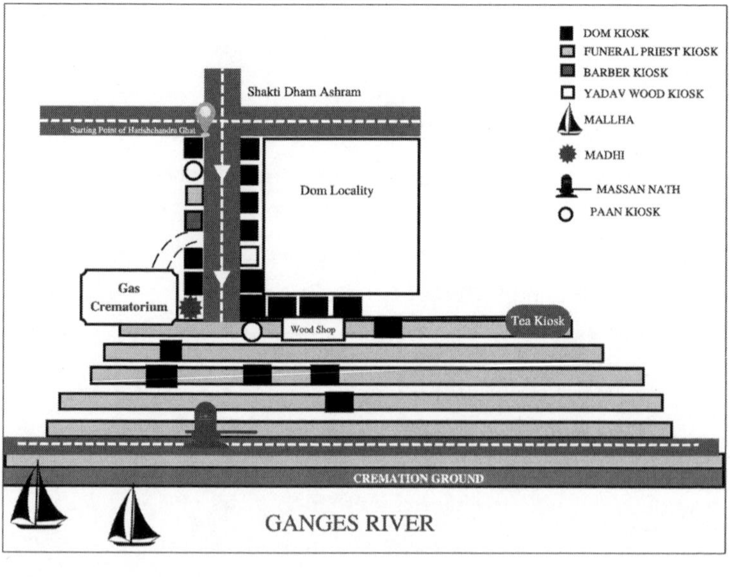

Figure 3.1 Working space of Harishchandra Ghat.

From this point onward, one can see many kiosks set up adjacent to one another. There are a total of thirty-one kiosks at Harishchandra Ghat. In these, the Dom stores essential items required for final rites, such as bamboo biers, shrouds and materials like *ghee*, red vermilion and incense sticks. The Dom estimates the family's economic status after acquiring general information regarding the dead body, such as the deceased's residence and the reason for death, along with other key information. He will inform the cost of cremation, which will be directly based on the estimated economic status of the customer. He will then inform them about different kinds of *theka* (services) and the facilities available within those services. Sharing one such incident:

After catching a customer, Bhola (Dom) explained that they would provide mango wood or sandalwood, fire, and one mazdoor to arrange and burn the pyre. It would cost around 10,000 rupees. But the mourner refused to pay this amount. Bhola further mentioned that, out of this total, 650 rupees would be the fee for the worker to burn the body, and this amount also included charges for wood and fire. While the bargaining was still ongoing, Sikander (Dom) intervened and said, 'For 10,000 rupees, they would provide wood to burn the body, fire, and one mazdoor. However, this amount would not include essential items required for funerals, such as ghee and roli, which could be purchased from his shop. Additionally, the mourner would have to pay the fees for the barber and the funeral priest out of pocket, as these were not included in the theka.' The mourner stated that he would only pay 7,000 rupees. Sikander then said that 7,200 rupees was the final amount.

Then the body is taken to the bank of the Ganges and placed with its feet pointing towards the east in such a way that half of the body is immersed in the river. Then all of the mourners take Ganges water in their hands and pour it over the mouth of the deceased five times. After that, the person who has verbally claimed this customer goes to the Yadav shop at the cremation *ghat*. Here, according to the deceased's family desires, such as five or seven *maunds*, wood is purchased. Meanwhile, the workers of Yadav handle the measuring and transfer of logs of wood, and the Dom *naukar* engages in arranging the pyre. A barber is approached, who tonsures the head of the chief mourner.

Then the chief mourner is sent to the *madhi* to fetch the sacred fire. If any *theka* is not accepted, then negotiations take place regarding the charge for the sacred fire. The Dom-Raja, the owner of the cremation *ghat*, will demand a high price for the fire depending on the condition of the family.[23] After the fire had been brought and the body placed over the pyre, a funeral priest[24] would come and talk with mourners and gather their details. He, along with the Dom, will ask the chief mourner to provide *mukhagni* to the body after completing five circumambulations of the pyre.

Then, mourners will rest in the sitting space available at the cremation *ghat* and observe the procedure of cremation performed by the Dom *naukar*. The act of cremation is called the 'ritual of burning' and the culmination of the 'last ritual' because it 'marks the closure of the series of rituals concerning the human body' (Madan 1987:135–6).

Some of the mourners drink tea at the tea stalls. Meanwhile, other mourners discuss how and when the person died and when and how they came to know about it. Other Dom males go back to the crossroads to look for other customers, while the Dom *naukars* to whom this body was allotted come and stroke the body with a bamboo shaft from time to time so that it can burn completely. Then, he calls the chief mourner to perform *kapal kriya* which involves hitting the skull with the bamboo. After around three hours, when the body has almost burned completely, a small piece of the body stump (*shesh*) remains unburnt.[25] The mourner offers that body mass into the flowing Ganges 'as the seed of future renewal' (Parry 1994:50). Then he circumambulates the cremated remains of the deceased with a pot kept on his shoulder filled with water and ends it by breaking the pot. This broken pot symbolizes the breaking of ties between the chief mourner and the dead person. The Dom man asks him to write

94 on the ashes, and my respondent informed me that '94 karmas are for Lord Rama and the rest are our own'. The numbers 9 and 4 resemble the shape of Vishnu's conch and shell (Parry 1994:177).

After this, mourners leave Harishchandra Ghat to go to a nearby *ghat*, which is Shivala Ghat, via the stairs, and bathe there. Then, they go to an eatery shop to have some refreshments and finally leave for their homes.

The above description portrays the division of labour at the cremation *ghat* among different occupational specialists. All of these castes have a *pari* system that contributes to the proper functioning of this workspace. Among these specialists, the Dom handles the deceased's physical remains, and the funeral priest deals with the marginal ghost (Parry 1994:75). Thus, the presence of these specialists is crucial for performing rites and rituals related to death.

Though each specialist has a specific role in the death industry, allotted based on their caste, the presence of conflict within these caste groups cannot be underestimated. These ritual specialists derive the importance of their occupation from the sacredness attached to Kashi. They use this sacredness as a tool for achieving the means of their livelihood, higher status and respect in society. Some of the ritual specialists continuing their caste-based occupations at the cremation *ghat* are the Dom, Mahapatra, Barber and Mallah castes.

Parry (1994) discussed in detail these ritual specialists who earn a livelihood by working at the cremation *ghat* through the *pari* system. He agreed with Dumont that 'the division of labour between castes is oriented towards the whole rather than toward the quest for individual profit institutionalised by the modern market', but there is a 'ruthless pursuit of egoistic advantages in which big fish swallow the little ones' (Parry 1994:115).

Table 3.1 provides a list of different kinds of work in which other caste groups are involved in the death industry.

Dom, as a specialist, neutralizes the danger emanating from dead bodies by cremating the physical remnants of the corpse. The barber separates the mourner from the living by tonsuring his head. The

Table 3.1 Service caste of cremation *ghat.*

Caste	Work	Price
Dom	• *Malik*: ownership of *ghat* • Manager: manages the workings of the *ghat.* • *Naukar*: burns corpses • Factor: measure wood for cremation under the Yadav caste. • deal with customers	• Sacred fire – above 1,300 rupees • Managing 10 per cent of total earnings. • Factor – ₹800 per day • Burning, sieving ashes, cleaning the ground – 650 rupees per body.
Mahapatra/ Funeral Priest	• performs last rites	• above 2,000 rupees
Nau/Barber	• tonsures head	• 100 rupees per person
Mallah/ Boatman	• ferries corpses for immersion	• between 1,500 and 2,000 rupees
Ahir/Yadav	• sells funeral wood	• 440 rupees for 40 kilograms

funeral priest acts as a mediator between the mourner and liminal entities and converts the malevolent ghost into ancestors (Kaushik 1976:288). Here, Yadavs are not engaged in their caste occupation and instead sell wood required for cremation.

The next section provides an account of these caste groups and attempts to provide an estimated period from when these castes worked at Harishchandra Ghat and, through it, tries to understand their respective claims of authority at the *ghat*. Details about the Dom have been elaborated on in the previous chapter. Besides them, another of the important ritual specialists in the death industry is the Mahapatra. Parry (1994) elaborated in depth on their *pari* system at Manikarnika Ghat. The Mahapatras working at Harishchandra Ghat had migrated from the Azamgarh district many years ago. Now, they have permanent residences in the Padao area (Banaras) with around 150 households.

They have distributed the *pari* for the areas of Barna/Varuna Ghat, Harishchandra Ghat, and Manikarnika Ghat. Among them, the *pari* starts with the sunrise. My informant has a total of three *paris* in a year, which are managed jointly by his family members. In a single day, they have *pari* at all *ghats* simultaneously. One of the three *paris* comes after ten months and twenty-four days, lasting for just one day.

In case anyone needs money, they can borrow it by keeping their *pari* on a lease, like Dom. The mechanism of keeping a *pari* on a leash is that half of the earnings belong to the person who gave the money, and the actual owner of the *pari* keeps the rest.

The Mahapatra usually sits at the cremation *ghat* and uses a notebook to jot down the details of the deceased's family, including the address and contact information. A list of only those bodies arriving from the boundary of Banaras city is made, with the dates on which further rites will be performed. On the tenth day after death, the Mahapatra will go to that house and perform *pinda-dan.*[26]

Besides looking at one's *pari*, there are other options too, such as working under those Mahapatras who have the maximum number of *pari*; these are referred to as *patidars* at Manikarnika Ghat. There are around twelve Mahapatras working under these *patidars.* It is done in two phases: in the first, a worker will sit at the cremation *ghat* on the *pari* of his *patidar* and jot down records of all bodies coming there. After providing all the information to *the patidar*, he will receive 25 per cent of the total earnings for that day.

Another phase is that on the tenth day, the *patidar* sends some Mahapatras to the houses of mourners to perform the ritual, for which they receive 10 per cent of the earnings. After returning, everyone shares the amount earned with the *patidars,* and then the profits are divided.

Mahapatra only goes to the house that has invited him on the day of cremation to preside over the offering of five rice balls made between the doors of the home and the funeral pyre. On the tenth day, the body of the *preta* is complete, it is fed, and it is ready to become an ancestor (Parry 1980:94). Besides these, Mahapatra at the cremation *ghat* also performs rituals to pacify the death which occurred at the time of *panchak*[27] or to perform *Narayani Bali*[28] in case of untimely death, and also the rites of *putla vidhan* is conducted in which an effigy of the deceased is made with flour, and is then cremated. It is performed for those dead bodies which were not found or were immersed in the Ganges River (Parry 1980:95).

Barber also continued their family tradition of caste-based occupation for many years. At Harishchandra Ghat, the barber had migrated some forty years ago with his family from a rural area of Banaras. For the past three generations, this barber has held onto the Harishchandra Ghat, and only this family has the right to this *ghat*, unlike at the Manikarnika Ghat, where the *pari* system also works among barbers (Parry 1994:93). Not all mourners accompanying dead bodies are tonsured, as some people from rural areas bring their own barbers. Mostly, the chief mourner is tonsured before cremating the body, and the rest of the family members will tonsure their hair after the tenth day of the death, so the majority of mourners perform this rite in their respective villages.

Mallah also earns a livelihood through the death ritual, in which bodies and the ashes of cremated individuals are immersed in the waters of the River Ganges. These immersed bodies, forbidden from cremation, are those of ascetics (Sadhu Baba), pregnant women, children below the age of five, and persons who died from smallpox or snake bite.

The allocation of rights among the Mallah has occurred over the last three generations, specifically since 1900. There are two main categories in the work system of boatmen: the first is resident boatmen (*ghatwars*), who have the right to operate boats at a particular *ghat*. The second category consists of non-resident boatmen (*Mallahsi* or drivers) of that *ghat*, who work as casual labourer under the *ghatwars* (Doron 2013:98).

The distinctive feature of their *pari* system is that, unlike Dom and Mahapatra, they cannot sell or rent their rights on the *ghat* to another boatman (Doron 2013:102). The *ghatwar* who has the right at Harishchandra Ghat is Sonu, a middle-aged man in his early forties. His family has been here since his great-grandfather's time. A ten-day rotation has been assigned in this *pari* for each brother within his family for immersing the dead bodies and ashes in the Ganges. But there is no *pari* for taking tourists on a ride.

Besides these, there is the presence of the Yadav caste owning businesses that supply wood required for cremation. This caste operates three shops at Harishchandra Ghat. They also follow a *pari* system, where each brother manages the business for a period of ten days. At Manikarnika Ghat, the wood business is dominated by Yadavs and Thakurs. There are a total of sixteen wood shops located at Manikarnika Ghat. In addition to these, tea kiosks and betel shops are present at both cremation *ghats*. Thus, all of these castes earn their livelihood through the death industry of Banaras.

A brief description of the caste groups that perform their ascribed occupations has been provided. The ritual specialists are essential for the proper functioning of the death industry in Banaras. The following section deals with the caste dynamics by examining the everyday interactions among these castes at the cremation *ghat*.

Caste Dynamics at the Cremation *Ghat*

The functioning of the death industry often encounters many disputes among different castes working at the Harishchandra Ghat. The major problem is interference by other castes in one's working domain. The decrease in the number of dead bodies at Harishchandra Ghat because of the higher cost of cremation has further exasperated workers. Unlike the Manikarnika Ghat, where the state has fixed the price, making the cremation process affordable for people across different sections.

For the proper functioning of the death industry, mourners and the Dom are crucial for the performance of cremation rites. Among ritual specialists, funeral priests and barbers have distinct work domains that reduce the chances of conflict with other caste groups working at the cremation *ghat*.

But the Dom, Mallah and Yadav castes have to interact with each other regularly. The Yadav sell wood for cremation, the Dom cremate bodies and the Mallah immerse bodies and ashes in the river. As interactions within these castes are higher, so are the chances of conflicts.

At Harishchandra Ghat, the Mallah caste earns a living by ferrying dead bodies for immersion in the Ganges, for which they charge a minimal amount of 1,500 rupees. However, in recent days, they have observed a decrease in the number of corpses for immersion as well. For instance, the location of the cremation *ghat* at the centre of this city makes the performance of the last rites noticeable.

To keep a dead body out of the sight of Aghoris,[29] mourners prefer to cremate their loved ones at isolated *ghats* named Raj Ghat or Samane Ghat. This deprives the Mallah of a suitable source of income.

Moreover, they blamed the Dom's greed for their loss and mentioned that these days the latter are cremating bodies that should be immersed. They are also charging a price for every corpse, irrespective of the method chosen for the last rites, such as cremation in the crematorium, cremation via wood, or immersion of bodies and ashes. The range of their fees varies, as they demand around 2,100 rupees from families who opt for the immersion of ashes in the Ganges.[30] Quoting the Mallah informant directly here

> These people (Dom) will charge the mourner around 10,000 to 15,000 rupees for the funeral items, whose actual cost is just 5,000. If the customer requests that the amount be reduced, they will suggest purchasing the materials from another shop. 'From where will they purchase those materials?' All the Dom are united in this. Another shopkeeper will tell the customer that their items are of original quality and will provide a bill for 15,000 rupees. In this helpless situation, customers are forced to pay 15,000 rupees. Although bargaining can happen for merely 500 rupees, you can see how much profit they make.

There are cases of conflict within the Dom community too. Whenever a Dom tries to deal with an already-fixed customer of another, it often results in a fight. Often, the affluent Dom families maintain their monopoly at the *ghat*. Here, power lies in the hands of those having the maximum *pari*.

Disputes between customers and the Dom are also often encountered. Customers often take their relatives' corpses to the Manikarnika Ghat due to higher demand and inappropriate behaviour by the Dom. If the customer is from a poor background, they are victims of verbal abuse, but if they are from affluent families, it often leads to police complaints against the Dom. Shambu Chaudhary's (a Dom) *pari* rarely comes, so he works under the *pari* of his *malik* to earn a livelihood.

He shares an incident that reflects the reality of the working system at the cremation *ghat*.

> On March 14, a dead body arrived, and these people (Dom *Malik*) provided everything required for the cremation. Customers often do not know what is essential for the process. If you hand over any packet to them and say it is crucial, they will accept it. After the cremation, they presented a bill to the mourner. It was realized that the customer was poor and did not have the money to pay. My caste people created such a scene and insulted them to such an extent that the woman among the mourners had to sell her gold jewellery to pay the cremation costs, after which they were allowed to leave.

There have been instances of police involvement in resolving disputes at cremation *ghats*. But when they are peeved that the voices of the Dom community remain unheard, they halt the cremation of dead bodies as a means of protest, after which the administration is compelled to act. This form of protest has even been employed at Manikarnika Ghat by Yadavs and Thakurs, particularly when officials ordered them to vacate illegally occupied land to construct the Vishwanath corridors. They protested by refusing to sell wood to mourners for cremation. Ultimately, these castes were compensated and instructed to store their wood supplies on boats in the Ganges. On this particular day, Harishchandra Ghat witnessed the cremation of around 250 bodies.

At Manikarnika Ghat, there is the dominance of the upper-caste group; at Harishchandra Ghat, there is the dominance of the Dom. Sharing another incident of tension between the police and the Dom, the Dom *naukar* recounted:

> It was monsoon season in 2013, and as the cremation *ghat* was submerged in river water, bodies were burned in the small area near our houses. Some mourners might have complained to the government authorities because there was no space to cremate the bodies. 'People should charge the rightful amount, but here, if the cost of wood is 6,000, they will demand 15,000 rupees.' So, people from municipal corporations came with police in plain clothes to check the situation, and they started removing our funeral kiosks. Only one policeman was on our side. They broke down two to three of our kiosks, and in return, we broke down their cars. Then the police arrested our people. The media came and covered the incident as we halted the burning of dead bodies, and eventually, the matter was resolved. At that time, authorities planned that a structure similar to the one at Manikarnika Ghat should be constructed here too, so that bodies could be burned easily during floods. However, Jamuna Devi refused to give her land to the government, so nothing happened.[31]

At Manikarnika Ghat, the business of selling funeral items, wood for cremation, dealing with customers, and providing the *theka* is handled mainly by the Yadav and Thakur communities. A Dom *naukar* working there said, 'We cannot deny burning bodies; if we do, it results in physical violence, and no one comes forward to support us.' Though the Dom treat the Chamar as inferior to themselves, under the shield of the upper caste, the Chamar command Dom *naukars* to fetch tobacco for them. One exasperated Dom *naukar* used abusive words to address them and told that 'these (Chamar) people even steal dead body ashes at night and remove jewellery. We cannot even question them for this.'

There was a time when the Yadavs feared the late Kailash Chaudhary, but after his demise, they expanded their complete authority. Kaushik (1979) shared an incident from her fieldwork where the Yadavs tried to encroach on the business of the Dom at

Manikarnika Ghat. Generally, the Dom provide fire by placing it on the *Sanai* (a kind of dry reed). One day, a shop owned by the Yadavs that supplied wood for cremation also started providing the *Sanai*. When one of the Dom's *naukars* argued with them, a fight broke out, leading to police intervention. The Dom was beaten up by the police. When the late Kailash Chaudhary heard about it, he ordered his *naukars* not to supply the sacred fire as a means of protest during his *pari* and said that 'people could take sacred fire from Ahir shopkeeper who had taken the supply of *Sanai*' (Kaushik 1979:1:37). As pandemonium broke out at the Manikarnika Ghat, the district magistrate intervened and restored the Dom's right to sell *Sanai*.

Though at Harishchandra Ghat, the Dom community has been able to maintain its authority because of its unity, this does not indicate any change in its social status, as they are still discriminated against and referred to as '*Chandala*'. The urban space provides an opportunity for them to interact with other caste groups, but it does not help them evade caste stigma. An informant from the Mallah caste asked me, 'Have you ever seen any upper-caste friends at any of their (Dom) marriage ceremonies? They would not come to these people's houses.' In rural areas, the Dom are not allowed to enter the houses of other castes. They must sit on the ground, maintaining a distance from members of other castes. A person running a tea stall at Harishchandra Ghat mentioned, 'It does not matter how much money one has. Even in our village, if people come to know that we eat and drink with the Dom, our "*hukka pani*"[32] will stop.'

That the Dom of Harishchandra Ghat have unity does not imply that other caste groups accept their dominance. Earlier, the work of selling funeral wood at Harishchandra Ghat was managed by Kashi Chaudhary. However, he failed to maintain his control due to being an alcoholic, and Yadav took advantage and obtained the licence to sell wood. Yadav has been indulging in the practice of encroaching on the businesses of other castes through their muscle and money power. They even captured the licence of the Mallah for mining sand from the banks of the Ganges (Doron 2013:114). Recently, Yadav tried to sell funeral items at Harishchandra Ghat as well but failed due to the unity of the Dom.

Despite the continuous claims made by the Dom of being the Dom-Raja and Chaudhary[33] of the cremation *ghat*, the actual reality of power dynamics becomes evident during the monsoon. As the water level increases in the Ganges River, the overall space of the cremation *ghat* simultaneously gets submerged. The water slowly reaches the crossroads from where the Harishchandra Ghat begins. In the absence of space and in order to earn a livelihood, the Dom cremate bodies in a smaller area just within their locality (see Figure 3.2).

In short, a microform of the death industry shifts to their locality. They relocate the funeral items from kiosks to their houses. The cremation work is already quite challenging, but the continuous rain and the task of cremating bodies in a congested space make it worse. Furthermore, plumes of smoke and the smell of burning bodies entering their houses become unbearable.

They already live in inadequate conditions and often adjust to the minimal space available. Dom males prefer to sleep at the cremation *ghat* itself during other seasons, but they do not have any other options during floods.

Figure 3.2 Space of temporary cremation within the Dom locality.

A temporary shift of the cremation ground, along with the working spaces of other caste groups, to the Dom locality for a few months further increases their hardships. The workers of the Yadav caste move the wood logs and place them outside the street of the Dom locality. The betel nut shopkeeper also relocates his temporary shop and sets it up outside their door. Due to the unavailability of space, mourners sit and wait on their doorsteps, creating a hurdle for the Dom in entering and exiting their houses. The women of the Dom community are strictly advised to keep the doors locked and are even restricted from peeking through the windows. All these restrictions have to be observed despite the lack of proper ventilation in these houses.

Death Pollution Validating Caste Pollution

The ideological basis of the caste system is the distinction between purity and impurity, which facilitates the ranking of castes in a hierarchical order (Dumont 1970:76). These two concepts are complementary poles; they complement one another, and neither can be understood without the other. This distinction plays an important role in structuring the basic framework of Hindu society (Shah 2007:356).

The myth of the origin of the four *varnas* from the primeval man and their hierarchical division has been based on concepts of purity and impurity. The emergence of the Brahmin from the head, Kshatriyas from the arms, Vaishyas from the thighs, and Shudras from the feet primeval man reflects this hierarchy. The head has been considered purer than the feet, thus providing higher status to the Brahmins and the lowest to the Shudras, while excluding the inferior ones from the *varna* system itself. The primary reason for one's caste ranking and affiliation with being polluted or unpolluted is linked to their traditional occupation, which had been decided based on their origin from the part of the primeval man.

Within the complementary pole, pollution signifies involvement with life substances and processes that should be avoided, including birth, death and bodily excretions, whereas purity means, in any event, the absence of biological involvement (Orenstein 1968:115).

Purity can be understood as a relative and temporary state (Harper 1964:194). Thus, there are several rules and regulations followed in order to maintain it.[34] For instance, a clear distance should be maintained between pure and impure things, as polluted things can defile the pure, but pure things 'cannot flow as it is an impermanent state that can be lost but not transferred' (Harper 1964:194). Hence, often, mechanisms are evolved to protect one's state of purity by following the basic features of the caste system, which are to maintain separation from other caste groups and indulge in the division of labour that also leads to interdependence within these castes. As Brahmins need to maintain their purity and are at risk of getting defiled easily, certain caste groups are made to indulge in polluted work through which the purity of the upper caste could be maintained, which is important for the functioning of society.

Besides occupation, certain food habits had also been taboo, such as eating carrion, meat, and drinking liquor, which further deteriorated their status, because these foods are categorized as polluted due to a linkage with the impurity of animal death (Randeria 1989:183). The practice of discrimination has been an integral part of the complex of purity and impurity (Shah 2007:357).

Lower castes are often engaged in menial work, either by force or voluntary means. The marked presence of these castes in considered polluted occupations, such as scavenging animal bodies, the removal of night soil, and cremation, is notable. Additionally, the engagement of females from the lower castes in professional weeping during the mourning phase,[35] the role of midwives during childbirth, the washing of menstruation-soiled clothes by the washermen caste, the announcement of death by barbers, the playing of *dhol* by the Chamar caste in north India and Vettiyans in Tamil Nadu. These works stigmatized them as inferior.

This stigmatization is often unavoidable even if one leaves their caste occupation, as the ranking of one's caste is an ascribed status. But when upper castes perform the same acts, it confers temporary pollution on them. Harper (1964), in his work on Havik Brahmins, highlighted some crucial instances, which I am quoting here directly regarding the role of a Havik woman.

> If a Havik woman assists in the delivery or the bathing of the mother and her child, she may not accept payment. This is but one of several examples of work that a Brahmin may perform as a friendly gesture for other Havik, but for which to accept payment is tantamount to following a ritually impure occupation, the penalty for which is caste ex-communication.
>
> (Harper 1964:168)

If anyone performs work labelled as polluted as a form of service for others, it is considered polluted, but if someone performs the same work for himself, it is not considered polluted.

> Some jobs that were performed exclusively by untouchables no longer are like removing dead cattle, cleaning Brahmin cattle sheds, cleaning the drainage ditch between houses that carries away bath water and into which children urinate and adults spit betel juice, cutting firewood for a funeral pyre, and sweeping the public road in front of the brahmin house. In many instances, Brahmins now do these jobs for themselves but not for others.
>
> (Harper 1964:170)

The barbers are allotted a lower status because they shave hair and cut nails as a form of service for people of other castes, thereby removing impurity from the client. However, if a Brahmin performs the same act for himself, it is not considered polluted.

> For the past thirty or forty years, some Brahmins have been shaving themselves. It is said that about forty years ago, the caste guru attempted to outcaste a Havik who defied caste custom by shaving himself, but, so the story goes, the guru's learned advisors discovered passages in the *shastras* which convinced him that Brahmin could

> perform this task for themselves (but not for another) without incurring severe pollution.
>
> (Harper 1964:170)

It could be concluded that the determining factor in labelling any caste as polluted is not based solely on the nature of the occupation but is also determined by whether the work has been performed in service for other caste groups by charging payment for the same. But does the same rule apply in the case of the upper caste performing death rituals?

Brahmins mostly burn the bodies of their caste members, and members of the lower caste are not allowed to touch their corpses. A touch from a lower caste can defile the purity of the Brahmin corpse. This practice is common among orthodox Brahmins, as in rural areas of Banaras, people still cremate their deceased relatives by themselves. Here, the role of the Dom remains limited to providing the sacred fire and arranging the wood for the pyre. However, this occupation of the Dom makes them permanently polluted and, as a result, categorized them as inferior in status. Even in Tamil Nadu, the Vettiyan have left the occupation of cremation due to their upward social mobility; hence, upper castes are cremating their deceased themselves (Arun 2007:101). So how can one understand the basis of the allocation of different categories of pollution, i.e., temporary and permanent pollution, based on caste ranking, when both upper and lower castes burn dead bodies?

Two kinds of pollution, mentioned by Orenstein (1968), are relational pollution and act pollution.

(i) Relation pollution occurs when a death or birth happens in one's kin groups. The person is defiled for a period that is dependent on his genealogical distance from the deceased or newborn. Here, the defilement of the one is inversely proportional to his caste ranking. This means that the higher the ranking of one's caste, the shorter the period of defilement for the person, after which they can attain purity. (ii) Act pollution occurs when the person comes into contact with a biological phenomenon that could involve external or internal pollution. In this case, there is a proportional relationship between one's caste ranking and the period of defilement. Hence, the higher the ranking of one's caste, the longer the period of defilement (Orenstein 1968:117).

Does it not mean that Brahmins touching and cremating corpses should be more polluted than other castes? Marriott (1959) raised crucial points that the attributional theories of caste ranking failed to answer, and the above question is one of them. The interactional theory explains this, as for the Dom, it is an occupation in which they render their service to another caste group, and 'he takes on the pollution or otherwise demonstrates his inferiority by the service, thus lowering his own caste rank', whereas the 'Brahmin renders non-occupationally on their behalf for their own caste fellow', which does not involve any inter-caste action. Thus no subordination or pollution is added to the performer (Marriott 1959:98).

Further, there is an association between the hierarchy of the caste system and the rationale of purity and pollution, so adopting the rituals prescribed by the Brahmins will automatically affiliate one with the upper caste. Bayly (1981) mentioned:

> Special funerary priests called *mahabrahmins* conducted the ceremony of cremation, while monitors of the scavenging Dom handled the corpses and tended the fire. One consequence of the cremation itself was to perpetuate ranking within the caste system through proximity to the pollution of death. So, the position of the Dom scavengers at the bottom of the caste hierarchy was reinforced, while the cremation priests, absorbing the sins and death of the deceased through the 'sacrifice' of the dead body, assured themselves of the lowest positions among Brahmins.
>
> (Bayly 1981:159)

Though this argument justifies the presence of caste hierarchy based on one's proximity to death pollution, is it not contradictory that other caste groups are also in proximity to death pollution while cremating the corpses of their relatives themselves? Or does the continuous presence of the Dom at the cremation *ghat* make their status permanently polluted? Generally, inferior castes across India are forced to stay in peripheral areas on the southern side of the village near the cremation grounds so that other castes can maintain their purity; hence, does proximity to the cremation grounds facilitate the determination of caste ranking?

Another reason for stigmatizing the Dom as permanently polluted could be that they earn a livelihood through the rites and rituals related to the deaths of other castes. However, at the Manikarnika Ghat, even Thakurs and Yadavs earn a livelihood by engaging in the death business of selling wood for cremation. Yet, these castes practice untouchability with the Dom by not permitting them to drink water from the same glass, refusing to give betel nuts into their hands, and using physical violence and abusive language against them.

Sudhir Chaudhary (Dom) works at Harishchandra Ghat and occasionally visits Manikarnika Ghat to meet his relatives. He recalls that about two years ago, he was thirsty, so he drank water from a glass kept outside a shop for this purpose. In the meantime, another Dom *naukar*, who works permanently at Manikarnika Ghat, came and started talking with him. When he left, the shopkeeper became suspicious and asked Sudhir his name. The moment he said 'Sudhir Chaudhary', the shopkeeper angrily threw the glass from his shop and began verbally abusing him. The primary reason for this discrimination was his livelihood, which involved burning dead bodies and coming into contact with corpses. However, as mentioned earlier, even the Dom community considers touching corpses derogatory. Other caste groups also earn from the death industry. Hence, even though upper castes also indirectly earn money from the same source, only the Dom are stigmatized.

There is a presence of inter-hierarchy within lower castes as well. Those at the top of this stratum attempt to relate to the upper castes through the process of Sanskritization and discriminate against those at the lowest rung. Randeria's (1989) work in Gujarat highlighted the presence of an internal hierarchy among the lower castes: Garo (priests), Vankar (weavers), Chamar (tanners), Tidagar (bow and arrow makers), Turi (musicians and genealogists), Senava (basket makers) and Bhangi (scavengers) (Randeria 1989:173). The Bhangi are considered the lowest among the inferior because they remove dead carcasses from the village and handle night soil. Furthermore, they deal with corpses at the cremation ground, which has further deteriorated their social condition (Randeria 1989:173).

During my field stay, I observed this inter-hierarchy among subcastes of the Dom in Banaras. But the difference is that the Chamar (sweepers and manual scavengers) are considered the lowest one instead of the Dom, who cremate the dead bodies. Since they are from the same subcaste, they do not purchase the sacred fire from the Dom. The difference in treatment is observable in the fact that they were allocated a separate space at the cremation ground for cremating their dead, and they cremate their relatives' bodies by themselves, as the Dom do not perform this task for them. There is an economic aspect attached too; among the Chamar, they remove all the jewellery from the dead body, and the price of the fire is given to the nephew of the deceased. This ensures that the Dom do not earn anything. That is why a separate area has been demarcated by the Dom to save themselves from the trouble of sieving those ashes.

Though Randeria (1989) mentioned that among the lower castes, their contact with dead bodies often results in associations with pollution, the situation is different in Banaras. The Chamar are considered lower in status by the Dom because they rear and consume pigs. Further, after their relative's death, the Chamar used to take out a funeral procession accompanied by both males and females. Men would play music from a clay pot with a drumhead stretched over the pothead (see Figure 3.3). The *dhol* is played until the cremation is complete, and mourners can be seen laughing and dancing to the sound of the *dhol* after consuming alcohol. The *dhol* is a drum made of calfskin that is tightly stretched on a circular wooden frame. The calfskin is further tightened to tune the drum by leather thongs attached to the circumference of the frame (Arun 2007:85). It is played by holding it upright between the arms and chest and beating it with a thick stick. The sound of the *dhol* is associated with death and funerals (Lillelund 2009:257).

Various works of literature have mentioned the playing of the drum by outcastes during funeral processions, including Clarke (1903), Moffatt (1979), Arun (2007) and Lillelund (2009). Arun (2007) noted that drumming at the funeral procession is performed because the drum, made of calfskin, is considered polluted and, due to its impure nature, has the power to drive away the evil spirits of the dead (Arun 2007:90).

The acts of playing the drum, dancing and getting drunk are considered derogatory by the Dom. The upper castes often mention these reasons to justify their claim of superiority over other castes and to assign them an inferior status. But, here, the Dom use the same reasons to maintain their superiority, even though they deal with dead bodies. Death pollution is considered more severe in comparison to other types of pollution, such as birth and menstrual pollution (Randeria 1989:185). The possible reason for the claim of

Figure 3.3 Funeral procession of Chamar.

superiority by the Dom is their known status as the Dom-Raja, as they are considered guardians of the sacred fire, without which salvation is not guaranteed. Still, this status of Dom-Raja is ephemeral, as for other castes, their perception of the Dom as inferior is regained after the cremation is over. As Srinivas (1952) pointed out:

> The inclusion of lower castes in rituals does not mean that the structural distance is abolished totally for the duration of the ritual occasion. Certain individuals belonging to low castes have ritual roles which place them temporarily in a superior position vis-à-vis the high caste.
>
> (Srinivas 1952:42)

As death rites do not 'form an integral part of domestic rituals' (Das 1977:9), the Dom are consequently degraded to a permanently polluted caste once the cremation process is over. People often laugh at their claim to be the 'Chaudhary' of the cremation *ghat*.

Further, the caste ranking of one's clients determines their status in the caste hierarchy (Randeri 1989:177; Shah 2007:360). Because of this, different castes provide the same service to other castes; for instance, the Mahapatra perform last rites for other higher castes, but barbers will perform those rituals for the Dom. Often, kin used to take the services of their own caste.

There are significant shifts observed in present times as the Vettiyans, a subcaste among the Paraiyas in Tamil Nadu, who used to perform the tasks of cremation and playing the drum, have now forsaken their caste occupation and become engaged in other respectable work. Only one Vettiyan man remains involved in this work, and he, too, is forced through physical violence to continue his caste occupation (Arun 2007; Lillelund 2009). Due to the absence of the lower caste to perform this work, now, in constrained situations, the upper caste started to cremate their dead bodies by themselves (Arun 2007:82).

In the case of Kashmiri Pandits, low-caste Muslims from Kashmir used to perform burials for them (Datta 2016:164). That is the reason we often hear that there are no Dom in other regions of India who engage in this work anymore, and people cremate their relatives' bodies by themselves or take them to an electric crematorium. Moreover, it is not mandatory to receive fire from the hand of the Dom in other parts of India, as is eulogized in Kashi. But what is important here is that even in crematoriums, lower castes have been assigned this work of cremation.

Interestingly, the Dom of Banaras become more important here, as this caste is still following its traditional occupation. Their literacy rate is still low, and their chances of engaging in another respected occupation without proper education are lower—another reason for being trapped at the cremation *ghat*.

Here, the religious importance of Kashi, as the bestower of salvation, attracts tourists from across the world to complete death rites, making the death industry a source of handsome earnings that is impossible in other non-religious areas across India. Kashi is called a microcosm of Hinduism, as even in the twenty-first century, old-age religious practices are still followed with ascribed occupations.

Another reason for the continuation of this occupation can be understood as the outcastes have been indoctrinated with various myths mentioned in the previous chapter, emphasizing their low status as being divinely ordained and eternal, and any attempts to change this would be met with divine retribution (Arun 2007:91).

Custodian of Salvation

Religious texts in Hinduism mention the gift of salvation to those dying in Kashi. For this, there is a need for specific ritual specialists to perform rites and rituals within their respective occupational domains. Every ritual specialist claims their own importance, without which salvation cannot be attained. In support of their claim, they often cite certain myths. In Banaras, three castes emphasize the importance of their caste's occupations in facilitating people to attain salvation: the Mahapatra, the Mallah and the Dom.

The Mahapatra perform the ritual of *pinda-dan* and facilitate the conversion of the malevolent ghost into an ancestor. After the completion of this ritual, the soul moves on the right *gati* (path and speed) instead of wandering in limbo, which helps in its attainment of salvation. Quoting the conversation with the Mahapatra of Harishchandra Ghat:

Question: What are your views on the attainment of salvation in Kashi?

Mahapatra: Dead persons have their *karma*, and we have our own *karma*. We perform *shraddha* (funeral rites) to help them attain salvation. Whether a person can attain salvation solely depends on God's will. He has sent us here as a medium to help the deceased in attaining salvation. We are Mahabrahmins, and our work is limited to the performance of rites on the 10th day and conducting the ritual of *pinda-dan;* for that, you can give us one rupee or ten rupees. Our work is in accordance with salvation.

Question: So, both Mahapatra and Dom are essential in helping the deceased attain salvation?

Mahapatra: There has been a system in place. It is written in the *Mahapuranas* that you can attain '*gati*' through Mahabrahman only. We are the supreme ones among all the Brahmins and are called Mahabrahman. (After that, he stopped the conversation and left.)

Here, the Mahapatra used references from the *Mahapuranas* to justify his claim about the importance of their role in death rites, in the absence of which the soul wanders in limbo.

The next important caste is the Mallah, who ferry dead bodies and, in some cases cremated remains of deceased for immersion in the flowing waters of the Ganges River. They support their claim with the story from the Ramayana, where they help the soul to cross over, as their ancestors did by assisting Lord Rama, Sita and Lakshma to cross the river. Here, the reference to crossing over could be understood as crossing the Vaitarani River. In another myth, it has been mentioned that Lord Shiva whispers the '*tarak mantra*' (ferry boatman mantra), through which the soul attains salvation. Both of these could be related, and they emphasize the importance of the Mallah in helping the soul cross over the Vaitarani River.

Lastly, to assert their importance, the Dom narrate the story of Raja Harishchandra as a testimonial to their significance in providing salvation. Here, these myths and rituals act as vehicles through which these castes reclaim their identity and importance in society. They enforce their role as ritual specialists and assert their importance in Kashi's spiritualized landscape to earn a respectful livelihood.

Though nearly all caste groups believe in the myth that underscores the importance of taking sacred fire from the hands of the Dom, it is interesting to note how different castes emphasize different sections of the same story. For instance, while narrating the story, a person from the Dom caste will often glorify the role of Kalu Dom and stress that he was capable enough to purchase a king and keep him as his servant. But whenever a person from another caste narrates the same story, they emphasize that it was because of Raja Harishchandra that God appeared and salvation was granted here. Meanwhile, ritual specialist castes working in the death industry believe that their caste plays a prime role in helping people attain salvation. Although other castes do not question the claims of the Mahapatra and the Mallah due to their respective caste rankings, the same level of acceptance does not apply to the assertions made by the Dom caste.

The reaction of other castes towards the claim made by the Dom to be the custodian of salvation is crucial. In the above narrative, the Mahapatra asserts the importance of his occupation by citing support from the religious text. However, his deliberate avoidance of the question regarding the role of the Dom in death rituals points towards his non-acceptance of the Dom's importance. The Mallah supports the Dom's claim to be descendants of Kalu Dom, but a man from the Yadav caste, who owns a wood business at Manikarnika Ghat, mentioned:

> People attain salvation by cremating bodies at the Manikarnika Ghat, as Lord Shiva and Parvati provided the boon of salvation here.

> For the role of the Dom, it is customary to pay a *kar* (fee) for the fire taken from them, as this tradition has been followed for generations.

Thus, a lower position within the caste hierarchy that leads to an inferior status hinders the Dom's acceptance as a custodian of salvation. But concurrently, people are not in a position to dismiss the importance of taking the sacred fire from a Dom's hand. Whether this is due to the presence of the infamous Raja Harishchandra myth supporting the Dom's claim or because of their own engagement in earning a livelihood through the death industry, it needs to be explored. Nonetheless, it highlights their incapability to completely repudiate the Dom's claim. Therefore, they stress that 'salvation is attained by dying in Kashi, and Dom merely provides the fire required for cremation'.

The death industry is functioning primarily due to people's firm beliefs in these myths. Furthermore, the glorification of this sacred space by ritual specialists contributes to an increase in devotees. It becomes important to understand their perspectives here. One elderly man, aged fifty years (mourner), working in the railway department in Banaras, shared his views on this matter as follows:

> Dom has been provided with this recognition, and we will get pure fire from their hand. I read in Harishchandra's story that even his wife could have taken fire from somewhere else; still, she chose to pay the *kar* (fee) by tearing her saree and taking fire from Raja Harishchandra, a servant of Dom Raja. So, we can say that Dom is the most crucial part of *daah-sanskar* (last rites).

Another man in his late forties, accompanying a dead body from a rural area, said, 'We can ourselves put fire through a matchstick, but then the soul will not get salvation, as it is not in accordance with the recognition mentioned in our traditions.' The third mourner from Banaras, a fifty-eight-year-old retired man from the post of assistant in the irrigation department, added that, as Raja Harishchandra had worked here, there is a belief that taking fire from these people's

(Dom) hands helps in attaining *mukti* (liberation). These mourners from different backgrounds were aware of the famous myth that emphasizes taking sacred fire only from the hands of the Dom. The old practices that have received recognition are continued as a matter of course, and people rarely question them.

People gather information from different sources, such as religious texts, ritual specialists and priests, which inform them about the story of Raja Harishchandra Ghat. Here, people can see this *ghat* in the same geographical space on the bank of the Ganges, where it is believed that Raja Harishchandra cremated dead bodies centuries ago.

Further, it is often argued that the fire provided by the Dom has never been extinguished since that time. Moreover, when the wife of Raja Harishchandra herself had to pay the fee for the fire in such a miserable condition, no matter how poor a person is, they should take fire from the hand of the Dom.

Out of twenty mourners interviewed, only one Brahmin objected to the importance of taking fire from the hand of the Dom, though he mentioned that they pay the amount asked by the Dom in exchange for fire but will not use that fire to cremate their deceased. Here, I am adding a few instances from the conversation.

Question: What is the reason behind taking fire from Chaudhary (Dom-Raja) to perform the cremation? Can the body also be cremated using other fire?

Temple Priest: As I am a Brahmin, the Brahmins will pay the complete *kar* (fee) for the fire, but we will not take their fire. The earlier tradition was that we ourselves used to churn fire with stones, as there used to be wood and all other essential elements. However, as all of these consume time, we now use camphor to kindle fire. We do this by taking permission from them (Dom), and we pay the full amount for the *kar*, but we will not use their fire.

A social milieu might have been established when Rishis and Maharishis created the varna system. In that social milieu, everyone was expected to have an occupation. Now, any rule or occupation could be adhered to only if there was some element of fear; hence, fear was instilled to ensure people followed the social structure. These people are referred to as Chaudhury here; if we do not take fire from them, then we will be indebted to them. And this is, after all, their domain, so you might consider it a debt that we have to repay, enabling them to earn a livelihood. Whether it is Banaras or any other place, to ensure that '*Varna-Vyavastha*' functions properly within the social milieu, all castes are intertwined like a garland, whether they are Pandit Ji or Chaudhary.

Question: So, do all the Brahmins not take fire from the Dom?

Temple Priest: I cannot speak for all Brahmins, but most of them do not. However, they will pay the fee and obtain permission from the Dom, and only after that will they kindle the fire with camphor.

Question: As you mentioned, Pandits do not take fire, but other people take sacred fire from the Dom, believing that it helps in attaining salvation.

Temple Priest: Yes

Question: So, what are your thoughts? Does Dom have an important role in helping the soul attain salvation?

Temple Priest: As per my knowledge, I have not seen it mentioned in any *Shastra* (holy book). Since you are researching, you can read the *Garuda Purana*, which has 16 chapters. However, even in that, there is no explanation for these people. It all depends on our social system. In many places, Doms are not available, so people themselves ignite the fire and complete the cremation.

Question: Okay, the dead body that you are accompanying here—who is cremating it now? Do you do it yourself, or does Dom burn the body?

Temple Priest: The rule for cremating a dead body is that you should burn it yourself. If someone cannot burn the dead body themselves, they can ask someone else. However, according to tradition, people should personally burn the body.

Question: But here, does Dom burn bodies?

Temple Priest: No, we burn ourselves. We will not let the Dom touch our dead bodies. We pay their *kar,* as they are the supreme ones of this place (cremation *ghat*), and take their permission. But we will complete all the rituals ourselves. They do not have any role here. Some people do not want to work or have mental delusions… they ask them to burn. (A *Dom servant was cremating the body that this Brahmin was accompanying*).

Question: Delusion-like?

Temple Priest: People will say that the person is dead, so do not touch him. These are delusions and not reality. The one who is dead is the only truth. At that time, the body is so pure that no one wants to touch it because it will get polluted. Similarly, Brahmins do not let Doms touch their dead bodies, so the corpse should not become impure by their touch. Therefore, we perform all rituals by ourselves. However, there are no fixed traditions, which is why people think, 'Who will take these troubles? Let us pay the money and get the work completed.' Even when I was a child, at that time, we used to burn the body by ourselves.

The above conversation illustrates a few modifications in the actual practice performed compared to the ones prescribed in myths. An important aspect is that the money charged for the sacred fire is referred to as *kar*, which means debt. The temple priest also added that they pay money to remove themselves from the debt of the Dom. This highlights the fact, which the priest even accepts, that those who do not pay the fee for the sacred fire remain in debt, which might hinder their attainment of salvation.

Moreover, it also alludes to the question of pollution from a lower caste. If a Brahmin touches a Dom, his purity will be compromised, even though, due to his relative's death, he is in a temporary phase of impurity. But, this does not mean they can compromise with the rules of the caste system. That is why they cannot allow a lower caste individual to touch even their corpses. Brahmins follow the rule of paying the *kar* as prescribed in the myth, but it is paid to free themselves from any debt.

Now, on the contradictory status of corpses as pure or impure, Das (1976) argues that the impure status of corpses denotes the matter of the corpse, which is its body and not its soul. 'The sacrificial fire destroys the corpse qua matter and carries the corpse qua spirit to God' (Das 1976:256). It is believed that, due to death, severe impurity is suffered by the living kin of the deceased. The impurity begins when *preta* is released from the dead body, and it decreases over time as *preta* is incorporated into ancestors through *pinda-dan*.

Parry (1982) argues that women's bodies that die during childbirth undergo special purificatory rituals to make them fit for sacrifice (Parry 1982:79). In such situations, there is a conflict about whether the corpse is pure or impure. Because if it is impure and dangerous, then why is it treated as a sacrificial object? Why must the chief mourner tonsure his head and maintain his purity before performing the *mukhagni*? Even the idea of not permitting a Dom to touch the corpse of a Brahmin also suggests the purity of the corpse. However, the mandatory ritual performance to free oneself from death pollution points towards the impurity of the corpse.

To resolve this contradiction, Parry (1981) used the idea of a time when the vital breath leaves the body. There are two different views: one believes that death pollution begins the moment physiological functioning stops and makes the corpse impure; the other, derived from theological beliefs, holds that the corpse is pure. Only after *kapal kriya*, does the vital breath leave the body, and the pollution begins. Hence, death pollution springs from the act of cremation rather than the physiological demise of the corpse (Parry 1981:361).

The commonality between both these views is the act of leaving off the vital breath, which incurs death pollution (Parry 1981). Further, though the corpse is an object of great sacredness, the theory of pollution argues that pollution is a consequence of 'the sin of burning the body hairs' and the violence perpetrated on the deceased at the rite of breaking the skull. Due to this, the regime of mourning is essentially a regime of atonement in which those who gave the fire play the part of principal penitents (Parry 1994:217).

To understand this, we need to delve further into theological discourse. The *Taittiriya Upanishad* mentions that the *atman* (self) is clothed with three bodies. The outermost, the physical body, consists of five elements: earth, water, fire, air and space. The second one is the *sukshma sharira* (subtle body). The self is associated with both the physical and subtle bodies. In the absence of a subtle body, the physical body has no capacity for independent functioning. According to Hindu belief, the subtle body does not get destroyed with the physical body. Instead, it remains associated with the self until liberation. The subtle body is understood as the repository of *karma*. The third body is the causal body, and it is manifested in the state of deep sleep (Rambachan 2003:641–2). From the above discussion, we can infer that the subtle body leaves the physical body during the breaking of the skull and hence incurs pollution. This clarifies that corpses are pure till cremation is performed (Das 1976; Parry 1982).

These works shed light on the impurity of death, which begins after the ritual of skull-breaking. Furthermore, corpses are also treated as objects of sacrifice to God via cremation (Das 1976:253). The literature highlights certain commonalities in the procedures carried out for cremation and sacrificial acts, such as the purification of the site and the prescribed use of pure wood. On the other hand, some corpses are immersed in water rather than cremated because their bodies are considered unfit as a sacrificial object[36] (Das 1976). Hence, it signifies that a corpse is an object of sacrifice to God, and a touch from lower caste could defile it. That is why they are not allowed to touch the corpses of Brahmins. So according to these circumstances, when the Dom are assigned an inferior status, it is impossible to provide them with the status of custodians of salvation by the upper-caste group.

The practice of discrimination based on caste is so prevalent in Banaras that lower castes were not allowed to stay at Kashi Mukti Bhawan, located at Godowlia Chowk, because the manager, from the Brahmin caste, did not think that lower castes were worthy enough to attain salvation. He held the view that these people might have done bad *karma* in their previous life, which is why they were born into this caste (Justice 1997:75). This idea aligns with Srinivas (1952), who argued, 'Caste hierarchy comes to be an index of the state of an individual's soul. It also represents certain milestones on the soul's journey to God' (Srinivas 1952:25). Now, if lower castes are not considered worthy enough to attain salvation by the upper castes, then how can they be provided with the status of custodians of salvation?

Further, Parry (1994) raised the issue of contestation between these myths. For instance, the Dom are believed to provide salvation through the sacred fire, and funeral priests are essential to complete the last rites, after which the soul will reach its final destination. However, certain myths highlight that simply dying in Kashi will enable the deceased to attain salvation (Parry 1994:28). In this, I would like to add that these different myths, which mention the roles of the Dom and the Mahapatra in death rites, are a smaller section of a larger myth that points towards salvation for those dying in Kashi. To justify this, let me provide some instances. At Harishchandra Ghat, I heard a catchy phrase used by the Dom: '*Mahabrahman se gati or Dom se mukti*' (Mahabrahman provides *gati,* and Dom provides *mukti*). This phrase emphasizes the role of both castes in the death industry.

Each caste has a specific role in helping people attain salvation. First, the Dom provide *mukti* (liberation) by giving the sacred fire. As the temple priest explains, liberation means getting rid of the bondage of birth and death, and salvation signifies that the soul becomes absorbed in God. The Dom assist in the attainment of liberation for the soul and helps break its bondages with this world; after that, the soul will be ready to enter another world. The story of Raja Harishchandra can help us comprehend this further. When he was cremating corpses as a servant under Kalu Dom, he refused to cremate his son in the absence of a fee for the sacred fire, despite witnessing his wife's destitute condition. In doing so, he had, in a way, freed himself from the bondage of worldly relationships. Thus, the sacred fire became significant in providing liberation to the other soul.

After the body is burned, the ashes are immersed in the Ganges. The Mallah considered themselves to be *Gangaputras* (sons of the Ganges) as they earned their livelihood through the Ganges (Doron 2013:22). Even some bodies that are not considered fit for sacrifices are immersed in the Ganges by the Mallah. Thus, their role could be understood as helping the soul to cross over the Vaitarani River.

Lastly, the Mahapatra perform rituals of *pinda-dan,* in which they provide a new body to the soul and helps it reach its final destination. Thus, all these separate myths that emphasize the roles of ritual specialists are subparts of a larger myth that mentions salvation for those dying in Kashi, as all these ritual specialists play their occupational roles in completing a larger picture.

Thus, the Dom have a crucial role as a custodian of salvation by being the keeper of the sacred fire, which must not be extinguished. The findings suggest that Dom *naukars* are not considered mandatory, as bodies can be cremated by family members too; however, the act of paying a fee for the fire is an undeniable norm in Banaras. Brahmins do not deny the necessity of paying the fee to the Dom in exchange for the sacred fire, as it removes them from the debt to a lower caste. This removal of debt signifies that, for the orthodox Brahmin, the fire from the hand of the Dom may not be important, but they accept that the act of not paying the fee can hinder their attainment of salvation. Though the upper caste cannot endure a lower caste person touching their corpse, they must accept the Dom's authority as the Dom-Raja at the cremation *ghat*. Here, the glorified myth of Raja Harishchandra and the myth of Lord Shiva punishing the Dom to cremate dead bodies assist the Dom in maintaining some authority.

4

Tradition versus Technology

Conflict and Convergence of Beliefs in Death Rituals

Old Man in a Gloomy Place

During the peak summer in May 2021, people were not seen on the stairs of the *ghat,* where they usually sit; a few were waiting under the shed of the gas crematorium. I went to the tea kiosk at Harishchandra Ghat, as there is an open sheltered space constructed by the government.

A skinny older man in his late sixties sat alone on a concrete bench. He had a dark complexion and wore a discoloured white *dhoti*[1] and *kurta* with dirt, dust patches and torn sleeves. Immersed in his thoughts, he seemed quite sad. He covered his head with a small piece of white cloth to avoid the scorching sun. His old flip-flops were covered in dry mud. His demeanour made his rural background obvious. I greeted him formally and immediately shaking off his sadness, he was willing to talk.

He came to the cremation *ghat* to provide a shoulder to the bier of his relative's deceased brother. A few days ago, he had lost his only son, who was in his early twenties. The son had been the sole breadwinner of their family. He was murdered in an act of revenge by some upper-caste men over an issue that was not disclosed. Since it was a sudden and untimely death, the old man had to cremate his son in the gas crematorium. Seeking justice for his son's death, which was a caste-based crime, he made several rounds to the police station, but his efforts were in vain, he said.

During our conversation about his preference between traditional and mechanized cremation, he immediately replied that wood cremation is better. He added, 'Here you can see what is happening with the dead body, unlike in a machine, where nothing can be seen, whether the body has burned properly or not. And it is only through wood cremation in an open space at the *ghat* that salvation can be attained.' Quite tragically, his only son was cremated in the machine, despite his preference for the traditional method.

The modernization of cremation practices has created a conflict in the minds of people regarding whether to opt for a crematorium, which goes against prescribed beliefs for the last rites. The fear of uncertainty after death pushes individuals to find solace in the justification provided by religion. This preference is influenced by the deep-rooted belief system often prescribed by one's religion. This is not only an instance of conflict between tradition and technology but also highlights a clash between one's religious beliefs and ecological concerns.

Death Rites and Rituals

The death of a close one often leads to a feeling of normlessness and chaos. A person's world of meaning suddenly turns into meaninglessness and unreality, highlighting the temporariness of social relationships. This loss of reality is perceived as anomic (Berger 1969:32). Death is not only a physiological phenomenon but is also understood as 'an object of collective consciousness' (Hertz 1960:54). The death of any member of society threatens the existence of its groups, and they are faced with the double-edged dilemma of preserving the body – keeping it intact – or preserving its remains while simultaneously getting rid of the corpse (Malinowski 1954:49). When survivors are struck by the emotional forces of fear, horror of annihilation and the supreme dilemma of life and death, religion provides a comforting view on 'culturally valuable belief in immortality, in the spirit independent of the body, and in the continuance of life after death' (Malinowski 1954:49). So, religion 'saves a man from surrender to death and destruction' and provides 'the desire of life' (Malinowski 1954:51). Society helps individuals by providing some belief in performing rites that leads to its proper functioning during the chaos. The belief that the soul enters a mythical society is constructed by society in its own image.

The performance of the last rites becomes crucial here as death threatens society by questioning the continuity of human relationships and challenging the basic assumption of order on which society rests. To control this chaos, society 'develops procedures to assist its members in remaining reality-oriented and returned to the socially established norms' (Berger 1969:32–3). And one such attempt that facilitates the individual in reconstructing reality and its meaning is cosmization (Kaushik 1976:265). As man creates the social order, he becomes its product through externalization, objectivation and internalisation.[2] Similarly, he creates sacred cosmos that shield a man from the anomy as it locates him within the wider ordering of reality. The symbolic systems help him link these two worlds that are man's empirical world to the cosmic world. Here, rituals act as a symbolic system that dramatizes man's movement from the social world (profane reality) to the cosmic world (sacred reality) (Kaushik 1976:266).

During the performance of rites and rituals, the whole society is involved. The performance of the final ceremony includes the burial, cremation or immersion of the last remains of the deceased. These rites ensure the soul's peace and a place in the realm of ancestors, which finally frees the living from the obligation of mourning (Hertz 1960:54). Feasts are arranged to mark the end of the mourning phase. This whole aspect portrays the collective representation of society (Hertz 1960).

The prescribed rites and rituals are crucial as they help incorporate the soul into ancestor realms and facilitate the individual mourner's reintegration into society. In Hindu theological discourse, the body and cosmos are equated, argued Parry (1982). During cosmic dissolution, conflagration destroys the world; similarly, cremation destroys the physical body. Furthermore, as water and fire are required for the annihilation of the world to re-create a new one, the body must similarly pass through fire (cremation) and water (immersion of ashes in a river) to restore the soul back to life (Parry 1982:76). Hertz (1960) also pointed out a similar belief in the reincarnation of the soul among the Dayak of Indonesia, Australians and the Arunta tribe. He noted:

> The painful psychological process expresses itself in the objective and mystical shape of the belief that the soul only gradually severs the ties binding it to this world. It finally has a stable existence again only when the representation of the deceased has acquired a final and pacified character in the consciousness of the survivors.
>
> (Hertz 1960:82)

The role of religion is to provide solace to man and help him face his fear of the unknown, thereby preventing chaos from disturbing the stability of society. The last rites performed after death and people's belief in the afterlife are crucial in helping bereaved families cope with the fear of death. Hence, funerary rites assist individuals during their period of distress as well as express the social loss of a member of society (Davis 2002:16). The next section deals with different types of final ceremonies for dead bodies prescribed by various religions and traces the history of cremation practices in India.

Ceremonial Methods

Dead bodies can be buried, cremated, immersed or mummified, depending on the beliefs prescribed by one's religion. The decision to choose any final ceremonial practice for dead bodies is influenced by religious beliefs, social customs and individual preferences (Gauthier et al. 2003).

Though there are ongoing debates regarding the preferred practice, different religious groups of people eulogized their religiously prescribed methods. Besides these common practices, there are other minor modes such as green burial, burial at sea and donation of bodies for scientific study. A few years ago, one professor from Banaras Hindu University donated his father's body to the hospital rather than opting for cremation.[3] Despite facing backlash from his relatives and friends, he stood firm on this decision. However, this trend of organ donation in India is still at a marginal level. The organ donation rate in India in 2021 was merely 0.01 per cent, creating a massive gap in the demand and supply rates. The primary reasons for this gap include a lack of awareness, negative attributes towards organ donation and spiritual belief in life after death.[4] The rate of organ donation from 2016 to 2022 shows that four states Delhi, Tamil Nadu, Maharashtra and Telangana, account for 53 per cent of organ donations in India.[5] There are possibilities that their geographical location near the major cities of India acts as a central medical hub and attracts more patients due to better medical infrastructure (Gauthier et al. 2003).

Moreover, this shift towards organ donation is gradual, as there have been crucial modifications in ceremonial methods since ancient times. For instance, there has been a practice of preserving bodies through embalming, as mentioned in the *Vishnu Purana*, which was performed in the cases Pandu[6] and King Dasaratha.[7] These bodies were embalmed in oil and sandal paste, respectively, to preserve the dead body from decaying till the time period final rites could be performed (Crooke 1899:272). The practice of mummification also aims to preserve the dead body.

The practice of burial is common in Islam and Christianity, whereas Hinduism and Buddhism are known for the practice of cremation. The cremation trend has been in practice since the Neolithic period and has been used in some parts of Southeast Asia, India, ancient China and by a few indigenous groups in South America (Davis 2003:767). Though in Europe, during the twentieth century, a shift from burial to cremation began, it was at the beginning of the twenty-first century that cremation took part in the traditional domains of death rites in North America (Davis 2003:767).

While tracing different modes of practices in India, Crooke (1899) suggested that earthen burial had been preceded by cremation. In the great epics, the Vedas suggest that, at least among the higher classes, both burial and cremation existed (Crooke 1899:278). After cremation, the remains of bones and ashes were collected and either buried or immersed in some sacred rivers (Crooke 1899).

Whereas the death rites of Zoroastrians or Parsees include building a 'tower of silence', where bodies were kept in an open space on a floor platform, as it was believed that dead bodies should not touch the earth. In the end vultures consume those flesh. Among them, cremation was not considered proper as they believed a polluted corpse would contaminate the sacred fire. They regard the dead body as extremely polluted because of their belief that evil must have been focused on bringing the person's death (Davis 2002:82–3). Slowly British Zoroastrians shifted towards both burial and cremation practices. Now, the earlier problem regarding the belief of sacred fire getting contaminated by the polluted corpse is catered by the view that in the crematorium, the body is cremated through electricity that causes intense heat and no actual fire is used (Davis 2002:83).

Shift in Cremation Practices over Time

Different regions adopt different last rites practices suited to their geographical locations. Mummification was suitable for Egypt, and cremation was an environmentally friendly approach in India due to its heavily forested areas. However, some factors have necessitated a shift from these traditional practices, leading to modifications. In the Indian context, conversion to Islam and colonial rule were among the contributing factors. The tribes of the Hindu Kush followed the practice of cremation until their conversion to Islam, after which they adopted burial. Similarly, the Khatik butchers buried their dead while following Lingayats, but after the advent of Maratha Hindu rule, they adopted the practice of burning their dead bodies (Crooke 1899:278).

Though the first indication of a jungle tribe being assimilated into the Hindu fold was evident in the replacement of burial practices with cremation (Crooke 1899). Yet it was not freely permitted to the lower castes. Cremation was not the universal practice among Hindus as members of lower castes, unless extremely rich, used to bury their deceased. An instance shows that there has been a rumour regarding the Dom in Bengal that they do not bury their dead but dismember the corpses at night, placing the pieces in a pot and sinking them in a river (Crooke 1899:278). This idea was generated because of the old Hindu Law, argued Risley (1892), that compelled them to bury their dead at night. The Dom of Dacca used to cast their dead into a river as only the bodies of the rich or influential were buried. At the same time, the Dom in western Bengal and Bihar used to cremate their dead (Risley 1892:248).

It is evident from the figures that in 1880, in Bombay, only 43 per cent of Hindus – that is, 5,569 out of a total of 13,037 deaths – were cremated (Arnold 2016:401). From 1873 to 1893, in Bombay, cremation rose slightly from 30 to 33 per cent as lower castes slowly began to adopt the ritual practices of higher castes (Arnold 2016:401).

From the mid-eighteenth century, the British often viewed Indian cremation practices with disgust. They even declared it a health hazard due to the smoke emanating from the open pyres in the burning *ghats*. In 1859, a Bengal jail inspector protested that the smell from the Hooghly burning *ghat* was so disgusting that the prisoners could not eat their food (Arnold 2016:397). This European disgust against Indian open cremation turned into an incentive for indoor cremation in England (Martin 1864:2). Slowly, cremation started gaining popularity from a sanitary viewpoint as a better and faster mode of decomposition of the body.

As many health problems were indicated by the practice of burial, such as the increase in population and the migration of people from rural areas to the cities in search of livelihood, a demand arose for more living space. Due to this, less space was left for burial grounds, which led to deteriorating conditions in terms of hygiene and public health.

The cities of England also shifted to cremation as a method for the decomposition of dead bodies. After the legalization of cremation in England, Sir Henry Thompson, a British surgeon, founded the Cremation Society of England in 1874. In 1875, the first crematorium was opened in Surrey (Davis 2002:232). Out of thirty bodies cremated in a working crematorium in Surrey, one was the corpse of a Brahmin woman (Thompson 1891:5). Major factors facilitating the shift from burial to cremation included public health concerns, decreasing availability of land, and the perception of cremation as the fastest and easiest method for the decomposition of the body (Thompson 1891).

During the same period in India, by 1880, the Indian Medical Gazette began campaigning for scientific cremation. In 1894, the Gazette argued that the risks emanating from the bodies of cholera, typhoid and other diseases were immense, and the only effective solution was the destruction of the germs via heat. By this time, cremation was seen as a 'speedy, effectual, and easy method' that could conveniently destroy the dead in comparison to burial (Arnold 2016:400). By 1920, cremation was described as the 'most sanitary method of disposal of the dead … when properly carried out the method is without objection' by *McNally Sanitary Handbook* (Arnold 2016:400).

In the mid-nineteenth century, there was a recommendation for an indoor crematorium in India. In 1864, a five-chambered crematorium was designed by Major Thomas Martin in Poona that could cremate ten bodies at a time. Martin had taken the caste dynamics of India into consideration, and his design permitted the cremation of bodies from different caste groups in separate spaces to avoid the mixing of ashes (Martin 1864:6). It was also used by municipal corporations for the disposal of unclaimed bodies. Moreover, the live telecast of the cremation of Gandhi, Nehru and other prominent figures during the national struggle for freedom in India led to the emergence of cremation as a Hindu identity, and acts of its denial were seen as questioning their dignity (Arnold 2016:404). After independence, crematoria began to gain acceptance among the secular elements of India, as the affordable cost of cremation and the increasing trend of cremation at that time facilitated its acceptance.

Significance of Cremation

In Hinduism, traditional cremation is the preferred method, performed using mango wood or sandalwood arranged in an open, purified space near the bank of a river, followed by the continuation of the prescribed rites and rituals performed by allocated caste specialists. Here, salvation is the highest and most valued goal, implying freedom from suffering and immortality (Rambachan 2003:640). Hence, cremation is not only a method of decomposition of a dead body, unlike in European countries, but also a means to achieve salvation. As per theological texts, in Hinduism, the act of cremation has been equated with a willing sacrifice of oneself to God (Das 1977; Parry 1982). Even many commonalities are illustrated between the sacrifice of a victim and rites of cremation as

> the site of cremation is prepared in exactly the same way as in fire sacrifice, i.e., the prescriptive use of ritually pure wood, the purification of the site, its consecration with holy water, and the establishment of *agni* with the proper *mantras* ... The dead body is prepared in the same manner as the victim of a sacrifice and is attributed with divinity.
>
> (Das 1977:122–3)

Death rites consist of two phases that include cremation/burial and the immersion of ashes, dealt with extensively in the work of Hertz (1960:41). He defined these phases as the 'wet' medium of the body and the 'dry' medium of the body. The first rite removes the deceased from the realm of daily social life, while the second phase places the dead into the supernatural world of ancestors. Due to this, 'cremation is usually neither a final act nor sufficient in itself; it calls for later and complementary rites' (Hertz 1960:42), which is followed by the practice of burial or immersion of ashes. By this act, the body of the deceased is destroyed and made capable of entering into a new life (Hertz 1960: 43). During the cremation, a set of ten substances are offered that are similar to those substances which are offered in fire sacrifices (Parry 1982:78). It is only after this that the deceased person is referred to as benevolent soul (Parry 1982).

But not all bodies are considered fit to be sacrificed through cremation, as discussed in the previous chapter. These bodies include those of victims of smallpox or leprosy, pregnant women, infants, ascetics and individuals who died from a snake bite. Such bodies are immersed in flowing water, as they are categorized as unfit for sacrifice (Das 1977:123). A possible explanation provided by Das (1977) is that these bodies could not be incorporated into society; for instance, an infant who has not cut their teeth is not yet incorporated into society. An ascetic had already performed their last rites and hence remained outside the system (Das 1976:260). A similar explanation applies to the pregnant woman with an unborn child in her womb. The person who died of smallpox is said to already be bearing the wrath of goddesses, so they cannot be sacrificed again to the fire (Das 1976:255). The person who died through the bite of a snake is believed to come back to life if received proper treatment, so his body is placed on a banana trunk and floated in a river.

In the above list, Parry (1982) also included those bodies that had died a violent or sudden death and mentioned that they were immersed rather than cremated. However, in my study, I observed that people who died suddenly were cremated either in the gas crematorium or even through the traditional mode. A boatman informed me about a recent phenomenon where the Dom have apparently been cremating children's bodies, which should ideally be immersed, to make more profit. Thus, a change can be seen in the prescribed traditional practices.

Besides the above-mentioned bodies, some are believed to have *akaal mirtyu* (untimely death), which means a sudden death due to illness, accident or suicide. It refers to the way or nature of death rather than just the deceased's age. In some places, *alp mirtyu* (death in youth) is used as a synonym for *akaal mirtyu* (Parry 1982:83). Thus, untimely death can be understood as a contrast to the notion of a timely death, in which one has control over their body's functioning and has prepared themselves for death. It should occur, most preferably, at any pilgrimage site, yet Banaras is considered the best. A person should die lying on purified ground under the open air. The whole idea of a timely death is about regeneration (Parry 1982).

To understand the concept of regeneration, let us examine the different kinds of births of a human being over a lifetime as described in the by *Satapathabrahmana* text. The first birth is the natural birth from the mother, the second birth occurs during the initiation ceremony and the third birth takes place after death, when the body is placed on the pyre and, through the fire, rises again and enters the realm of the ancestors (Davis 1988:41). To illustrate regeneration following a timely death, Parry (1982) draws an analogy between the last birth and the birth of a newborn. The corpse is taken to the cremation ground in such a way that its head points towards the cremation ground, similar to how, during birth, a child's head emerges first followed by the rest of the body. After five months, the vital breath is believed to enter the embryo through the suture at the top of the head, and thus the rite of breaking the skull is performed to release it from the body. Furthermore, just as the child survives in the womb through the digestive fire, the body is cremated in fire. During birth, the child must pass through the uterine wall, which is full of blood and mucus; similarly, the soul is believed to cross the Vaitarani River, which is also full of blood and mucus. Moreover, in both processes, the lower caste plays a mediating role: a midwife cuts the umbilical cord of a newborn child, and in death, it is the Dom who play a crucial role in cremation (Parry 1982:81). The underlying belief is that, in the case of a timely death, these rituals regenerate the soul back to life.

It is often said that death is celebrated in Banaras. On some occasions, in the case of a timely death, people can be seen celebrating it. The celebrations include decorating the bier with balloons and men dancing to songs. But, during other deaths, when the chief mourner is grieving the loss of their loved one, other mourners console them with reassuring words, saying that the deceased had lived their life to the fullest, for which they will attain salvation.

In contrast, those who die untimely are grieved more, and prescribed elaborate rituals are not followed. The reason for this is the fear that the soul may not attain peace and that there is a possibility of it haunting the living. In Banaras, these bodies are cremated in the gas crematorium, where family members are often in a hurry to do away with the rituals. From an ecological perspective, this modern technology came into existence to lessen environmental damage. But, how much the State has succeeded in this endeavour needs to be explored. The following section provides a brief introduction to the emergence of crematorium technology in the death industry of Banaras and the way it affects the livelihoods of ritual specialist castes.

Coming of Crematorium

The scientific crematorium is a 'post-modern structure that collapses both space and time' (Davis 2002:230). It destroys a complete body within a short duration and leaves only ashes. The final installation of the electric crematorium at Harishchandra Ghat, right from the passing of this proposal, had been quite dramatic. People from different sections of society critiqued and protested against it. The late Dom-Raja Kailash Chaudhary handled the situation until 1985, before his death. Simultaneously, conservative Hindus were against this crematorium and argued that it 'would detract from the cremation ground as a place which provides an education in detachment' (Parry 1994:67). However, the state viewed the installation of the crematorium as a cheaper and more efficient alternative to combat river pollution. It was finally constructed in 1986, during the tenure of then prime minister of India, Rajiv Gandhi, under the Ganga Action Plan (GAP), but it became functional only in 1989. However, it was soon closed down after six months following complaints of smoke affecting the residents, as the height of the chimney was insufficient (Parry 1994). Udit Chaudhary, from Dom, recalls the incident of 1989 when the first body was cremated in the electric crematorium.

> One day, we were sitting at the *ghat* as usual, and our people were engaged in manually cremating bodies. Some babus (authorities) came and asked one of us to fetch a dead body from the Ganges (as some bodies were immersed). The six of us brought a body from the Ganges. Those babus asked us to put the body in the machine, and we followed their instructions. That body was burnt in one hour. At that time, the cost of cremation in machines was fixed at 50 rupees per body. The six people – Gopal, Ramavatar, Ramesh, Udit, Kalki, and Bhairav – who helped in the trial run were given permanent jobs operating this crematorium. Initially, as the cost of traditional cremation was higher than that of the electrical crematorium, many bodies came and waited in queues. People preferred the machine, as it allowed mourners to have some refreshments for the same amount of money. However, over time, its cost increased to 150 rupees, and now its current price is 500 rupees per body.

Besides Dom workers, there is an operator, a secretary to maintain recorded files, and a security person. There are three shifts in a day: the first shift runs from 6 a.m. to 2 p.m., the second from 2 p.m. to 10 p.m., and the last from 10 p.m. to 6 a.m. In one shift, five people must be present in the office: two Dom men, a secretary, a security person, and an operator.

This crematorium is under the management of the Municipal Corporation of Banaras and leases out a tender for five years to private companies. In 2014–15, the Jalan group won the tender and promised to provide free services to the people, but later it was revealed that they were charging money, so government authorities cancelled their tender. Currently, the Gas Authority of India Limited (GAIL) is working on it. It has converted the electric crematorium into a gas crematorium as the latter is more eco-friendly than the former. And the electrical crematorium remained mostly dysfunctional due to the re-occurrence of technical snags. Because of this shift from electricity to gas, the crematorium remained dysfunctional for a period of two years, from 2016 to the mid of 2018.

But despite this, the crematorium has remained closed for months. One instance was shared by Ankit Chaudhary.[8] During the flood season as he was burning a body, the gas got blocked in the pipelines because of excessive water. The gas pressure increased leaving him injured. After this incident, they closed the crematorium and sent an application to the Municipal Corporation, but no one came for inspection for some months. The crematorium workers were also not under any pressure as they get a monthly salary of around 30,000 rupees on the basis of their daily attendance, even if the crematorium remains dysfunctional. Mostly during the flood season, this crematorium remains close.

But one thing is certain: this crematorium poses a threat to the livelihoods of ritual specialists engaged in the death industry. As Freeman and Luc (1994) notes, in the 'long-run, technical changes generate new employment to compensate for the loss of old jobs, but it does not always do so quickly or in a way that is agreeable to the unemployed and their families' (Freeman; Luc 1994:1). Furthermore, among the types of technology, product-oriented innovations tend to have positive effects on employment, whereas process-oriented technology adoption is expected to have a negative impact on employment (Ugur and Mitra 2017:11). Workers in the death industry view technology as a potential competitor, offering numerous benefits to consumers (mourners) that are difficult to replicate through human skills. Work performed by machines remains cost-effective, efficient, consumes less time and minimizes environmental pollution. But, it threatens the employment of these low-skilled workers and simultaneously exacerbates income inequality across classes.

The crematorium is a process-oriented technology that employs a limited number of workers and threatens all those caste groups who directly earn from the death industry by selling funeral wood or performing death rites. These groups will remain unemployed if they do not engage in manual cremation or find other means of livelihood. For instance, the Mallahs are experiencing challenges; as one respondent put it:

> We are facing problems because of this machine, as it performs cremations at a cheaper rate. Within 1,000 rupees–1500 rupees, the whole cremation procedure is completed. With that money, they (mourners) pay fee to Dom of around 400 rupees to 500 rupees.
>
> For the immersion of a body, we will not ask for just 100 or 200 rupees but will demand 1,000 or 2,000 rupees. Additionally, the Doms will demand their fee of 2,100 rupees, and the cost of the stone, amounting to 500 rupees, will also be added. (Here, the stone is required to tie down the body so that it sinks.) If people have to pay this much money to immerse one body, they will obviously choose machine cremation.

Funeral priests highlight prescribed beliefs and traditions in Hinduism.

> There is no provision for cremating bodies using the machine. It has been introduced to reduce pollution, and the government has enforced its use. People who do not have money often opt for cremation through the machine. However, according to *Sanatana Dharma*,[9] nine pieces of wood are traditionally meant for the cremation of dead bodies. Those who lack money or time are increasingly turning to machines. Some people, however, interfere and suggest that bodies should be cremated using wood, regardless of whether one has money.

> In wood cremation, the body is burned in front of your eyes, and you can see whether it is completely burned or not, as there is always doubt after cremating bodies in the machine. Though you receive ashes from the machine as well, you cannot differentiate whether the ashes are of your own deceased or of some other person.

Though the establishment of the crematorium led to an increase in the popularity of Harishchandra Ghat and caused a spike in the number of dead bodies arriving at the *ghat,* the Dom community also complained about facing losses due to this crematorium. To compensate for their losses, they have adopted different strategies. For instance, earlier the *madhi* was located near the cremation ground, but when the electric crematorium was introduced, the Dom community collectively constructed a new *madhi* near the gate of the electric crematorium. It became mandatory for every mourner coming to the cremation *ghat* to pay a fee to the Dom for the sacred fire, irrespective of the method chosen for the body's last rites. The state fixed an amount of 220 rupees payable to the Dom for the exchange of the sacred fire for bodies being cremated in the crematorium.

Dead bodies brought for immersion in the river require one shroud and a stone to tie it. However, it is now also requisite for the mourners to purchase all the materials of *havan samgiri*, which are used in cremation. These materials are tied to the body and then immersed. Logically, there is no requirement for these materials, but they can be understood as different means to compensate for one's loss due to technological intervention.

The Yadav also face losses as wood is not required in the crematorium. Recently, there has been a proposal by the government to install a green crematorium at Manikarnika Ghat as well. People were protesting against it, but as informed by an executive officer of the Municipal Corporation, this new crematorium will use wood rather than electricity or gas. The functioning of the crematorium will be handed over to the Dom.

It raises a few concerns: first, opting for wood cremation is already a problem from an ecological perspective. Secondly, it will mostly benefit the Yadav and Thakur caste groups owning this wood business at the Manikarnika Ghat, as they are influential here due to their numerical dominance and caste status.

Lastly, there is a need to understand the role of the State in introducing the crematorium – both the gas crematorium at Harishchandra Ghat and the crematorium at Manikarnika Ghat. From an environmental perspective, the initiative of introducing the crematorium is an appreciable effort, but it is threatening the livelihood of people engaged in the death industry, as the crematorium can provide work to only a handful of people, as happened at Harishchandra Ghat. The cremation grounds of Banaras city are a means to prosperous earnings in comparison to any other cremation grounds in India. No other cremation grounds see such thriving business in India due to the idea of salvation associated with Banaras. The emergence of technology as a potential competitor to the Dom threatens their livelihoods. The state should provide alternative employment or rehabilitation to this marginalized group.

The above section highlighted the disagreements of ritual specialists regarding the intervention of technology in cremation rituals, which are supported by their religious beliefs and concerns about economic losses. The next section will present mourners' (consumers') perspectives to explore the contention between religious beliefs and technological intervention.

Preference of Mourners

To gain in-depth information on the reasons behind choosing the traditional method or opting for a crematorium to conduct last rites, twenty in-depth interviews with mourners who accompanied their relatives' bodies at Harishchandra Ghat were analysed. Table 4.1 provides details of these mourners. Out of these, four mourners cremated their deceased in the gas crematorium, while the rest opted for traditional cremation. As it was inappropriate to question people who had just lost their loved ones, I interviewed distant mourners who were not closely related to the deceased. At the cremation *ghat*, it was not difficult to distinguish between closer and distant relatives, as close ones were grieving their loss and were engaged in performing the essential rituals, while the distant relatives were seated in groups at a distance, discussing among themselves the incident of death and waiting for the completion of the cremation.

Here, the sample size of respondents who opted for the gas crematorium is smaller, as it was difficult to interview these mourners. Prominent reasons included the fact that, generally, in the gas crematorium, there were often fewer mourners accompanying the deceased, and those present were usually close relatives of the deceased. These close relatives were often in a state of despair. Secondly, the cremation process in the gas crematorium took around one hour to complete, so people were less willing to talk, unlike in the traditional cremation process, where distant relatives often feel bored while waiting for three hours. The third reason was that most of the bodies were Covid-infected, so I did not interview those mourners who were accompanied by workers wearing PPE (Personal Protective Equipment) kits for safety reasons.

The paragraph below briefly describes the people who opted for the gas crematorium. Here, I am referring to the mourners based on the numbers allotted to them rather than their names. Mourner 13 accompanied the dead body of his colleague's brother. The deceased was thirty-five years old and had committed suicide by hanging himself in his office in Banaras. Though his home was in the outskirts of a village near Banaras, after the post-mortem, his body was brought directly to the gas crematorium rather than being taken back home. Relatives were informed, and they all gathered at Harishchandra Ghat.[10]

Here, the decision to choose the gas crematorium was made by the eldest son, and the reason mentioned was:

> It was an untimely death at a young age. Secondly, it was peak winter in the month of January, and cremation rites had to be performed in

Table 4.1 Details of dead bodies whose last rites were performed at Harishchandra Ghat.

S.No.	Mourners Details (Occupation & Age)	Relation with deceased	Age of deceased	Reason of death	Body coming from Hospital/ Home	Place from where body came	Mode of last rites	Reason of preference
1	Guard (40)	Uncle	55	Disease	Hospital	Banaras	Traditional	Custom
2	Retired Railway Employee (63)	Sister's Mother in-law	80	Age	Home	Banaras	Traditional	Custom
3	Engineer (35)	Uncle	53	Covid	Hospital	Madhya Pradesh	Traditional	Custom
4	Railway Employee (60)	Colleague son	32	Disease	Home	Banaras	Traditional	Custom
5	Government Job (32)	Relative	45	Disease	Hospital	Mirzapur	Traditional	Custom
6	Contractor (48)	Sister in-law	60	Accident	Hospital	Sant Ravidas Nagar	Traditional	Custom
7	Retired Engineer (65)	Uncle	78	Age	Home	Banaras	Traditional	Custom
8	Labourer (55)	Relative	65	Disease	Home	Banaras	Traditional	Custom
9	Shopkeeper (45)	Mother in-law	85	Age	Home	Mirzapur	Traditional	Custom
10	Priest (45)	Relative	56	Disease	Home	Banaras	Traditional	Custom

S.No.	Mourners Details (Occupation & Age)	Relation with deceased	Age of deceased	Reason of death	Body coming from Hospital/ Home	Place from where body came	Mode of last rites	Reason of preference
11	Contractual Job (35)	Neighbour	60	Disease	Home	Banaras	Traditional	Custom
12	Lecturer (27)	Teacher father	70	Disease	Hospital	Banaras	Traditional	Custom
13	Scholar (30)	Friend Brother	35	Suicide	Office	Banaras	Gas Crematorium	Untimely death
14	Scholar (30)	Colleague Sister in-law	35	Suicide	Hospital	Banaras	Gas Crematorium	Untimely death
15	Retired (69)	Nephew	48	Disease	Hospital	Madhya Pradesh	Traditional	Custom
16	Labourer (52)	Colleague	48	Disease	Home	Banaras	Gas Crematorium	Cheaper
17	Tea shop (40)	Friend Nephew	Infant	Delivery	Hospital	Banaras	Immersed in river	Custom
18	Lecturer (52)	Colleague	83	Age	Home	Banaras	Gas Crematorium	No family member of Deceased
19	Parlour(30)	Mother	55	Covid	Home	Banaras	Traditional	Custom
20	Shop (28)	Uncle	42	Covid	Hospital	Banaras	Traditional	Custom

the evening. It would be difficult for elderly relatives to travel back to their villages, so the gas crematorium was considered the best choice as it consumes less time.

Mourner 14 attended the funeral of his colleague's sister-in-law. She had committed suicide by consuming poison and was immediately admitted to Sir Sundar Lal Hospital in Banaras Hindu University (BHU) but could not survive. Consequently, she was taken directly to the gas crematorium due to the nature of her death. Mourner 16 was a labourer waiting for his colleague's cremation at the gas crematorium. The deceased, aged forty-eight, was his friend and had been unwell for the past three months due to a damaged liver. Only three to four people attended his funeral, including the deceased's son, who was around ten years old. When asked about the reason for choosing the gas crematorium, the mourner replied, 'It's our constrained situation.'

Mourner 18 accompanied the dead body of his colleague—an eighty-three-year-old woman – a professor who had done a lot of charity work in her life. She did not have any family members or relatives, so her colleagues brought her body to the gas crematorium for her last rites. Mourner 17 accompanied the body of his colleague's newborn nephew, who died a few hours after birth. His body was wrapped in a white shroud, tied with stones, and immersed in the flowing water of the river.

These cases were mostly of untimely deaths; three had opted for the gas crematorium, and one chose immersion of the body as recommended in Hinduism. Besides the nature of death, the explicit factors for choosing the gas crematorium were the unaffordability of the cost of traditional methods and the lesser time required to complete cremation rites. In one case, as there were no family members for the deceased, the mourners opted for the gas crematorium to save time. Moreover, unexpected death is more shocking for family members, so they opt for a quicker means to cremate the body, unlike those cases where an elderly person had lived a full life and awaited death for salvation. In the latter cases, families are willing to perform all rituals and spend their money on a grand cremation, such as choosing *charan paduka* for the cremation, decorated with rangolis and flowers. In these cases, the Dom-Raja is also provided with a handsome amount.

Among all the mourners, only Mourner 19[11] was a female, thirty years old, who runs a parlour for a living. She is the only child of her parents. She lost her father at a young age, and her mother died due to Covid. The respondent, along with her friends, cremated her mother through traditional methods. As they were just four people, she gave a shoulder to her mother's bier and even performed the *mukhagni* ritual. When asked who made the decision to opt for traditional cremation, she replied:

> Even if it was just for fun, I used to tell my mother that I would give her body to the Nagar Nigam (Municipal corporation-gas crematorium). She would immediately say, 'Do not give my body to the machine because if my body remains unburnt, then my soul will roam here in this world, and I will come to trouble you'. Money did not matter in this situation. It was my mother's wish, so I borrowed 25,000 rupees from my friend and completed her cremation.

This narrative emphasizes that death is another rite of passage. Though for better-off families the cost of cremation does not matter, there are cases where people even take money on loan to arrange a proper cremation as prescribed in Hinduism. Furthermore, age is not the only determining factor that influences one's choice of cremation method; the nature of death also matters. Deaths due to suicide or murder are prominent reasons for opting for the crematorium.

The reluctance of people in opting for crematoriums was due to difficulties in conducting specific prescribed rites, which were hindered by the machine. For instance, one of the prominent reasons is the assimilation of body elements back into nature. In Hinduism, it is often believed that the human body consists of five elements: earth, water, air, space and fire. Cremation through traditional means, that is, burning a body on a wooden pyre in an open space near the bank of a river, facilitates the assimilation of these elements back into nature. As the pyre is arranged in an open space on the earth's surface, the fire used in cremation consumes the body, the ground assimilates the body into the earth, and the open space provides ascension of the smoke into the sky. Finally, the ritual of immersing the last part of the body remains into the Ganges River, along with the immersion of ashes, leads to the assimilation of the body parts into the water.

The second is the belief in the reincarnation of the soul through the rites of immersion of the remaining body parts and ashes in flowing water. The third is the performance of the *kapal kriya* ritual, which helps release the trapped vital breath from the head of the body, without which the soul will not be liberated. Moreover, another important factor that motivates people to opt for the traditional method is ending the attachment with the deceased and acknowledging the truth of life, which helps the mourners to continue with their lives, as revealed by Mourner 4.

> When we look at the body burning slowly in an open space, it helps in the dissolution of our attachment. Observing the transformation of the body into ashes and its integration back into the five elements of life reinforces this perspective. These traditions are rooted in a psychological view of ending our attachment.

Besides these reasons, the economic expenditure involved in the performance of death rites also reflects an individual's social status, similar to birth and marriage ceremonies. Thus, in addition to cultural values, these rites also have economic aspects associated with them. This is highlighted by Mourner 2.

> There is a social recognition attached to wood cremation. Earlier, resources were easily available, but not anymore. Now, this machine, as part of modern technologies, has come into use. Though the cost of cremation is lower with it, you will not be able to explain the science behind it to everyone. If a family is poor, they say, 'Let's go to Harishchandra Ghat; the body will be cremated via electricity'. However, wood cremation is preferred because of the social status

> attached to it, along with age-old traditions and beliefs. Even though wood is available here at 460 rupees per maund, in rural areas, the same wood can be purchased for 300 to 350 rupees per quintal. (stressing this point emphatically)

The above-mentioned factors influence the decision-making of people in choosing the mode of last rites, with the freedom to perform all prescribed rites for the liberation of the soul.

Though gas crematoriums have positive implications from an environmental perspective, there has been a failure in creating awareness about this among the masses. In the present time, technological innovation is advancing rapidly. Is there no possibility of assimilating both the beliefs of people and environmental concerns simultaneously while designing modern crematoriums? Martin, in 1864, designed the first crematorium by taking caste dynamics into consideration. Modern-day technology does not provide options for mourners to perform the aforementioned rites. To justify their rejection of gas crematoriums, people often refer to the recognition of wood cremation provided by traditions and *dharma.* Mourner 2 mentioned that 'fire is considered pure in Hinduism, but in the machine, they use a coil that is heated up; hence, actual fire is absent. Moreover, there is a fear of mixing up ashes with those of other dead bodies'.

Despite knowing the reason for the installation of the gas crematorium, people merely used it for sudden and untimely deaths. It is often argued by mourners that the gas crematorium is for unclaimed bodies, poorer families and those constrained by time. Some situations force individuals to confront a conflict between their traditionally rooted belief systems and actions based on rationality. The following instance illustrates this: a mourner in his late sixties accompanied the dead body of his colleague's son, which was cremated using wood, but he had opted for the gas crematorium for his own grandmother.

> Question: What is the need for this crematorium when most people prefer traditional cremation?

Mourner: It is cheaper, and the pollution is less. Cremation via wood is expensive, and pollution is greater. To reduce pollution, a gas crematorium was installed.

Question: How much did it cost you for the traditional cremation?

Mourner: I am not sure, but approximately 10,000 rupees to 12,000 rupees. I do not know the cost at a gas crematorium, but I think it could be arranged within 1,200 rupees – 1,300 rupees.

Question: 500 rupees are fixed there.

Mourner: Yes, it is fixed. I cremated my grandmother's body at the crematorium.

Question: Why did you choose the gas crematorium for your grandmother?

Mourner: That time, it was the rainy season, and the water level was too high, so, due to the circumstances, we had chosen this crematorium.

Question: Okay. As you have used both methods, which method do you prefer?

Mourner: In Hinduism, people give more recognition to traditional cremation as the Hindu religion emphasizes recognition and belief. If we do something new, there is fear in our minds that there will be repercussions. It is said that fear leads to devotion. The day that fear is gone, we will not believe in anything.

The above narrative from an educated and experienced individual working in the government sector illustrates that people went to the crematorium in constrained situations despite being fully aware of its benefits. The gas crematorium has been used primarily for unclaimed bodies and untimely deaths.

I have observed that some unclaimed bodies are also cremated through the traditional method after the non-governmental organization (NGO) named 'Banaras Mukti Dhaini', which started in 2014, took responsibility for these bodies. But, no separate pyres are arranged for these bodies; in fact, they are thrown onto an already burning pyre.

The findings suggest that neither ritual specialists nor mourners are ready to completely accept the interference of technology in cremation rites and rituals. As ritual specialists have their economic interests, they are engaged in propagating the glorification of Banaras and are concerned that mandatory rules related to death rites and rituals are followed by people; otherwise, it will affect their own means of livelihood.

On the other hand, people are following these rites and rituals as prescribed by religious texts in the name of tradition. They are reluctant to use technology instead of traditional methods due to the fear of the unseen. Here, religion acts as the saviour of the individual when they are trying to deal with this fear of uncertainty and the threat of existence caused by the loss of their loved ones. It provides hope and a belief in life after death. Certain rites and rituals are prescribed, allowing the soul to be liberated and enter into their ancestors' realm. However, the advent of technology has challenged this whole concept, and there is a continuous fear that the soul will not be liberated in the gas crematorium in the absence of prescribed rites. People cannot trust the technology as they cannot see what is happening to the body inside the machine. Their mind remains perplexed, unaware of whether the bodies are getting completely burned and the ashes are mixing with other people's ashes. As a result, they choose to trust the ritual specialists, the experts in this domain. This has led to another belief that crematoriums are meant for unclaimed bodies, those who do not have anyone to perform their rites.

Hence, the death industry is shifting towards a mixed approach, using traditional means on one hand and technology on the other, with the use of each alternative depending on the circumstances. It can be understood as a continuum on a spectrum, where one end represents dominant traditional practices and the other end represents technological practices inextricably linked to the environment at both local and global levels, albeit in different ways (Singh 2022:114).

There are crucial alterations in the dominant traditional practices, either through the use of the permanent fixed iron-grill platform to burn the pyre, which consumes less wood in comparison to makeshift pyres, or the use of 'Royal', a chemical that induces flames (Singh

2022:121). Comparing the situation of technological acceptance in migrated Hindus staying in other countries and Hindus of India, it is rightly argued that 'if in Britain, cremation progressed down the social scale from the upper and middle classes, in India, this western style (in-door) cremation began with the low caste poor and struggled to gain acceptance among high-status communities' (Arnold 2016:402).

We had discussed the conflict and convergence of traditional beliefs and technology, representing two separate ends of a continuum axis. The following section will address the environmental concern of Ganges pollution, which is inextricably linked with technological intervention.

River Ganges as 'Cosmic Sink'[12]

The Ganges holds an important position in Hinduism as a purifier of sins, but in Banaras, it becomes the epitome of auspiciousness because of the amalgamation of sacred spots: Banaras, the beloved city of Lord Shiva, and *mahashamshan* (great cremation ground).

Hindus consider the Ganges the most auspicious river and offer their prayers not to the visible form of the water but to the life within it (Darian 1978:17). Ganges water has been used on numerous occasions, sometimes as a cure to ward off evil spirits, or at other times as a medium of purification by sprinkling it at weddings over the bride and bridegroom, and feeding it into the mouths of dying persons, besides serving as an oath-taking medium (Mahajan 1994:11).

Pilgrims from across India come to this *tirtha* for a holy bath to wash away their sins. The Ganges occupies a position of incongruence between the religious model of removing ritual pollution (to attain spiritual purity) and the accumulation of biological pollution (removal of physical impurities) (Barrett 2008:40). The Ganges embraces everything, ranging from carcasses, corpses, untreated sewage, garlands, offerings and lamps, thus being treated similar to a dumping ground. People can be seen bathing, washing clothes and enjoying boat rides, seemingly unbothered by the rotting smell of carcasses floating in the water. These activities illustrate how the Ganges has become a 'sacred cosmic sink' for disposing of both physical and metaphysical refuses (Barrett 2008:31). There is a need to understand the agency of the Ganges in performing the reabsorption of these materials. Reabsorbing is understood as both 'possessing the grace and being involved with negotiating the abject and poisonous' (Singh 2022:117).

For centuries, corpses unfit for cremation have been immersed in the flowing waters of the Ganges. However, a sharp decline in these numbers was noticed in the 1980s due to the Swachh Ganga Abhiyan – the 'Pure Ganges Campaign' started by the Chief Priest of the Sankat Mochan temple. But the situation returned to square one after patrols by the river police became easy to evade (Parry 1994:69). The government also released flesh-eating turtles and Gharial crocodiles into the river, but nothing improved. Even the coronavirus pandemic witnessed a number of dead bodies floating in rivers. This reflects the incongruence of the Ganges as the provider of purity (spiritual) when she is engulfed in physical pollution. Banaras itself daily produces 450 million litres of sewage, out of which it partially treats only 250 million litres; the rest is poured into the holy river.[13] Besides, there are spiritual activities that have their share in making the Ganges a cosmic sink.

As mentioned in an earlier chapter, myth plays a central role in strengthening the beliefs of people, and here this river has been assigned the image of a deity and allocated the status of a mother, thus referred to as 'Ganga *ma*'. In the past, it was called 'Forshwul', the *river of religious merit*, which can wash away countless sins (Mahajan 1994:15). The Ganges has been thought of as a mother who purifies the sins of her children and possesses life-giving properties. The famous myth of Bhagiratha, who indulged in ascetic practice for years, describes the sole purpose of bringing the Ganges to earth as taking the souls of the deceased to God's abode (Darian 1978:17–19). Myths always carry a message that attributes certain traits to the described God. Those traits became the reason for worshipping God to get blessings from them. Besides being the purifier of sins, the life-attributing property of the Ganges is one such trait described by this myth from the tale of *Mahabharata*.

Myth 8

> One day, a king named Shantanu was walking by the river when he saw a lovely woman. Unknown to him, she was the Goddess Ganga. Completely enchanted, he asked her to be his wife. She accepted but on one condition: 'You must not interfere with anything I do, no matter what. I will be your wife, but the moment you reproach me, I will leave you'.
>
> The King, while enjoying himself with his wife for years, had eight children born to him who, in beauty, were like the celestials themselves. But at birth, each child was thrown into the river by his wife. He remained silent for the fear of losing her but with the birth of the eighth child, he could not restrain himself any longer, 'Why have you done these terrible deeds, murdering your own children?' he demanded. 'There is no blame in what I do', she replied demurely. I am the Goddess Ganga, and these children I have borne to you, they are Vasus, celestials who were cursed to appear in human form as punishment for their misdeeds against Sage Vasishtha. It is a terrible fate to live as a man once you have known immortality; and out of compassion, I agreed to bear them on earth and restore them to paradise the moment they were born. And now according to our compact, I must leave you. She left leaving Shantanu with the eighth child who later was known as *Gangadatta*. (Darian 1978:31–2)

Hence, the Ganges has been regarded as the one who purifies one's sins and takes the souls of the departed to heaven. Due to this belief, basil leaves and a few drops of its water are poured into the mouth of the dead body immediately after death. Travellers who visited India wrote interesting descriptions of life around the Ganges. Some of those writings provide us with a glimpse of past times and the way religious practices have changed over time. They were baffled to see how the ashes of the deceased were immersed in the Ganges to attain redemption from their sins, along with how half-burnt bodies or people who had just died were immersed in the river.

> At one place where we halted for a while, the foul gush from a sewer was making the water turbid and murky all around, and there was a random corpse slopping around in it that had followed down from up country. Ten steps below that place stood a crowd of men and women, and comely young maidens waist deeps in the water – and they were scooping it up in their hands and drinking it. Faith can certainly do wonders, and this is an instance of it. Those people were not drinking that fearful stuff to assuage thirst, but in order to purify their souls and their interior of the bodies … When we went to Agra, by and by, we happened there just in time to be in at the birth of a marvel – a memorable scientific discovery – the discovery that in certain ways the foul and derided Ganges water is the most puissant purifier in the world ! … Mr Henkin, the scientist, went to Benares and made his test, he got water at the mouths of the sewers where they empty into the river at the bathing *ghats*; a cubic centimetre of it contained millions of germs; at the end of six hours, they were all dead. He caught a floating corpse, towed it to the shore, and from beside it he dipped up water that was swarming with cholera germs; at the end of six hours, they were all dead. He added swarm after swarm of cholera germs to this water; within six hours they always died, to the last sample … The Hindus have been laughed at, these many generations, but the laughter will need to modify itself a little from now on. How did they find out the water's secret in those ancient ages? Had they been germ scientists then? We do not know that they had a civilisation long before we emerged from savagery. (Mark Twain: *Following the Equator* 1897)[14]

These incidents exemplify the way myths and beliefs facilitate these rituals among Hindus. These actions were quite shocking for outsiders who did not understand the actual belief behind those practices, which were performed on such a large scale and, in fact, continue to this day. The degrading water quality of the Ganges raises the question of whether she, who herself is an emblem of purity in Hinduism, can become polluted. Here is a different perspective to look at the same problem. In 1809, Heber was told about a Hindu-Muslim riot in Banaras, and the following passage provides his witty description of the episode, bringing out the great importance of the Ganges and Banaras in the life of Hindus.

> One-half of the population was literally armed against the others, and the fury which actuated both was more like that of demoniacs than rational enemies. It began with the Mussulmans breaking down a famous pillar, named Siva's walking-staff (the Lat Bhairon) held in high veneration by the Hindoos. These last in revenge burnt and broke down a mosque, and the retort of the first aggressors was to kill a cow and pour her blood into the sacred well. Both parties then took to arms, several lives were lost and Benares was in a state of turmoil for several hours until the British authorities intervened and the disturbance was put down.
>
> After the tumult was quelled, a very curious and impressive scene succeeded; the holy city had been profaned; the blood of a cow had been mixed with the purest water of Ganga, and salvation was to be obtained at Benares no longer. All the brahmins in the city, amounting to many thousands, went down in melancholy procession, with ashes on their heads, naked and fasting, to the principal *ghats* leading to the river, and sat there with their hands folded, their heads hanging down, to all appearance inconsolable, and refusing to enter a house or to taste food. Two or three days of this abstinence, however, began to tire them, and a hint was given to the magistrate and other public men, that a visit of condolence and an expression of sympathy with these holy mourners would sufficiently comfort them, and give them an ostensible reason for return to their usual employment. Accordingly, all the Britisher functionaries went to the principal *ghats*, expressed their sorrow for the distress which they saw in them, but reasoned with them on the absurdity of punishing themselves for an act in which they had no

> share, and which they had done their utmost to prevent or avenge. This prevailed, and after much bitter weeping, it was resolved that the Ganges was the Ganges still, that a succession of costly offerings from the laity Benares might wipe out the stain which their religion had received … (Reginald Heber: *Narratives of a Journey through the Upper Province of India* (1828)[15]

It is an interesting incident where Banaras and the Ganges, considered the epitome of sacredness and purity, turned profane. The spiritual purity of the Ganges came under the radar of doubt. That, too, due to the spilling of the blood of a holy cow in the river. In Hinduism, a cow is also treated as a mother, similar to the Ganges. The death of the holy animal profaned the status of another mother, due to which Brahmins literally mourned the death of the Ganges. This implies two things: firstly, due to the death of another sacred being, the Ganges involuntarily lost its sacredness and turned profane. Secondly, the proximity of a sacred being to a dead sacred entity led to its own symbolic death. This further resulted in the loss of its attributes of providing salvation. Hence, both Banaras and the Ganges lost their sacredness as a result of the mixing of blood with the Ganges' water. Furthermore, as this incident happened in Banaras, it turned both the city and the river profane, thus causing them to lose their respective attributes of being salvation providers. If both these epitomes, which bestow salvation, were to remain profane, it could pose a significant challenge for attaining salvation in Hinduism. To resolve this dilemma, religion was brought forth as a saviour and rituals were performed to mitigate the negative effects of the act.

But then, what about the carcasses of floating cows that are still immersed in the Ganges? Do these not compromise the sacredness and purity of the Ganges? It rather questions the distinction between spiritual purity and physical pollution. The incident of spilling the blood of a cow into the Ganges is different from immersing its dead carcasses, in the sense of how death had occurred. In the earlier incident, the cow was killed in revenge for hurting Hindu sentiments. In other cases, animal carcasses are immersed as they are forbidden from cremation and cannot be sacrificed. Though the religious perspective argues that bodies unfit for cremation should be immersed in water, some people prefer to dump bodies into the Ganges due to their inability to afford the cost of cremation (Alley 1998:309). Though the crematorium was constructed to cremate the corpses flowing in the Ganges along with animal carcasses. I noticed animal bodies floating freely on the river, emanating a foul smell, on which stray dogs attempt to feed. Due to the deterioration of the Ganges' water quality, the Allahabad High Court, as part of anti-pollution measures, banned the immersion of idols into the Ganges in 2013. Instead, immersion was permitted into certain water bodies or wells (*pokhara*). But, many Hindus protested against it. One of the boatmen mentioned:

> Earlier, idols were immersed in Ganga Ji, but now the government has banned this practice and instructed people to perform the immersion in *Pokhara* (pond). It does not look good, but what can we do? Government employees only come and chant slogans about keeping Ganga clean when the weather is favorable. Why do they not come during the flood season, when all the garbage from the streets is floating in Ganga Ji? They ask us not to bathe or wash clothes here, but they fail to realise that they live in bungalows, while many of us do not even have roofs over our heads or food to eat. (He took out his phone and showed me a picture of a floating corpse in Ganga) and asked, 'Now, is Ganga not getting polluted?'

Natives of Banaras daily encounter floating corpses and carcasses in the river, but they do not believe that these threaten the Ganges' spiritual integrity, as they firmly believe that the Ganges' sole purpose of coming to the earth was to provide liberation to these souls. They, in fact, point out that bodies which are unfit for cremation are anyway immersed in the Ganges'. Moreover, for unclaimed bodies that float in the river after committing suicide, there is no sense of disgust; instead, people laugh it off, saying, 'He attained salvation.'

Common life does not seem to be affected much by these bodies, as people walk normally around the *ghat* and continue their day-to-day activities. Dogs' attempts to feed on these floating bodies are not surprising either. Mourner 12 shares:...

> Once, when I was sitting at Tulsi Ghat with my friend, I saw two dogs fighting with each other over a child's dead body immersed in Ganga Ji. Perhaps it was not tied properly with a stone, so it was floating and had drifted to the bank of the *ghat*. Local people shooed away the dogs and threw the body back into the Ganga again.

Despite being aware of the benefits of gas crematoriums, people are still reluctant to change their practices. As Mourner 3 puts it, 'Rites and rituals can only be performed in wood cremation. Additionally, I think the gas crematorium is eco-friendly and involves no wastage of wood. The gas crematorium positively impacts our environment, but as per rituals, people continue to follow the traditional method.'

There is a dissonance between the physical pollution and the spiritual purity of the Ganges. Hindu devotees believe that the Ganges can clean herself and purify any person despite being physically polluted. Many believers hold that while Mother *Ganga* could, unfortunately, become unclean (*asvaccha*), she could never be impure (*asuddha*) or ever die.

From the perspective of the government, physical pollution is believed to be the result of public activity on the river bank and sewage treatment plants. In contrast, people blame government policies that failed to take into consideration the common masses who earn a livelihood from the Ganges and the role of the State in supporting corruption. Thus, 'religious images have no parallel in materialist interpretations of space and create symbolic dissonance with spatial meanings constructed by scientific and official governmental worldviews' (Alley 1998:298).

Coming back to our earlier question, there is a difference between spiritual purity and physical pollution of the Ganges. From a spiritual perspective, floating bodies do not contribute to the spiritual pollution of the Ganges, as its main attribution is to carry souls to heaven. The physical pollution of the Ganges is majorly attributed to untreated sewage, besides the construction of dams that decreased the river flow. It makes sense, as the dilution of water through increased flow will reduce the damaging effects of pollution, even if it does not eliminate the problem entirely (Mallet 2017:72).

According to Jal Nigam officer:

> Banaras produces 450 MLD (million litres a day) of sewage daily, but we treat only 250 MLD. The remaining 200 MLD flows directly into the river. This is because the five sewage treatment plants here do not work at full capacity. The dredging to set up a cruise service and widespread construction for a riverfront tourism programme are two ongoing government projects affecting the flow of the Ganga.[16]

About 95 per cent of the pollution is caused by sewage flowing into the river from thirty source points in Banaras. The level of pollution is quantified by Biochemical Oxygen Demand (BOD) in mg/L of the river water, which is a measure of organic matter present in the water, and the faecal coliform counts (FCC) per 100 mL of the water sample (Singh et al. 2018:244).

Studies show that maximum BOD was recorded at Manikarnika Ghat, indicating irreparable damage due to the discharge of organic waste and religious activities (Singh 2018). The water quality index reveals that Ganges water is moderately polluted and is unfit for human consumption. This points that Banaras itself is a major contributor in the increased pollution. Besides these, McNeill's work mentioned that in 1980, the official crematoria of Banaras burned 30 million bodies a year and deposited several million tonnes of human ashes into the Ganges every month (McNeill 2000:129).

Further, many additional bodies, partly cremated, were shoved into the river, accounting for roughly 60,000 animal carcasses (McNeill 2000). In the 1960s, the Ganges was a bacteriological nightmare when the first systematic pollution studies took place and worsened further. The government's clean-up efforts began in 1960 and coordinated into the Ganga Action Plan in 1985, which had little discernible effect. Here important changes were the intensification of bacteriological pollution, not the problem derived from the industrial emissions, which the river's huge flow masked until about 1990 (McNeill 2000:135). These conditions have not changed much.

At both the cremation *ghats*, Harishchandra Ghat and Manikarnika Ghat, nearly 32,000 bodies are cremated every year with the help of 10,000 tonnes of wood.[17] On an average, daily around 250 dead bodies come to Manikarnika Ghat because of its mythological importance. It is important to note that the human body produces 800 tonnes of ashes which are released into the river (Singh 2017). Ashes of dead bodies consist of bone, enamel, cartilage and traces of dentine. These are composed of carbon dioxide, calcium phosphate, magnesium phosphate, sulphur dioxide and traces of nitrogen dioxide, nitrate oxide and nitrogen monoxide. Sulphur dioxide is a harmful compound which has adverse effects on the lungs (Maurya and Sharma 2016:11). These ashes contain nitrogen 77,000 kg, phosphorus 48,000 kg and potassium 5,000 kg, leading to water composition changes (PTI 2016).

Moreover, about 200 tonnes of half-burnt flesh are released into the Ganges, increasing the BOD and decreasing Oxygen Demand levels (PTI 2016). As the cremation process continues round the clock, bodies are burned in an unorganized and haphazard manner. Shrouds, wood logs, ashes and garlands can be seen floating in the water near the cremation *ghats*. However, under the 'Namami Ganges Programme', workers are now engaged in removing garbage from the cremation *ghats* on a daily basis early in the morning. In most cases, unclaimed bodies and those who have committed suicide are seen floating in the Ganges. The analysis of water samples from seven *ghats* shows that the river's pollution level is higher at Harishchandra Ghat in comparison to other *ghats* due to the large quantity of industrial and sewage discharge, along with the performance of cremation activities (Ali and Kumar 2017:237).

Besides water pollution, open cremation has contributed to air pollution as well. Hazardous air pollutants emitted during this process include particulate matter, gaseous pollutants such as CO, NOx, NH_3, SO_2 etc., and heavy metals like Hg, Pb, As (Ali and Kumar, 2017). In addition, the most dangerous polychlorinated dibenzo-p-dioxins and dibenzofurans (PCDD/Fs), mercury and polycyclic aromatic hydrocarbons, as well as other organic pollutants, have been proven dangerous for human health (Ali and Kumar 2017). Out of the various route of direct exposure to these pollutants, inhalation seems to be the usual route (Cruz et al. 2017:24130). Excessive ozone and carbon monoxide can cause breathing problems, trigger asthma and cause lung diseases. Sulphur dioxide can cause acid rain, which can negatively impact water quality. It can cause irritations in the eyes and respiratory tract infections. Thus, higher concentrations of these air pollutants are dangerous to health (Singh et al. 2018:844).

Open cremation becomes problematic as its combustion processes involve the production of gases deemed harmful to the environment. Even the presence of mercury in the tooth fillings of people in the mid and late-twentieth century served as example of substances producing dangerous gases (Davis 2003:768).

Many affidavits have been filed by people to the National Green Tribunal, urging the government to step into the matter of dumping dead bodies in the Ganges. Through the Press Information Bureau, the government had directed states to prevent the dumping of corpses into the river, the burying of bodies in the sand near the river, and to provide dignified cremation for the bodies, but these directions have been limited only to paper (Maria 2022).

What could be a possible solution? There are differences in the functioning of the official gas crematorium and the traditional open cremation *ghats* at Banaras. It takes about three to four hours in an open cremation to burn the body with around 500 to 600 kilograms of wood.[18] There is no option for a filtering system or to keep a minimum incineration temperature, so that the emission of mercury can be tackled safely. In addition, due to the lack of any safety and preventive measures in handling dead bodies, Dom *naukars* are more vulnerable. Moreover, the bursting of pacemakers during cremation is dangerous for these *naukars* as it leads to injuries to their eyes and body burn (Kumari 2018:124).

Further, the Dom can be seen sieving the ashes in the Ganges for hours in search of jewellery. This practice pollutes the river water and impacts Dom *naukars,* who stand in the polluted water for five to six hours. As a result, they are more prone to diseases, as cremations are known to produce cancer-causing dioxins, trace metals, hydrochloric acid, carbon dioxide and sulphur dioxide (Maurya and Sharma 2016:12).

Though Western countries had developed scientific indoor crematoria by observing traditional cremation practices, in India, Western technology failed to displace the ancient practice. It is not the first time that 'tradition' and 'modern' technology have competed, contested and intersected with each other (Arnold 2016:404). When Martin designed the crematorium in 1864, he took into consideration the requirements of people from their religious perspectives. He examined the traditional cremation costs and noted that orthodox Brahmins practising untouchability were reluctant to use crematoriums due to fears of mixing ashes with those of other caste groups, as well as concerns about not being able to follow the rites prescribed by Hinduism. To address these issues, Martin (1864) designed a machine where ten bodies from different castes could burn separately at the same time. Since Brahmins preferred to collect their ashes after the third day, this division and the increased number of chambers resolved the problem. Moreover, he left some space at the back of the chamber so that Brahmins could complete the ritual of circumambulating around the pyre. He also suggested that the crematorium should be under government supervision and that a market selling essential supplies required for funerals should be organized near the crematorium to save time (Martin 1864: 6–8).

In order to tackle environmental damage, it is important to consider people's beliefs and gain their trust before implementing any changes. Recently, the Indian Institute of Technology (IIT) Delhi redefined the ritual of cremation by using cow dung to make logs and performing cremation with them (PTI, 2022). This can save wood, and has religious alignment and does not generate comparable emissions in burning. But people must be made aware to be ready and accept these changes.

Religious beliefs and practices determine certain cremation rituals, such as the immersion of ashes and the exclusion of dead bodies that are not considered fit for cremation. These religious beliefs also influence the number of dead bodies brought to Banaras for their last rites due to the notion of salvation associated with the city. These practices play a crucial role in the degradation of the Ganges, which is further compounded by activities such as worshipping the river with garlands, bathing, brushing teeth, and washing clothes in it. As a result of the declining water quality, families residing near the cremation *ghats* face serious health hazards. Consequently, the Ganges, which is the epitome of purity, has been continually abused by the masses.

Even the crematorium at Harishchandra Ghat, which was built in 1989 as part of the GAP, does not function properly due to frequent technical snags and a lack of resources for its maintenance. Thus, most bodies are burned on traditional pyres. Even in the crematorium, after the bodies are burned, the ashes are handed over to the Dom to sieve in search of jewellery.

Whether a person adopts the gas crematorium, manual cremation, immersion or burial depends on religious preferences, but there is a requirement for a space where the bereaved family members can express their grief and pain. For instance, the gas crematorium does not provide the space to perform all the mandatory rites prescribed by Hinduism, so many people opt for wood cremation, where crucial rites and rituals can be performed. Thus, the State should consider religious beliefs and sentiments of people, along with those working in the death industry, for properly implementing its policy to tackle pollution.

The next chapter discusses the emergence of pathological conditions due to the coronavirus, when unmanageable bodies were arriving and technology intervened much more than before. It attempts to analyse alterations, if any, in the prescribed Hindu rites and rituals during the normlessness, to understand how people adapted to the 'new normal' in death rites. It also examines the effect of the pandemic on the Dom, the mourner and the role of the state in dealing with the catastrophe.

5

Coronavirus and Cremation Ground

A Transition from Normal to Pathological

Waves of Fear

The Covid-19 pandemic wreaked havoc across the world. To control the spread of the virus, India announced a complete lockdown starting from 25 March 2020. There was widespread fear about the newly discovered virus. The first Covid-infected dead body in Banaras reached Harishchandra Ghat on 22 April 2020.[1] The sole purpose of bringing dead bodies here was the availability of a gas crematorium. In the initial days of the pandemic, all Covid-infected bodies were cremated here.

As a mortuary van carrying the first Covid-infected body reached Harishchandra Ghat, two people wearing Personal Protective Equipment (PPE) kits moved a body out and placed it on the ground. Within minutes, the news had spread throughout the locality that a Covid-infected body had arrived. People from the neighbourhood came out of their homes and gathered on their verandas, balconies and rooftops to see the body. Policemen warned them not to step out of their homes due to existing lockdown norms. Yet, people defied orders and stepped out to catch a glimpse of the dead body. However, the road leading to the cremation ground was empty.

Meanwhile, twenty-five-year-old Raj Chaudhary was sleeping in his house when the dead body arrived. His grandmother hurriedly woke him up to inform him about the Covid-infected body and asked him not to go near the *ghat*. He woke up and, within no time, ran upstairs to the terrace to get a glimpse of what exactly was happening.

He saw some of his fellows recording the incident on video when the policemen ordered them to come down to cremate the body. None dared to go downstairs due to the fear of infection.

Shamu Chaudhary, intoxicated at the time and resting in the *madhi*, decided to provide the sacred fire for a charge of 1,400 rupees. A family member was handed the sacred fire, which was then taken around the dead body to perform *mukhagni*. The face of the deceased was not visible as it was wrapped in a PPE kit.

Shamu offered a share of the money he had received for the sacred fire to his *malik*, but he refused to take it due to fear of infection. Mourners carried the Covid-infected body to the gas crematorium and placed it inside. Then, Ranjit Chaudhary cremated the first Covid-infected body in the machine.

As days went on, it had by then become the norm that Covid-infected bodies would be cremated in the gas crematorium, whilst for other bodies the traditional method would be followed.

Slowly, the cremation grounds turned into a terrifying sight as a plethora of pyres burned next to each other. During this period, the number of bodies reaching the cremation grounds daily surpassed the usual count. Plumes of dark smoke rose upward into the air. At the same time, around thirty dead bodies were waiting for their last rites – some were partially immersed in the Ganges, while others lay on bamboo biers. Not only were the family members of the deceased devastated by the sudden loss of their loved ones, but many of them were simultaneously fearful of getting infected.

Men from the Dom community were struggling to cremate the steady stream of dead bodies. They had been working tirelessly around the clock to maintain the pace. The sudden rise in the number of dead bodies led to a space crunch in the cremation ground. Bodies were thrown over other burning pyres to cope with this paucity of space and the increasing workload. The Dom were seen wearing masks to protect themselves from infection while hastily attending to multiple pyres at once.

The Covid-19 pandemic brought about unprecedented turbulence in everyone's life, leading to despair. The surge in deaths contributed to pathological[2] conditions due to accelerating death rates. Only dead bodies were seen across streets and morgues, waiting for their last rites. The normlessness created a chaotic situation where individuals were left baffled and helpless.

To mitigate this disastrous situation, a complete lockdown was observed throughout the world. Various measures were taken in different countries; for instance, in Italy, the army was brought in to move Covid-infected bodies to funeral services. Moreover, at the beginning of the lockdown period, China, Brazil, Ecuador and Ghana discouraged funeral gatherings, while South Korea, India and France put a cap on the number of people attending such events. Meanwhile, some countries adopted forceful cremation of dead bodies across all religions (Bear et al. 2020; Singh 2020).

During this time, technology turned out to be a boon, facilitating the visual participation of family members in the cremation of their loved ones. As the pandemic's debilitating effects lingered on, the masses slowly accepted the 'new normal' after a phase of uncertainty. This is evident from the shift towards an online mode of education, the move to online consultations with doctors, and the continuous use of masks and sanitizers as safety measures.

This chapter provides glimpses of the conditions at Harishchandra Ghat during this catastrophe. It attempts to analyse alterations, if any, in the prescribed Hindu rites and rituals during this phase of normlessness. This study seeks to shed light on possible ways through which mourners adapted to the 'new normal' in the last rites. Particularly, I aim to offer insights into the effect of the pandemic on the ritual specialists and the Dom. Lastly, it examines the role played by the state in handling this situation.

Onset of the First Wave

Generally, when a dead body arrives at the Harishchandra Ghat, the Dom enquire about the cause of death. A mortuary van reached the *ghat,* and an enquiry was made. The men in the mortuary van, who were unaware that the body was Covid-infected, panicked realizing this and dumped the body in a haphazard manner from the van onto the road before leaving. The covering sheet on the body partially came off, with the hands and legs of the body jutting out. Blood oozed from the dead body.

A family member – the younger brother of the deceased – who was accompanying the body, pleaded with the Dom's men to help him cremate it. The Dom were terrified, and one of them pointed out that 'the coronavirus could spread merely by touching infected people. Here it is a pool of blood from a Covid-infected patient. How can we touch it?'. So, they called another person who usually handled unclaimed bodies. He charged 4,000 rupees for putting the body back in the PPE kit and moving it to the gas crematorium. He later cleaned and sanitized the whole area where the body had been dumped. At last, the body was cremated.

Instances such as these show how the pandemic threatened humanity, as even family members were scared to touch their relatives' bodies. They were willing to pay money for cremations, and the poor and marginalized sections were forced to carry out the task, putting their lives at risk.

But there were also cases where family members performed the last rites of their loved ones despite facing situations that were not conducive. In May 2020, the body of an elderly man who died due to Coronavirus was brought to the *ghat,* accompanied by his son, daughter-in-law and granddaughter. As it was a peak summer day and given that they were all wearing PPE kits, both his son and daughter-in-law collapsed and became unconscious. The granddaughter, who was in her twenties, single-handedly dragged the dead body from the road to the gas crematorium. There were a few people standing nearby, but they did not come forward to help the woman. The Dom, who watched the scene unfold, said that 'the family members were wearing lots of gold and were even ready to pay a handsome amount to get help for the woman, but no one was willing to assist due to the fear of Covid'.[3]

During those days, even a seven-month-old child who died of Covid and should have been immersed in the river was cremated in the gas crematorium. While the above-mentioned cases had become common, some mourners forced the Dom to cremate bodies using wood, as per tradition, in a conventional way and tried to lure them with money.

One day, the dead body of a businessman who had died of Covid was brought to the Harishchandra Ghat from Kolkata. His family was willing to pay 50,000 rupees—far more than the existing rates – to ensure that the body was cremated on a wooden pyre, following all rituals. Despite being offered a hefty sum, the Dom refused to give in, as they feared getting infected. Finally, the body was cremated in the gas crematorium. Raj Chaudhary said:

> People are asking to cremate bodies with wood, but we do not have any safety equipment. And as our houses are near the cremation grounds, what if the virus reaches our homes through the smoke? At least in the gas crematorium, the smoke goes up. Will our families not get infected? If people want to burn bodies on wood, then the government should allow us to burn the bodies on the other bank of the Ganga, because no one stays there. If more bodies come, then we will have to burn them on wood; what else can we do? If we do not burn those bodies, who will? Willingly or unwillingly, we have to do it. We only have this piece of cloth to cover our faces as a safety measure. Though the staff of the gas crematorium are provided with equipment, we have not been informed about it.[4]

But the efforts of mourners did not cease, as most of them believed that salvation could be attained only through wood cremation. On a particular day during that period, Harish Chaudhary, who is in his late teens, was approached by some mourners and a policeman to cremate a dead body. The bereaved family offered Chaudhary 25,000 rupees to carry out a wood cremation. Chaudhary could not resist the temptation of being paid 25,000 rupees—far more than what he earns on a daily basis.

He agreed and cremated the body without the knowledge of other Dom. However, all the while, he feared getting infected.

After the cremation, he went to Shivala Ghat, where some workers were busy sanitizing the area. He had himself completely sanitized and returned to Harishchandra Ghat. Still not convinced, he went for another round of sanitization. However, he continued to feel restless. He then took off his clothes and bathed in the Ganges. Before stepping out, he discarded his clothes and wrapped himself in a new towel. He went home but remained scared throughout the night of catching the infection.

The next day, around 7:30 a.m., the same policeman accompanied another Covid-infected body for wood cremation. When the Dom refused to do it, they were shown the video of Harish cremating a Covid-infected body with wood the previous day. They were left shocked. Harish was then summoned from home to the *ghat*. Harish's elder brother thrashed him badly with a belt as soon as he arrived. He pleaded and apologized while he was being beaten up.

At that time, the gas crematorium also stopped functioning, and around ten to fifteen Covid-infected bodies were waiting in queue for cremation. Soon the matter reached the higher authorities, and the district magistrate ordered the Dom to either cremate Covid-infected body through wood or leave the cremation *ghat*. He added that the pandemic had hit the whole country and was not limited to their areas. Having no other option, the Dom agreed to cremate all bodies. So, they bought 10 litres of petrol and kept it at the *ghat*. After the bodies were placed on the pyres with petrol doused, they lit the fire. PPE kits of accompanying mourners were burnt near *Massan Nath* temple. In reply to a question about the fear of infection after cremating so many Covid-infected bodies, Vishal shared an incident:

> My grandmother once told me about another epidemic (Cholera) when the situation was so bad that only dead bodies were visible everywhere. Even people who accompanied the dead bodies to cremation grounds collapsed and died. Those who were coming

> with dead bodies were themselves ending up getting cremated. At that time, we also survived, and Coronavirus does not seem that dangerous now. The rest of our life and death are in the hands of Mahadeva (Lord Shiva).

The non-functioning crematorium and the steady demand from mourners for the traditional method forced the Dom into involuntarily cremating infected bodies. In the absence of proper dissemination of information regarding safety protocols and protective equipment, their safety has been ignored. Their labour is utilized extensively in crises, like the Covid pandemic, but their role has not been treated with the seriousness it deserved.

Coming back to the previous point, it must be noted that people prefer to follow the prescribed rites and rituals despite the pandemic and the higher costs of cremation. This becomes more evident from the case of Kalpana, a female mourner aged thirty, who is the single child of her late parents. Her father passed away during her childhood, and her mother succumbed to Covid in August 2020. As she was not on speaking terms with her relatives, she informed her cousin about her mother's death and managed everything independently. The cousin in question arrived at the cremation ground with two of his friends. Kalpana sanitized her mother's body after it was handed over from the mortuary van, followed by sanitizing herself and her friends. The four of them became the pallbearers and carried the body to the cremation ground. It was challenging to procure wood during those days due to increased demand and supply shortages. Observing her situation, people at the *ghat* persuaded the wood seller to arrange wood for her. At that time, Kalpana had only 3,000 rupees, but it was her mother's last wish to be cremated through traditional means. Determined to honour her mother's wish, she borrowed the remaining money to cover the expenses, which were significantly higher than the usual cost. The cremation ultimately cost her around 25,000 rupees, but she was content knowing she had fulfilled her mother's last wish.

The act of performing last rites according to a traditionally prescribed set of norms provides a sense of satisfaction to bereaved families, as they feel they have managed to give a fitting farewell to their loved ones despite being in a crisis. But, the pandemic snatched away this possibility of performing last rites for many of the departed. Many bodies went missing due to negligence by hospitals. There were also instances of bereaved families being unable to locate the mortal remains of their loved ones, as bodies were haphazardly disposed off in hospitals and mortuaries, wrapped in PPE kits, making it difficult for people to search for a particular body, which led to widespread confusion.

There was a case at Harishchandra Ghat where a mourner cremated a dead body, believing it to be his daughter, only to realize later that it was someone else's body. The person learned about this after someone related to that body revealed what had happened. The mourner was left startled. The other family, to whom the dead body belonged, compensated him for the cremation costs. He then searched again for his daughter's body in the hospital and cremated it once he finally found it.

It is evident that, despite going through the pandemic, people still preferred wood cremation due to their belief in salvation. Those from more affluent backgrounds strove to follow their traditions by offering hefty amounts of money for wood cremation, which led to a sudden increase in the cost of cremation. Those specialized in performing rituals also demanded more than the usual amount of money due to the rise in the mortality rate, the risk of infection, the increasing workload and the opportunity to make a huge profit. Bodies had been kept waiting in long queues in morgues, crematoria and burial sites before being attended to (Kumari 2023:1441).

Due to technical snags cropping up in crematoria nationwide, the government has been forced to shift to wood cremation. Furthermore, the rise in the death rate has also affected the wood supply. As a result, cremation *ghats* across India have been struggling without sufficient wood (Kumari 2023:1444). In these circumstances, some people have found dumping bodies in flowing rivers to be an easier alternative.

The sudden imposition of the lockdown also caused trouble for the masses, as they could not earn their livelihoods. It was difficult to survive in such circumstances with mouths to feed. The same was the case for the Mallah caste. Tourists did not turn up in Banaras due to the pandemic, which affected their livelihoods. Looking at the condition of the members of his caste, Sambhu Majhi, one of the richest among them from the Dashashwamedh Ghat, gathered some people to deliver cooked food to all the families of the Mallah community.

The lockdown was different for everyone. The death industry was prospering due to the increase in dead bodies, and it became beneficial for those specializing in performing rituals. For the Yadav and the Dom, it was the best time for their business, as five maunds of wood were sold at prices ranging from 11,000 to 20,000 rupees, with demand dictating the price. The same occurred with the cost of cremation as well. Even Ramesh, who runs a tea kiosk at the cremation *ghat*, earned a good amount by opening his shop for a single day during the lockdown and then keeping it closed for three consecutive days.

Gradually, the peak of the first wave began to subside, and so did the fear of the virus. There came a time when the situation transitioned to a 'new normal', as Covid-infected bodies were treated and cremated like any other deceased individuals. The immersion of the Covid-positive body of a baby who died just two days after birth indicates the return to normal practices.

Even though, during this period, around two to three Covid-positive people were staying in the Harishchandra Ghat locality,[5] no one seemed worried. Instead, the people of Harishchandra Ghat began to question the very existence of the coronavirus. Some blamed the government for enforcing a lockdown and making it difficult for the poor to earn a livelihood. A vast majority of them also blamed doctors for false diagnoses, accusing them of greed for the incentive of two hundred thousand rupees promised by the government for treating Covid patients. Udit Chaudhary, a Dom *naukar*, said:

> We had asked mourners about the causes of death. They revealed that the deceased had suffered from liver damage for the past five years, and today the doctor said that he died due to Covid. Even the person who had died in an accident was reported to be Covid-positive. My mother has been a diabetic patient for the past 20 years. Recently, she fell ill. I took her to a doctor, and she was declared Covid-positive. We kept her in quarantine for 30 days, and then she recovered and was normal again.

Even Ranjit Chaudhary, a worker at the gas crematorium, said, 'I had cremated the first Covid body that came from Gangapur. That person was a wealthy businessman who had died of a heart attack, but the doctor reported it as a Covid death.'

These factors contributed to reducing the fear that people had during the initial days of the Covid waves. By now, the Dom had begun cremating bodies in the absence of any safety measures. Things were back to normal for those working at the cremation *ghat*. In fact, everyone began to exert pressure on me to remove my mask, and when I resisted, they made fun of me for wearing it. In their words, *there is nothing like Corona; this is an illusion*.

Impending Second Wave

As the second wave approached, the situation began to limp back to normalcy (as the earlier fear of Covid had largely subsided by then). The second wave began in March 2021 and peaked in April 2021. It had worn off by June 2021 (Bogam et al. 2021). The rise in the number of infected people and the higher number of dead bodies were alarming signs of these waves. But this time, people working at the cremation *ghats* did not perceive it as something to be feared.

On 26 March 2021, around 11 a.m., while sitting on the stairs of Harishchandra Ghat, I noticed that Shamu Chaudhary was managing the mourners of a Covid-infected body. He was instructing two men wearing PPE kits to place the body on the pyre. Generally, while placing the body on the pyre, it is lifted directly by the hands and legs. However, since it was a Covid-infected body, Shamu suggested they lift the entire bamboo bier along with the body and then flip it over the wooden pyre.[6] Shamu was wearing a mask, and the bereaved family members were standing at a distance, watching the scene unfold. Another Dom fetched Ganges water from the river in a bucket and poured it over the corpse lying on the pyre. Both men who lifted the body removed their PPE kits, placed them inside the pyre, and left. Then, the ritual of *mukhagni* was performed by a family member. By this time, Shamu had left, and the Dom *naukar* cremated the body while wearing only a mask for safety. Thus, despite the second wave, the last rites were performed as prescribed in Hinduism, with slight modifications (see Figure 5.1).

In mid-April 2021, the peak of the second wave led to panic in Banaras. By then, conditions in Lucknow, Delhi and Mumbai had

Figure 5.1 Covid-infected body cremated by traditional method.

worsened. Though Covid vaccinations were now available, there was confusion and uncertainty among the masses. People were hesitant to get vaccinated as there was doubt about whether the vaccine was truly a lifesaver. Amid all this confusion, I got myself vaccinated, and Sahil Chaudhary tensely asked me, 'Why did you take the vaccine? People getting vaccinated are the ones dying more.'

I grew anxious by now, and the hot summers worsened it. One fine day in the early morning, I went to a shopkeeper near where I stayed, and he informed me that around eight people had died in our street the previous day. By afternoon, another man who delivered drinking water to my room revealed that one of his friends had died and that he would be attending his funeral. Later, I went to the cremation *ghat* and met Sujata Chaudhary, who informed me that the washerman from her street had died too. Slowly, it felt like a horror film, as it did not matter to whom I was talking; everyone was sharing news of death with fear. I vividly imagined the number of deaths taking place in the whole city. By this time, the media was flooded with death updates and was focusing on how the situation had gone out of control in Lucknow, showing pictures of cremation *ghats* blazing with fires.

During those days, around 200 to 250 bodies were being burned in a single day at Harishchandra Ghat. As the second wave had far exceeded the mortality rate of the first wave, the distribution of a token system for the cremation of dead bodies started. Families had to wait for hours after collecting tokens. One of the mourners said:

> I came to Harishchandra Ghat at around 1 p.m. Around 10 to 15 bodies were burning on the cremation ground using wood at that time, and the gas crematorium had cremated around 20 bodies in the last 24 hours. There were queues of dead bodies with allotted tokens, waiting for their turn. In one day, more than 80–90 bodies are burnt at Harishchandra Ghat alone. You might not have seen such a sight. It can hardly be imagined.[7]

While mourners were devastated and shocked by the sudden loss of their loved ones, they were still trying to hide the actual cause of death due to the fear that the Covid-infected body might not be cremated using wood if the actual cause was revealed. On 14 April 2021, a body was cremated at around 3 p.m. Below is the conversation with one of the mourners.

Question: Can you please provide details about the deceased?

Mourner: His name was Ramesh Baranwal, and he was around 42 years old. He was the owner of a factory that produced sugar.

Question: What was the cause of death?

Mourner: He had been ill since Holi. Due to viral fever, his whole family had fallen ill. For the past 10 days, he had been bedridden. His family members had taken him to a general physician and had continued his treatment there. However, on the night of the 13th, when his condition deteriorated further, he was admitted to Kapil Chowraha Hospital. There, he was diagnosed with typhoid fever. The next day, it was revealed that he had Covid.

Question: Who gave you the report that he had Covid?

Mourner: The hospital staff sent the report to us via WhatsApp. They did not provide us with a hard copy.

Question: So, what happened after that?

Mourner: In that hospital, oxygen was not available, so the family went to BHU Hospital. At BHU Hospital, oxygen was available. However, the family of the deceased believed that since it was a government hospital, if the doctor discovered the patient had Corona, the entire family would be admitted to the hospital. Consequently, they decided to go to another hospital on the highway named Janta Hospital. They were informed that oxygen was available there, but after admitting the patient, there was no oxygen supply, so they had to arrange for an oxygen cylinder.

Question: Did they inform this hospital that he had been diagnosed with Covid-19?

Mourner: Yes, in the private hospital, it was reported. The patient's condition was such that, in his restlessness, he was removing the syringe needle from his hand, as a result of which his hands were covered with blood. He even broke the oxygen pipe twice. Consequently, the hospital staff had to tie his hands and legs, and then he was connected to an oxygen cylinder. At 6:30 a.m., his lungs stopped functioning, and he passed away between 6:30 a.m. and 7 a.m. The hospital discharged his body at 12 p.m.

Question: Did the family members encounter any issues while discharging the body from the hospital?

Mourner: No, there would have been a problem if the family had asked for a Covid certificate.

Question: So, they didn't ask for it?

Mourner: The hospital denied it, so both family members and hospital staff discussed the matter with each other. Ultimately, the family members decided not to take the report because they feared facing problems due to the stigma of Covid. The body was wrapped in a bed sheet and handed over to us.

Question: Was it disclosed at the cremation *ghat* that the person had died due to Covid-19?

Mourner: No. I was observing the situation from the beginning, and I think even while making a deal with the Dom on the phone, they did not disclose the actual cause of death.

Question: While family members were discussing it, did this issue arise that if the body were to be cremated using wood, the virus might transmit to other people as well?

Mourner: When family members were discussing how to proceed with rituals, I suggested that burning the body on wood would not be a good idea. However, the deceased's son insisted *that we would cremate with wood only*. People in Banaras believe that the body should be cremated on wood during the final rites. I think even in the gas crematorium, smoke is released into the open area after a Covid-infected body is burned. It is not going somewhere else. So, if there is a problem with burning wood, then the gas crematorium might also have the same issue. Additionally, I feel that in the gas crematorium, more smoke is emitted.

Question: Have you seen any dead bodies, diagnosed by doctors as Covid-positive, being cremated at the cremation ground?

Mourner: Yes, I saw one dead body being carried by four people wearing PPE kits. The mourners were shouting to maintain distance. That body was taken to the cremation ground and

> dipped in Ganga water before the cremation was performed. There is a belief that a dead body should be dipped in Ganga water.

The above conversation highlights certain crucial facts, such as the tendency of family members to hide the actual cause of death due to fear of stigmatization, which could have possibly hindered cremation through traditional means. Secondly, family members followed all prescribed rites and rituals despite the Covid-related death. Thirdly, there was a lack of awareness among relatives and workers in the death industry on how to handle a Covid-infected dead body. There also seems to be an issue on the hospital's side, as they were reluctant to hand over Covid-positive certificates. Lastly, although the pandemic could not stop people from following traditional rituals, it significantly increased the demand for gas crematoriums. The gas crematorium, which had previously been the last option for people, was now in high demand, as evidenced by long queues waiting in front of them. People waited for five to six hours to have their loved ones cremated. However, it cannot be ignored that this was primarily due to the difficulty in performing traditional cremations.

Due to the increase in the number of dead bodies, the burning area of Harishchandra Ghat cremation ground has now been expanded, as bodies are also being cremated in the area that belongs to other *ghats* located at the extreme end of Harishchandra Ghat (see Figure 5.2).

Further, the Municipal Corporation of Banaras had officially recognized two *ghats* specifically for cremating Covid-infected bodies, namely Samane Ghat and Harishchandra Ghat, to maintain a record of the bodies cremated. The executive officer of the Municipal Corporation shared his experience at the cremation ground.

> There was a queue of 40 corpses awaiting cremation. Huge numbers of corpses were burning. Our gas crematorium had stopped functioning, so it was important to get the bodies cremated using wood. Besides these, there were fire and smoke on the cremation ground. You could see only ashes and black smoke. You could get

Figure 5.2 Extended area of Harishchandra Ghat cremation ground.

> infected by staying there. I went into depression after witnessing such a scene that day.[8]

As the number of bodies kept increasing, to tackle the situation, Covid-infected bodies were permitted to be cremated at a total of five *ghats*: Manikarnika Ghat, Rajghat Ghat, and Domri Ghat, including both Harishchandra Ghat and Samane Ghat.

As there were long queues of dead bodies, these bodies were now left half-immersed in the river for a minimum of thirty minutes, thus completing the ritual of immersion in the Ganges for purification. In attending to these bodies, the Dom had hectic schedules and could afford only smaller breaks for drinking water and chewing tobacco. A Dom *naukar* said:

> A large number of corpses are coming this time. They had to wait in queue as they were provided with a token to get cremated by wood. No space is left; only burning pyres are visible. It is too hot; we cannot eat anything, so we are just drinking water, consuming

> tobacco, and working tirelessly. We do not have time to have food; we quickly run home, eat, and return to work.[9]

It has been challenging to cremate numerous bodies at once. But not everyone seemed equally afraid of getting infected this time, as shared by Shobha Chaudhary.

> So many people are dying this time; if Corona is nothing, why are so many dying? My husband is not coming home at night these days; he eats outside. In the mornings, he bathes in the Ganga. After that, he comes home for some time. He is scared because of our young children - what if they get infected? But others in our community are coming without washing their hands and feet, and we cannot stop them. Our children also mingle with other children in the street. There is a fear of Covid, but what can be done?

The above narratives highlight the challenges faced by the members of the Dom community in particular. The pandemic affected everyone, and despite being in shock at losing their loved ones, family members had to struggle at cremation *ghats* to have their deceased cremated.

The situation was similar all over the country; family members could not touch the bodies of their loved ones. It was disheartening. They had to cough up large sums to follow rites and rituals and get the bodies cremated. Some families could not afford the exponential rise in prices, and many dead were denied a dignified farewell. Due to the shortage of wood, some bodies were half-cremated and then dumped in rivers as the cost of cremation had shot up (Kumari 2023:1444). Pictures of bodies floating in water bodies created outrage across India. Consequently, the Municipal Corporation of Banaras decided to cremate Covid-infected bodies free of cost for the months of April–May 2021.

In the midst of the pathological circumstances, the significant role of the Dom remained unacknowledged; their hard work in handling a large number of corpses was never recognized, unlike other frontline workers. It was not the first time that such treatment was meted out to them. For centuries, India has witnessed many epidemics and pandemics, and officials have treated it as the sole responsibility of the Dom to cremate the dead. This time too, no vaccination drive was conducted for them; instead, a Municipal Corporation official said that 'the Dom could go to the Primary Health Care (PHC) center to get vaccinated'. However, he failed to realize how technical and cumbersome the process was to get vaccinated in those days. Additionally, most of the Dom were illiterate, making it difficult for them to register themselves on the online portal. How would it have been possible for those who were working round the clock to cremate piles of Covid-infected bodies to get themselves vaccinated? After facing numerous difficulties, many Dom approached me to help them with the vaccination procedure.

Concluding Notes and Way Forward

This book on the Gotakhor Dom staying at Harishchandra Ghat shows that their consciousness contains both opposing elements, as argued by Gramsci (1971), which are autonomous (they are the custodians of salvation) and borrowed (they belong to a lower caste destined to cremate dead bodies). Their stronger assertion of being the Dom-Raja and custodian of salvation due to their role in providing unextinguished sacred fire is cited as support from the legendary myth of Raja Harishchandra. Further, the claim of keeping a Kshatriya king as their servant by their ancestor Kalu Dom provides them with a sense of superiority.

Secondly, in an incident where the late Dom-Raja Kailash Chaudhary was summoned by Kashi *Naresh* (King) to remove the tiger statue from the former's rooftop, he denied this order and even won the legal case. The Dom often glamorized this particular incident by quoting the late Kailash Chaudhary's words: 'If he is the king of that side of the river, then I am the Dom-Raja of this side.'

But despite having this conception of being a custodian of salvation, they adopt the borrowed consciousness of a caste destined by their past *karma* to cremate corpses. Here, one position within the class hierarchy also affects this consciousness formation, as illustrated in Chapter 2.

The caste system has made them dependent on the misfortune of other people for their livelihood. Daily, they have to witness people crying over the loss of their loved ones and work amidst the burning smell of flesh. Their engagement in the ritual aspects of death makes them distinct from other caste groups. Furthermore, their claim of superiority over other subcastes, such as Chamar and Valmiki, demonstrates how they are 'continuously recreating a microcosm of the larger system in their own cultural system' by 'complementing and replicating' the same hierarchical caste differentiation based on the transaction of food and service providers from which they have been excluded (Moffatt 1979:5). But as Jodhka (1997) argued, 'attempt to claim higher ritual states through, what Srinivas called Sanskritization, was not a simple process. It could not be achieved only through a ritual and lifestyle imitation and had to be also negotiated with the local power structure' (Jodhka 1997:35).

Different caste groups are engaged in the death industries to earn a livelihood from the business of death through direct or indirect means (refer to Chapter 3). But due to the power structure of the cremation *ghats,* only the Dom caste is categorized as 'Chandala', earning from the dead. Vaid (2014) pointed out, 'the significant chances the upper caste has of usurping social and economic capital that provides them a leg up in labor market' (Vaid 2014:403). Here, the upper castes are expanding their dominance in this industry. Despite the fact that these caste groups (Yadav, Thakurs, Mallah) are not forced to engage in this business, unlike the Dom caste, for whom this is an ascribed and stigmatized work. Thus, though the ritual aspect is connected with their traditional occupation, the economic aspect cannot be underestimated in the functioning of the death industry. Here the Dom become important momentarily only for providing the sacred fire, which is the ritual aspect. However, in the economic aspect, as the findings suggest, Dom *workers* are vulnerable to discrimination, exclusion and violence. Even though some Dom families are economically strong, they still yearn for respect, which they fail to achieve. Vaid (2014) argues that 'a mere imitation without a simultaneous change in economic position will not result in successful upward caste mobility' (Vaid 2014:396). Yet, despite having better economic conditions, they are still referred to as '*Domwa*' or 'Chandala'. For instance, the late Kailash Chaudhary used to walk with a *Trishul* shaft, its points designed with gold, politely requesting space on the road because of his lower caste status, as his touch could be defiling for other castes. The Dom caste is vocal about being recognized as the Dom-Raja and Chaudhary of the cremation *ghats,* but they cannot raise their voice in front of other caste groups.

The class difference among the Dom affects their consciousness formation, as the study highlights the difference between the Dom of Harishchandra Ghat and those coming from the rural areas of Banaras City in Chapter 2. They are well aware that in rural areas, they are not allowed to enter the houses of other castes. They are even discriminated against by shopkeepers selling betel nuts in the city area and at Manikarnika Ghat shops. Because of their caste status, they are conscious of the fact that if the name of Harishchandra Ghat is changed to Kalu Dom, devotees might stop cremating bodies there. They use myths to glorify their cremation *ghat* through the name of Raja Harishchandra.

The sacred geography and ritual specialists constitute major elements of the sacred complex of Kashi, which is sustained by traditions of myths. There is a link between the role of ritual specialists engaged in the rites and rituals of death and their continuing role as facilitators of the deceased in attaining salvation. Moreover, different ritual specialists make use of these glorified myths to earn a livelihood, especially those that justify their work. Thus, separate myths emphasizing the role of ritual specialists serve as a subpart of a larger myth. Ritual specialists play crucial roles in completing the larger picture of salvation in Kashi.

The study suggests that the upper castes (the Brahmin, the Thakur and the Yadav) are not ready to accept the importance of the Dom's role in Hindu last rites as custodians of salvation. However, they do not deny the necessity of paying a fee to the Dom to absolve themselves of debt in exchange for the sacred fire. This act of absolving oneself from the debt owed to a lower caste signifies that, for the orthodox Brahmin, the fire provided by the Dom may not hold intrinsic importance, but they acknowledge that failing to pay the fee can hinder their attainment of salvation. Although the upper castes cannot endure a lower caste person touching their corpse, they are compelled to accept the Dom's authority as the Dom-Raja at the cremation *ghat*. Here, the glorified myth of Raja Harishchandra and the myth of Lord Shiva punishing the Dom for cremating dead bodies have assisted the Dom in maintaining some degree of authority.

I will take this space to mention that it is not mandatory for everyone to believe in or want salvation, as some prefer crematoriums and even donate their bodies. However, the study has shown that the percentage of organ donation is still low in India. Furthermore, the study focused on people coming to these spiritualized spaces for their last rites. In short, this study investigated the ritual aspects methodologically and theoretically, constructing a kind of discourse, and examined how the caste question in their everyday lives reproduces the same circumstances whereby the Dom are unable to understand how it is acting upon them.

Parry (1994) argued that the sacredness of Kashi makes it a more preferred destination for the last rites by people, but it could be understood as a back-and-forth situation because the continuous flow of people to Kashi contributes to its sacredness (Parry 1994:32). The arrival of people in Kashi even during the pandemic points to their deep-rooted faith. Chapter 4 showed that despite the presence of a gas crematorium at Harishchandra Ghat, people are still reluctant to cremate bodies there and, in fact, are using it as an alternative for unclaimed and untimely deaths. The Covid-19 pandemic is a relevant example to show that, despite being faced with severe waves, when piles of bodies were on the roads, and in hospitals and morgues, families still tried to get the last rites performed through traditional means. They adopted various mechanisms, whether it was luring workers by paying more money or facing threats from policemen. The gas crematorium was definitely useful, but because of waiting in long queues for a minimum of four hours, its efficiency was limited. Though the crematorium served as an easy alternative, even here, dead bodies were waiting for their last rites with a token system. This completely failed the basic purpose of installing the crematorium to control pollution.

During the pandemic, everyone was terrified by the loss of their loved ones and the risk of getting infected. But, the most ignored were the workers of the death industry. Although the pandemic provided them with a huge number of bodies and, consequently, better income, it simultaneously put them at a higher risk. The Dom community bore the responsibility of managing and freeing society from infected bodies. Despite their significant responsibilities, no one considered it important to make them aware of possible risks and precautionary measures. Verbal threats were used to force them to cremate Covid-infected bodies using wood when the crematorium was dysfunctional, yet they were not deemed worthy of being considered equal to other frontline workers. No separate efforts were made to provide them with vaccinations or educate them about its benefits. Thus, this pandemic highlighted that, despite being in the twenty-first century, casteism still persists in modern India, where some castes are still discriminated against and excluded. One recalls Harriss (2012), who argued that caste 'entails an ideology that explains and legitimates the material differences of class and power relations. Furthermore, even, if the importance of caste as an ideology is waning with regard to its importance to the acquisition and usurpation of "cultural capital" remains significant.' The ignorant attitude towards the Dom highlights the discriminatory attitude of the society.

Though the crematorium was installed to address the problem of Ganges pollution, its intervention in a spiritualized space is viewed as a potential threat to people earning a livelihood in the death industry. Dom *naukars,* who are engaged in manual labour, face continuous danger of encountering accidents in the workspace, along with the risk of infections due to prolonged exposure to infected dead bodies (Kumari 2018:115). But, they do not have other job alternatives where they could be accepted without caste-based discrimination and exclusion.

As the state faces a major challenge in controlling environmental pollution, it can take into consideration the beliefs of people who are opting for cremation and provide an alternative, as was done by Martin (1864). Simultaneously, it can provide rehabilitation and respectful work to the Dom community, who are still engaged in this traditional occupation. This will ensure that people are not forced to compromise their beliefs and are provided with a dignified livelihood. Consequently, the challenges posed by environmental problems arising from cremation could be effectively addressed.

In a nutshell, this book attempts to address the following points: First, the Dom of Banaras are in a better position than their counterparts in other areas in terms of earning a livelihood and gaining some recognition through the myths. But if the aspect of taking the sacred fire is removed, their condition remains unchanged despite being in an urban space. The religious beliefs of people facilitate the continuation of Kashi's status as the bestower of salvation. Due to this belief, people across the country come to Banaras for their last rites. The purpose of the crematorium seems to fail in altering people's beliefs, due to the fear of failure in the attainment of salvation in the absence of prescribed rites and rituals, which are not possible in the crematorium. Instead, the crematorium has been used for sudden and untimely deaths. Surprisingly, mourners were reluctant to use crematoriums even during the pandemic and forced Dom *naukars* to cremate Covid-infected bodies through traditional means.

Notes

Introduction

1 Cremation ground is the spot where bodies are cremated near the bank of the Ganges, whereas a cremation *ghat* refers to the overall area.

2 Towels, often in red colour.

3 It is often mentioned that tax is paid to free oneself from the Dom debt.

4 An open space under a shed or roof, where the sacred fire is burnt.

5 Throne of Dom: here, an old mattress is used for seating and resting purposes.

6 In this book, the author does not hold the view that the Dom are inferior, untouchable or of a lower caste. The sole purpose of referring to them in this context is, as mentioned in various pieces of literature, that the basis of the caste system is rooted in historical and social constructs. The system lies in the hierarchical arrangement of ranking various caste groups on the basis of the notion of purity and pollution with ascribed occupations. The author tries to question this dichotomy, where the caste system provided the Dom with an inferior rank and simultaneously a status as custodian of salvation in Hinduism.

7 The Dom are located in many northern Indian states. This book focuses on the Dom working at the cremation ground of Harishchandra Ghat in the Banaras district. Varanasi is referred to by three different names: Benares, Banaras and Kashi. However, this research uses Banaras, as it is commonly referred to by the local people.

8 As elsewhere, I have tried to locate how they have been ignored by the government and its policies (Kumari 2022).

9 Representation of Lord Shiva: the word *Jyoti* (radiance) and *Linga* (sign) means the radiant sign of Lord Shiva. There are twelve *Jyotirlingas* located across India.

10 Religious sites dedicated to Goddess Sati, the divine feminine deity of Hinduism.

11 Eulogistic text on Kashi.

12 Residence in Kashi by migration from respective places to die in Kashi for salvation.

13 Profit of Kashi: promise of salvation for those who die in Kashi.
14 *Mahapatras* (funeral priests) are the lowest Brahmins involved in performing death rites.
15 *Chamar* are a subcaste of Dom engaged in leatherwork in northern India.
16 Here, the social sphere is understood as an area of activity at the cremation *ghat* where the actors are able to unite in sharing understandings, rules and principles regarding the activities within the death industry. These understandings influence the way individuals engage in such activities.
17 For further information, see Chapter 2.
18 Holy religious texts in Hinduism.
19 Framework of reference for one's caste ranking. Ghurye (1932) defines it as the division of social groups on the basis of colour (see Ghurye 1932).
20 Dalits is a sociological category based on the experiences of lower-caste untouchables, who are officially categorized as Scheduled Castes. Therefore, Dalit has more political and social connotations than the hierarchical term 'untouchable'.

Chapter 1

1 Documentary directed by Rajesh S. Jala in 2008.
2 Name of Lord Rama is the ultimate truth.
3 Lord Shiva.
4 Figure 1.1 shows the presence of both traditional and modern cremation methods (gas crematorium – yellow building) at Harishchandra Ghat.
5 Concept given by Elias (1956).
6 Pseudonym have been used in the book for all the respondents to maintain their confidentiality.

Chapter 2

1 One of the early poems on Dalits, composed by Heera Dom and titled '*Achhuth ki Shikayat*', was originally written in the Bhojpuri language.

It was published in *Saraswati* in the year 1914 and later translated in the *Shared Mirror* on 1 June 2011, http://roundtableindia.co.in/lit-blogs/?p=1790.

2 Banarasi Doms are known by different names, such as Gotakhor and Harischanni Dom.

3 The idea of this division of myths has been taken from the work of Srinivas (1952). Here, he categorized Hinduism as All-India Hinduism, Peninsular Hinduism, Regional Hinduism and Local Hinduism (Srinivas 1952:214–15).

4 *Let* is a subcaste of the Bagdis in Murshidabad (Risley 1891).

5 Gotakhor Dom (divers), my informants reveal that, earlier used to jump into the river and retrieve coins. After the construction of the electric crematorium at Harishchandra Ghat, the Municipal Corporation allocated some Dom males the task of fishing out floating corpses from the Ganges and cremating them in the crematorium. However, they abandoned this work as it is considered stigmatized. Even Cape (1924:35) mentioned that the Dom do not touch corpses.

6 In Hinduism, ceremonial worship of gods and goddesses involves offering flowers and fruits.

7 Food offered to God is consumed as a form of blessing by devotees after concluding worship.

8 The Dom use the Chaudhary surname; it could be understood as a form of Sanskritization to uplift their status. By adopting the surname 'Chaudhary', they assert their claim to being the owners of the cremation *ghat*.

9 For further information, see Moffatt (1979:196).

10 One rupee is equal to 16 *annas*.

11 For further details, refer to Chapter 4.

12 Saiyer Mata is a Dom deity, and only the head of the community can offer sacrifices to her. The propitiation is carried out every three years, between 11 November and 11 December.

13 Veblen (1899) introduced the term 'conspicuous consumption' to describe the excessive expenditure of money on luxurious items as a means of displaying one's wealth.

14 Vernacular terms used by informants are retained here rather than using the alternative word 'workers', which may not have an exact meaning.

15 During data collection, gender neutrality was kept in consideration; however, as the work of cremation is traditionally considered a men's domain, it frequently mentions them. In other areas, wherever females were present, they are equally referred to.
16 Second wife of Kailash Chaudhary.
17 Original names are used for deceased original *patidars* and pseudo names are used for living individuals.
18 House is the area of land that is a shared and undivided property among the households.
19 The Dom get used items of the deceased person, such as clothes, bedsheets and blankets.
20 Working of cremation *ghat.*
21 I visited the following locations: Domri Ghat, Harishchandra Ghat, Manikarnika Ghat, Koniya, Varuna Ghat, Chandauli, Saidpur, Chunar and Narayanpur. Other places were not visited because, as a female researcher, I did not consider it safe due to the greater distance from the city of Banaras.
22 One *maund* equals 49 kilograms of wood.
23 Immersion of dead bodies that are not considered suitable for cremation, such as those of pregnant women, infants, sadhus or persons who died due to small pox or snake bite.
24 Mixtures of ingredients required for the fire offering.
25 Only while conversing with mourners, *naukars* were referred to as *mazdoor*. Both terms have different meanings. The word *naukar* seems more appropriate in the wider context of this book, so *naukar* is used.
26 Marriage procession of Lord Shiva.
27 Hindu festivals are celebrated in honour of the deity Shiva.
28 Caste that sells vegetables and fruits.
29 Lord of the cremation ground refers to Lord Shiva.
30 A diety in Hinduism known as God Shani.
31 In the cremation ground, Holi is played with the ashes of dead bodies.

Chapter 3

1 Traditional dress of Indian villagers.
2 Locality of Brahmins.

3 For further information, see Chapter 5.

4 I am using Kashi as a 'spiritualized landscape'. The area of Kashi is demarcated as one that grants the boon of salvation. Outside that area, I will use the name Banaras for the city.

5 Bestower of salvation.

6 Mahajan (1994:84).

7 Mahajan (1994:27–8).

8 For further information, refer to Chapter 4.

9 Small natural tanks filled with water.

10 Praising hymns.

11 *Tarak Mantra*: the word *tarak* means an aid in crossing the river of birth and rebirth. *Mantra* stands for hymns. Thus, it is believed that Shiva whispers the *Tarak Mantra* into the ear of the deceased, by which the soul attains salvation.

12 Cycles of birth and rebirth.

13 *Karma* affirms that a result is produced from every action, which is determined by the nature and motive of the action (Rambachan 2003:641).

14 Singh (2010) elaborated on the terminology and difference between *Pravaha* and *Parvaha.*

15 An individual is deemed to pay the *karmic* debt for the sins committed by their forefathers by experiencing different punishments.

16 Data provided by the Municipal Corporation of Banaras.

17 The tea shopkeeper mentioned that the area is called Vyas Kashi or Maghar.

18 Manikarnika *Kund* is a pond located at Manikarnika Ghat, which is believed to have been dug by Vishnu to perform austerities.

19 https://anthyesti.com/about/.

20 Shark Tank India on 12 January 2022, https://fb.watch/jpnLgQuT1Z/?mibextid=1YhcI9R.

21 http://www.kashimoksha.com/about.php.

22 CEO of The Last Journey, Rishabh Jalan, discusses digitizing India's death care industry. -industry-119792.html

23 Generally, if the *theka* is taken, mourners wait at the cremation *ghat,* and the Dom arranges everything for them. If mourners do not choose the *theka,* they have to cremate the body themselves.

24 Funeral priests' work began after the tenth day of death.

25 From the male body, the shoulder portion remains unburnt, and from the female body, the hip portion remains unburnt.

26 Some people also perform this rite on the third day after death.

27 It is a block of five consecutive *nakshatras* (lunar mansions) in each cycle (Parry 1980:94). It is believed that death at this time will lead to five more deaths in the family.

28 In cases of untimely death, it is performed to prevent the soul from remaining in the *preta* form.

29 I was informed that Aghoris stay at the isolated Chet Singh Fort near Harishchandra Ghat. They practice cannibalism and hunt for immersed corpses in the Ganges.

30 Interviewed boatman on 23 March 2021.

31 Arjun (Dom *naukar*) in November 2019.

32 To be banished from society.

33 Head or owner of the cremation *ghat.*

34 See Harper's (1964) article on 'Ritual Pollution as an Integrator of Caste and Religion'. In this work on Havik Brahmins in the Malnad region of South India, Harper argues that Havik Brahmins must follow many rules and practices to maintain their '*madi*' (ritually pure state).

35 Greene (1999).

36 For further details, refer to Chapter 4.

Chapter 4

1 Indian traditional attire.

2 For further elaboration, see Berger (1969).

3 Informed during a formal conversation.

4 Financial Express (2021). Retrieved from https://www.financialexpress.com/lifestyle/health/india-needs-more-organ-donations-as-only-0-01-indians-have-given-consent-to-donate-their-organs-after-death/2300173/.

5 Kancharla (2022), https://factly.in/data-between-2016-2021-four-states-accounted-for-53-of-the-organ-donations-reported-from-across-the-country/.

6 Pandu was the father of the five Pandavas in the epic Mahabharata.

7 King Dasharatha was the ruler of Ayodhya and the father of Lord Rama in the epic Ramayana.
8 Dom staff work in the crematorium.
9 Endonym of Hinduism: it refers to the 'eternal' truth and teachings of Hinduism.
10 Generally, women do not come to the cremation *ghat*. They sit in the vehicle at the crossroad near Harishchandra Ghat. I noticed women from one family who came to pay their last respects to the deceased and afterwards asked to go and wait in the car. In some cases, when the son is not present to provide *mukhagni*, the daughter performs *mukhagn*i for her deceased father. The reason mentioned for not allowing women to perform this ritual is the belief that women have weak hearts and there is a fear that malevolent spirits might attack them. During a conversation with a temple priest, he told me that women are not considered 'pure' for these rituals due to menstruation, and that is why they are not allowed to come to the cremation *ghat*. However, women from the Dom community visit the cremation *ghat*, pay their respects and then wait by sitting on a nearby *ghat* until the cremation is over.
11 This interview was not conducted at the cremation *ghat*. I met her one month after her mother's death and then interviewed her.
12 The cosmic sink concept is taken from Barrett (2008).
13 Water Digest (2022), https://thewaterdigest.com/slower-flow-of-ganga-in-Banaras-worsens-sewage-problem/.
14 Mahajan (1994:18–20).
15 Mahajan (1994:91–2).
16 Water Digest (2022), https://thewaterdigest.com/slower-flow-of-ganga-in-Banaras-worsens-sewage-problem/.
17 Singh (2017), https://timesofindia.indiatimes.com/city/Banaras/cow-dung-cakes-for-ecofriendly cremation/article show/60286270.cms.
18 Key informants reported this.

Chapter 5

1 Informed by respondents.
2 Here, 'normal' and 'pathological' are derived from Émile Durkheim's (1982) concept of normal and pathological facts.

3 I was mostly present at the *ghat,* but when death rates were at their peak, I conducted telephonic interviews. Then, after returning to the field, I gathered information by interviewing people about their experiences during the first wave.

4 For further details, see Kumari (2022:64–5).

5 Informed by Ramesh *Bhaiya.*

6 The Dom of Harishchandra Ghat do not touch any corpse. They consider it stigmatized to touch a dead body. It is either the family members or an attendee, in the case of unclaimed bodies, who shift and arrange the body on the pyre.

7 Mourners were interviewed on 22 April 2021. For further details, refer to Kumari (2022:66).

8 Kumari (2022:66).

9 Kumari (2022:65).

References

Ali, N. and Kumar, U. (2017), 'Study and Evaluation of Water Quality of River Ganga at Different Ghats of Varanasi City', *International Journal for Scientific Research & Development*, 5(3): 678–84.

Alley, K.D. (1998), 'Idioms of Degeneracy: Assessing Ganga's Purity and Pollution', in Nelson E. Lance (eds), *Purifying the Earthly Bodies of God: Religion and Ecology in Hindu India*, 297–330, Albany, NY: State University of New York.

Alley, K.D. (2000), 'Separate Domains: Hinduism, Politics and Environmental Pollution', in Christopher Chapple and Mary Tucker (eds), *Hinduism and Ecology: The Intersection of Earth, Sky and Water*, 355–78, Cambridge, MA: Harvard University Press.

Arnold, D. (2016), 'Burning Issues: Cremation and Incineration in Modern India', *NTM International Journal of History & Ethics of Natural Sciences Technology & Medicine*, 24(4): 393–419.

Arun, J.C. (2007), 'From Stigma to Self-Assertion: Paraiyars and the Symbolism of the Parai Drum', *Contribution to Indian Sociology*, 41(1): 81–104.

Ashforth, B. and Kreiner, G. (1999), 'How Can You Do It?: Dirty Work and the Challenge of Constructing a Positive Identity', *Academy of Management Review*, 24(3): 413–34.

Ashforth, B. and Kreiner, G. (2013), 'Profane or Profound? Finding Meaning in Dirty Work', in Michael F. Steger, Zinta Byme, Bryan J. Dik (eds), *Purpose and Meaning in the Workplace*, 127–50, Washington, DC: American Psychological Association.

Bailey, F.G. (1993), 'Closed Social Stratification in India', *European Journal of Sociology*, 4(1): 107–24.

Bailey, T. and Walter, T. (2016), 'Funerals against Death', *Mortality*, 2(2): 149–66.

Bandyopadhyay, S. (1997), *Caste, Protest and Identity in Colonial India: The Namasudras of Bengal, 1872–1947*, Surrey: Curzon Press.

Barrett, R.L. (2008), *Aghor Medicine: Pollution, Death and Healing in Northern India*, Berkeley, CA: University of California Press.

Bayly, C.A. (1981), 'From Ritual to Ceremony: Death Ritual and Society in Hindu North India since 1600*', in Joachim Whaley (eds), *Mirrors of*

Mortality Studies in the Social History of Death, 154–86, London: Europa Publications.

Bear, L., Simpson, N., Angland, M., Bhogal, J.K., Bowers, R.E., Cannell, F., Gardner, K., Lohiya, A.G., James, D., Jivraj, N., Koch, I., Laws, M., Lipton, J., Long, N,J., Vieira, J., Watt, C., Whittle, C., and Zidaru-Barbulescu, T. (2020), 'A Good Death during the Covid-19 Pandemic in the UK: A Report on Key Findings and Recommendations', Available online: https://eprints.lse.ac.uk/104143/.

Beck, B. (1976), 'The Symbolic Merger of Body, Space and Cosmos in Hindu Tamilnadu', *Contributions to Indian Sociology*, 10: 213–44.

Berger, P.L. (1969), *The Social Reality of Religion*, Harmondsworth: Penguin University Books.

Berreman, G.D. (1963), *Hindus of the Himalayas*, Berkeley, CA: University of California Press.

Beteille, A. (1965), *Caste, Class, and Power: Changing Patterns of Stratification in a Tanjore Village*, Berkeley, CA: The University of California Press.

Beteille, A. (1969), *Caste: Old and New: Essay in Social Structure and Social Stratification*, Bombay: Asia Publishing House.

Beteille, A. (1972), 'Pollution and Poverty', in Michael J. Mahar (eds), *The Untouchables in Contemporary India*, 411–20, Tucson, AZ: The University of Arizona Press.

Bogam, P., Joshi, A., Nagarkar, S., Jain, D., Gupte, N., Shashidhara, L., Monteiro, J., and Mave, V. (2021), 'Burden of COVID-19 and Case Fatality Rate in Pune India: An Analysis of First and Second Waves of the Pandemic', *MedRxiv BMJ*, 2 Yale: 1–22.

Bougle, C. (1971), *Essays on the Caste System Celestin Bougle*, trans. D.F. Pocock, Cambridge: Cambridge University Press.

Briggs, G.W. (1953), *The Doms and Their Near Relations*, Mysore: Wesley Press.

Briggs, J. (1970), 'Kapluna Daughter', in Peggy Golde (eds), *Women in the Field: Anthropological Experience*, 19–46, Chicago, IL: Aldine Publishing.

Buitenen, J.V. (1957), 'Dharma and Moksha', *Philosophy East and West*, 7(1/2): 33–40.

Cape, P. (1924), *Prisoners Released: The Redemption of a Criminal Tribe*, London: Wesleyan Methodist Missionary Society.

Census of India (2011), 'District Census Handbook of Varanasi: Village and Town Wise Primary Census Abstract (PCA)', Directorate of Census Operation Uttar Pradesh, Part XII-B, Series 10.

Charmaz, K. (2005), 'Grounded Theory in the 21st Century: Applications for Advancing Social Justice', in N.K. Denzin and Y.S. Lincoln (eds), *The Sage Handbook of Qualitative Research*, 507–36, Thousand Oaks, CA: Sage Publication.

Chatterjee, P. (1989), 'Caste and Subaltern Consciousness', in Ranajit Guha (eds), *Subaltern Studies VI: Writings on South Asian History and Society*, 169–209, Delhi: Oxford University Press.

Clarke, G.R. (1903), *The Outcaste Being: A Brief Account of the Maghaya Doms*, Calcutta: Indian Civil Service Thacker, Spink.

Clarke, M. (1975), 'Survival in the Field: Implications of Personal Experiences in Fieldwork', *Theory and Society*, 2(1): 95–123.

Clive, S. (1998), *Constructing Death: The Sociology of Dying and Bereavement*, Cambridge: Cambridge University Press.

Coffey, A. (1999), *The Ethnographic Self: Fieldwork and the Representation of Identity*, London: Sage Publication.

Coffey, A., Atkinson, P., Delamont, S., Lofland, J., and Lofland, L. (2002), *Handbook of Ethnography*, London: Sage Publication.

Cohen, B. (1987), 'The Census, Social Structure and Objectification in South Asia', in Bernard Cohen (eds), *An Anthropologist among the Historians and Other Essays*, 224–54, Delhi: Oxford University Press.

Cohn, B.S. (1958), 'Changing Traditions of a Low Caste', *The Journal of American Folklore*, 71(281) (July–September): 413–21.

Coward, H. (2000), 'Hinduism in Canada', in H. Coward, J.R. Hinnells, and R. Williams(eds), *The South Asian Diaspora in Britain, Canada, and the United States*, 151–72, Albany, NY: State University of New York Press.

Crooke, W. (1899), 'Primitive Rites of Disposal of the Dead with Special Reference to India', *The Journal of the Anthropological Institute of Great Britain and Ireland*, 29(3/4): 271–94.

Da Cruz, Lezana, N., Santos, P., Pinto, I., Zancan, C., and Souza, G. (2017), 'Environmental Impacts Caused by Cemeteries and Crematoria, New Funeral Technologies, and Preferences of the North Eastern and Southern Brazilian Population as for the Funeral Process', *Environmental Science and Pollution Research*, 24(31): 24121–34.

Darian, S. (1978), *The Ganges in Myth and History*, Delhi: Motilal Banarsidas Publishers.

Das, V. (1976), 'The Uses of Liminality: Society and Cosmos in Hinduism', *Contributions to Indian Sociology*, 10(2): 245–63.

Das, V. (1977), *Structure and Cognition: Aspects of Hindu Caste and Rituals*, Delhi: Oxford University Press.

Das, V. and Uberoi, J.S. (1971), 'The Elementary Structure of Caste', *Contribution to Indian Sociology*, 5(1): 33–43.

Datta, A. (2016), *On Uncertain Ground-Displaced Kashmiri Pandits in Jammu and Kashmir*, New York: Oxford University Press.

Davis, D.J. (2002), *Death, Ritual and Belief: The Rhetoric of Funerary Rites*, London: Continuum.

Davis, D.J. (2003), 'Cremation', in Clifton Bryan (eds), *Handbook of Death and Dying*, Vol. II, 767–74, Thousand Oaks, CA: Sage Publication.

Davis, R. (1988), 'Cremation and Liberation: The Revision of a Hindu Ritual', *History of Religions*, 28(1): 37–53.

Deliege, R. (1993), 'The Myths of Origin of the Indian Untouchables', *Man*, 28(3): 533–49.

Deliege, R. (1999), *The Untouchables of India*, trans. Nora Scott, Guildford: Berg Publishers.

Dirk, N.B. (1987), *The Hollow Crown: Ethnohistory of an Indian Kingdom*, Cambridge: Cambridge University Press.

Doron, A. (2013), *Life on the Ganga: Boatmen and the Ritual Economy of Banaras*, Delhi: Foundation Books.

Douglas, M. (1966), *Purity and Danger: An Analysis of Concepts of Pollution and Taboo*, New York: Routledge.

Dumont, L. (1970), *Homo Hierarchicus: The Caste System and Its Implications*, London: Weidenfeld Nicolson. The University of Chicago.

Durkheim, E. (1982), *The Rules of Sociological Method*, trans. W.D. Halls, New York: The Macmillan Press.

Eck, D.L. (1981), 'India's "*Tirthas*": Crossings in Sacred Geography', *History of Religions*, 20(4): 323–44.

Eck, D.L. (1983), *Banaras: City of Light*, London: Routledge and Kegan Paul.

Elias, N. (1956), 'Problems of Involvements and Detachment', *The British Journal of Sociology*, 7(3): 226–52.

Ellis, C. (2007), 'Telling Secrets, Revealing Lives: Relational Ethics in Research with Intimate Others', *Qualitative Inquiry*, 13(1): 3–29.

Etherington, K. (2007), 'Ethical Research in Reflexive Relationships', *Qualitative Relationships*, 13(5): 599–616.

Financial Express (2021), 'India Needs More Organ Donations as Only 0.01% Indians Have Given Consent to Donate Their Organs after Death', *Financial Express*, 29 July. Available online: https://www.

financialexpress.com/lifestyle/health/india-needs-more-organ-donations-as-only-0-01-indians-have-given-consent-to-donate-their-organs-after-death/2300173/ (accessed 20 February 2023).

Fisher, H. (1884), *Statistical Descriptive and Historical Account of the Northern Western Province of India*, Vol. XIV, Part I- Benares.

Freeman, C. and Luc, S. (1994), *Work for All or Mass Unemployment?: Computerised Technical Changes into the Twenty-First Century*, London: Pinter Publishers.

Gauthier, D., Chaudoir, N.K., and Rhonda, D.E. (2003), 'Disposing of the Dead: Minor Modes', in Clifton Bryant (eds), *Handbook of Death and Dying*, Vol. II, 792–800, Thousand Oaks, CA: Sage Publication.

Ghuyre, G.S. (1932), *Caste and Race in India*, London: Kegan Paul.

Glaser, G.B. and Strauss, A.L. (1967), *The Discovery of Grounded Theory: Strategies for Qualitative Research*, Chicago, IL: Aldine Publishing House.

Gobo, G. (2008), *Doing Ethnography*, trans. Adrian Belton, London: Sage Publication.

Goffman, E. (1963), *Stigma: Notes on the Management of Spoiled Identity*, New Jersey: Prentice-Hall Inc.

Gokhale, J. (1993), *From Concession to Confrontation: The Politics of an Indian Untouchable Community*, Bombay: Popular Prakashan.

Golde, P. (1970), 'Odyssey of Encounter', in Peggy Golde (eds), *Women in the Field: Anthropological Experience*, 67–96, Chicago, IL: Aldine Publishing.

Gould, H.A. (1963), 'The Adaptive Functions of Caste in Contemporary Indian Society', *Asian Survey*, 3(9): 427–38.

Gramsci, A. (1971), *Selections from the Prison Notebooks of Antonio Gramsci*, trans. and eds. Quintin Hoare and Geoffrey Nowell-Smith, New York: International Publishers.

Greene, P. (1999), 'Professional Weeping: Music, Affect, and Hierarchy in a South Indian Folk Performance Art', *Indian Folklore Research Journal*, 1(2): 1–26.

Greetz, C. (1973), *The Interpretation of Cultures: Selected Essay*, New York: Basic Books Inc Publishers.

Gupta, A and Ferguson, J. (1997), 'Discipline and Practice: "The Field" as Site, Method, and Location in Anthropology', in Akhil Gupta and James Ferguson (eds), *Anthropological Locations: Boundaries and Ground of a Field Science*, 1–46, Berkeley, CA: The University of California.

Gurney, J.N. (1985), 'Not One of the Guys: The Female Researcher in a Male-Dominated Settings', *Qualitative Sociology*, 8(1): 42–62.

Hammersley, M. (2006), 'Ethnography: Problem and Prospects', *Ethnography and Education*, 1(1): 3–14.

Hammmesley, M. and Atkinson, P. (1995), *Ethnography: Principles in Practice*, London: Sage Publication.

Harper, E. (1964), 'Ritual Pollution as an Integrator of Caste and Religion', *The Journal of Asian Studies*, 23: 151–97.

Harriss, J. (2012), 'Reflections on Caste and Class, Hierarchy and Dominance', *Seminar, Issue* 633. Available online: https://www.india-seminar.com/2012/633/633_john_harriss.html.

Hertz, R. (1960), *Death and the Right Hand*, trans. Rodney Needham, Claudia Needham, Illinois: Routledge.

Ibbetson, D. (1883), 'Panjab Castes: Being a Reprint of the Chapter on the Races, Caste and Tribes of the People', in the Report on the Census of the Panjab, Government Printing Punjab, Lahore.

Ingalls, D.H. (1957), 'Dharma and Moksha', *Philosophy East and West*, 7(1/2): 41–8.

Jodhka, S. (1997), 'From "Book-view" to "Field-view": Social Anthropological Construction of the Indian Village', Working Paper No.5, QEHWPS05, Queen Elizabeth. House, Oxford Dep. Int. Dev., University of Oxford. Available online: http://www.unipune.ac.in/snc/cssh/HistorySociology/A%20DOCUMENTS%20ON%20HISORY%20OF%20SOCIOLOGY%20IN%20INDIA/A%203%20IEG%20Workshop%20papers%202000/A%203%2007.pdf.

Jodhka, S. and Manor, S.J. (2018), *Contested Hierarchies, Persisting Influence: Caste and Power in Twenty-First Century India*, Hyderabad: Orient Black Swan.

Jordan, P., Ward, J., and McMurray, R. (2019), 'Dealing with the Dead: Life as a Third-Generation Independent Funeral Director', *Work, Employment and Society*, 33(4): 700–708.

Justice, C. (1997), *Dying the Good Death: The Pilgrimage to Die in India's Holy City*, Albany, NY: State University of New York.

Kancharla, B. (2022), 'Data between 2016 and 2021, Four States Accounted for 53% of the Organ Donation Reported from across the Country', *Factly*, 22 December. Available online: https://factly.in/data-between-2016-2021-four-states-accounted-for-53-of-the-organ-donations-reported-from-across-the-country/ (accessed 20 February 2023).

Kane, P.V. (1973), *History of Dharmasastra*, Vol. IV, Poona: Bhandarkar Oriental Research Institute.

Kaushik, M. (1976), 'The Symbolic Representation of Death', *Contributions to Indian Sociology*, 10(2): 256–92.

Kaushik, M. (1979), 'Religion and Social Structure: A Case Study of the Doms of Banaras', PhD thesis, University of Delhi, New Delhi, India.

Kolenda, P.M. (1964), 'Religious Anxiety and Hindu Fate', *Journal of Asian Studies*, 23: 71–81.

Kumar, V. (2014), 'Inequality in India: Caste and Hindu Social Order', *Transcience*, 5(1): 36–52.

Kumari, S. (2018), 'Caste-Based Occupation and Health: A Study of Dom Caste in Varanasi District, Uttar Pradesh', MPhil dissertation, Jawaharlal Nehru University, New Delhi, India.

Kumari, S. (2022), 'On the Margins: A Tale of the Pandemic and the Funeral Workers in Benares', *Social Trends: Journal of the Department of Sociology of North Bengal University*, 9: 54–74.

Kumari, S. (2023), 'Understanding of Stigmatization and Death amid COVID-19 in India: A Sociological Exploration', *OMEGA-Journal of Death and Dying*, 86(4): 1432–48.

Laungani, P. (1997), 'Death in a Hindu Family', in Parkes Colin, Pittu Laungani, and Bill Young (eds), *Death and Bereavement across Cultures*, 52–72, London: Routledge Publication.

Li, J. (2008), 'Ethical Challenges in Participant Observation: A Reflection on Ethnographic Fieldwork', *The Qualitative Report*, 13(1) (March): 100–15.

Lillelund, C. (2009), 'The Last Vettiyan: A Musical Tradition and a Degraded Low Caste Profession', *Review of Development and Change*, 14(1&2): 251–69.

Lyche, H.T. (2017), *Transaction and Hierarchy: Elements for a Theory of Caste*, New Delhi: Manohar.

Lynch, O.M. (1969), *The Politics of Untouchability: Social Mobility and Social Change in a City of India*, New York: Columbia University Press.

Madan, T.N. (1987), *Non-renunciation: Themes and Interpretations of Hindu Culture*, New York: Oxford University Press.

Mahajan, J. (1994), *Ganga Observed: Foreign Accounts of the River*, Varanasi: Indica Books.

Malinowski, B. (1954), *Magic, Science and Religion and Other Essays*, New York: Doubleday Anchor Books.

Mallet, V. (2017), *River of Life, River of Death: The Ganges and India's Future*, New Delhi: Oxford University Press.

Maria (2022), 'NGT Agrees Early Hearing on Plea on Unscientific Disposal of Bodies Near Ganga River', *Indo-Asian News Service*, 11 August. Available online: https://www.siasat.com/ngt-agrees-early-hearing-on-plea-on-unscientific-disposal-of-bodies-near-ganga-river-2387633/ (accessed 14 November 2022).

Marriott, M. (1959), 'Interactional and Attributional Theories of Caste Ranking', *Man in India*, 39(2): 92–107.

Marriott, M. (1968), 'Caste Ranking and Food Transactions: A Matrix Analysis', in B. Cohn and M. Singer (eds), *Structure and Change in Indian Society*, 133–71, Chicago, IL: Aldine Publishing.

Martin, T. (1864), *Specification of a Cinerator for the Use of Brahmins and Other Hindoo Castes*, Bombay: Regimental Press.

Maurya, U. and Sharma, A. (2016), 'Impact of Cremation Centers in River Pollution: A Case Study from Gomti River, Lucknow, Uttar Pradesh, India', *International Journal of Geology, Earth & Environmental Sciences*, 6(3): 8–15.

McNeill, R.J. (2000), *Something New under the Sun: An Environment History of the Twentieth Century World*, New York: W.W. Norton.

Mencher, J.P. (1974), 'The Caste System Upside Down, or the Not-So-Mysterious East', *Current Anthropology*, 15(4): 469–93.

Moffatt, M. (1979), *An Untouchable Community in South India: Structure and Consensus*, New Jersey: Princeton University Press.

Morson, G.S. (1998), 'Sideshadowing and Tempies', *New Literary History: Critics without Schools*, 29(4): 599–624.

Murthy, U.R. (1978), *Samskara: A Rite for a Dead Man*, trans. Ramanujan, New York: Oxford University Press.

Nesfield, J.C. (1885), *Brief View of the Caste System of the North-Western Province and Oudh*, Allahabad: Government Press, United Province.

Nevill, H.R. (1909), *Benares: A Gazetteer.* Vol. XXVI *of the district Gazetteers of the United Provinces of Agra and Oudh*, Allahabad: Government Press, United Province.

Obeyesekere, G. (1980), 'The Rebirth Eschatology and Its Transformations: A Contribution to the Sociology of Early Buddhism', in W.D. O'Flaherty (eds), *Karma and Rebirth in Classical Indian Traditions*, 137–64, Berkeley, CA: University of California Press.

Oommen, T.K. (1984), 'Sources of Deprivation and Styles of Protest: The Case of the Dalits in India', *Contribution to Indian Sociology*, 18(1): 45–61.

Orenstein, H. (1968), 'Toward a Grammer of Defilement in Hindu Sacred Law', in B. Cohn and M. Singer (eds), *Structure and Changes in Indian Society*, 115–30, Chicago, IL: Aldine Publishing.

Pal, A. (2021), 'In Search of a Neighbourhood among the Kashivasis: An Ethnographic Account of an Ashram in Banaras', in Pathak Jha and Das (eds), *Neighbourhoods in Urban India: In between Home and the City*, 63–91, New Delhi: Bloomsbury.

Parry, J.P. (1980), 'Ghost, Greed and Sin: The Occupational Identity of Benares Funeral Priests', *Man*, 15(1) (March): 88–111.

Parry, J.P. (1981), 'Death and Cosmogony in Kashi', *Contributions to Indian Sociology*, 15(1–2): 337–65.

Parry, J.P. (1982), 'Sacrificial Death and the Necrophagous Ascetic', in Maurice Bloch and J.P. Parry (eds), *Death and the Regeneration of Life*, 74–110, Cambridge: Cambridge University Press.

Parry, J.P. (1991), 'The Hindu Lexicographer? A Note on Auspiciousness and Purity', *Contribution to Indian Sociology*, 25(2): 267–85.

Parry, J.P. (1994), *Death in Banaras*, Cambridge: Cambridge University Press.

Pathak, D.N. (2018), *Living Dying: Meanings in Maithili Folklore*, New Delhi: Primus Books.

Press Trust of India (2016), 'Floating Human Bodies Polluting Ganga in UP, NGT Told', *Press Trust of India*, 27 January. Available Online: https://www.business-standard.com/article/pti-stories/floating-human-bodies-polluting-ganga-in-up-ngt-told116012700925_1.html (accessed 14 November 2022).

Press Trust of India (2022), 'IIT-Delhi Gets Machine for Making Cow Dung Logs for Cremations', *Press Trust of India*, 6 May. Available online: https://www.deccanherald.com/national/north-and-central/iit-delhi-gets-machine-for-making-cow-dung-logs-for-cremations-1107005.html (accessed 14 November 2022).

Quigley, D. (1993), *The Interpretation of Caste*, Oxford: Clarendon Press.

Radhakrishna, M. (2000), 'Colonial Construction of a Criminal Tribe: Yerukulas of Madras Presidency', *Economic Political Weekly*, 35(28/29) (July): 2553–63.

Rambachan, A. (2003), '*The Hindu Way of Death*', in Clifton Bryant (eds), *Handbook of Death and Dying*, Vol. II, 640–8, Thousand Oaks, CA: Sage Publication.

Randeria, S. (1989), 'Carrion and Corpses: Conflict in Categorizing Untouchability in Gujarat', *European Journal of Sociology*, 30(2): 171–91.

Risley, H.H. (1891), *Tribes and Caste of Bengal: Ethnographic Glossary*, Vol. I, Calcutta: Bengal Secretariat Press.

Risley, H.H. (1892), *The Tribes and Caste of Bengal: Ethnographic Glossary*, Vol II, Calcutta: Bengal Secretariat Press.

Risley, H.H. (1915), *The People of India*. Calcutta: Thacker Spink.

Rousselet, L. (1876), *India and Its Native Princes: Travels in Central India and in the Presidencies of Bombay and Bengal*, London: Chapman and Hall, 193. Piccadilly.

Saraswati, B. (1975), *Kashi: Myth and Reality of a Classical Cultural Tradition*, Shimla: Indian Institute of Advance Study.

Sarkar, S. (1984), 'The Conditions and Nature of Subaltern Militancy: Bengal from Swadeshi to Non-co-operation, c.1905–22', in Ranajit Guha (eds), *Subaltern Studies III: Writings on South Asian History and Society*, 271–320, Delhi: Oxford University Press.

Schutz, A. (1972), *The Phenomenology of the Social World*, trans. George Walsh and Fredrick Lehnert (1967), Illinois: North Western University Press.

Shah, A.M. (2007), 'Purity, Impurity, Untouchability: Then and Now', *Sociological Bulletin*, 56(2): 355–68.

Shah, A.M. (2014), *The Household and Family in India: A Field Study in a Gujarat Village, and a Review of Other Studies*, Orient. Longman, New Delhi: University of California Press.

Sharma, S. (2005), 'Dom', in K.S. Singh (eds), *People of India: Uttar Pradesh, Vol. XLII, Part I Anthropological Survey of India*, 457–9, New Delhi: Manohar Publisher.

Sherring, M.A. (1868), *The Sacred City of the Hindus: An Account of Benares in Ancient and Modern Times*, London: Trubner.

Sherring, M.A. (1872), *Hindu Castes and Tribes as Represented in Benares*, Calcutta: Thacker, Spink.

Singh, A.N., Shrivastava, R., Devendra, M., and Kumar, P. (2018), 'Assessment of Spatial and Temporal Variations in Water Quality Dynamics of River Ganga in Varanasi', *Pollution*, 4(2): 239–50.

Singh, B. (2017), 'Cow Dung Cakes for Eco-friendly Cremation', *Times of India*, 30 August. Available online: https://timesofindia.indiatimes.com/city/varanasi/cow-dung-cakes-for-eco-friendly-cremation/articleshow/60286270.cms (accessed 8 May 2023).

Singh, L. (2020), 'BMC Issues Circular: Bodies Must Be Cremated Irrespective of Religion', *The Indian Express Online*, 31 March. Available online: https://indianexpress.com/article/coronavirus/coronavirus-deaths-mumbai-bmc-6339687/ (accessed 20 November 2022).

Singh, R.N. (2010), 'Representation of Death in Benaras', PhD thesis, Jawaharlal Nehru University, New Delhi, India.

Singh, R.N. (2022), *Dead in Banaras: An Ethnography of Funeral Travelling*, New Delhi: Oxford University Press.

Singh, R.P.B. (1993), 'Cosmic Layout of the Hindus Sacred City, Varanasi (Benares)', *Architecture & Comportement/Architecture & Behaviour*, 9(2): 239–49.

Singh, R.P.B. (2004), *Cultural Landscape and the Lifeworld: Literary Images of Banaras*, Varanasi: Indica Books.

Singh, R.P.B. (2008), *Banaras, The Heritage City of India: Geography, History, and Bibliography*, Varanasi: Indica Books.

Singh, R.P.B. and Pravin, S.P. (2016), 'Kashi and Cosmos: Spatial Manifestation and the Five Pilgrimage Journeys of Banaras', *International Journal of Religious Tourism and Pilgrimage*, 4(6): 1–15.

Srinivas, M.N. (1952), *Religion and Society among the Coorgs of South India*, Oxford: Clarendon Press.

Srinivas, M.N. (1975), 'Villages Studies, Participant Observation and Social Science Research in India', *Economic and Political Weekly*, 10(3/35): 1387–94.

Srinivas, M.N. (1976), *The Remembered Village*, Berkeley, CA: University of California Press.

Srinivas, M.N. (1984), 'Some Reflections on the Nature of Caste Hierarchy', *Contribution to Indian Sociology*, 18(2): 151–67.

Srivastava, K., Kumar, N., and Khwairakpam, D. (2018), 'Environment Impact of Cremation Activities in Manikarnika Ghat, Varanasi, Uttar Pradesh', *International Journal for Scientific Research & Development*, 6(4): 842–45.

Stanton, W.J. (1984), *Fundamentals of Marketing*, New York: McGraw-Hill Book.

Strauss, L. (1968), 'The Story of Asdiwal', trans. Nicholas Mann in Edmund Leach (eds), *The Structural Study of Myth and Totemism*, 1–48, New York: Barnes and Noble.

Sukul, K. (1977), *Varaṇasi Vaibhav*, Paṭna: Bihar Raṣṭrabhaṣa Parişad.

Thompson, H. (1891), *Modern Cremation; Its History and Practice: With Information Relating to the Recently Improved Arrangements Made by the Cremation Society of England*, London: Kegan Paul, Trench, Trubner.

Thompson, W.E. (1991), 'Handling the Stigma of Handling the Dead: Morticians and Funeral Directors', *Deviant Behavior*, 12(4): 403–29.

Turner, N. and Caswell, G. (2020), 'A Relative Absence: Exploring Professional Experiences of Funerals without Mourners', *OMEGA – Journal of Death and Dying*, 85(4): 1–19.

Turner, V. (1969), *The Ritual Process: Structure and Anti-structure*, Chicago, IL: Aldine Publishing.

Turner, V. (1974), *Dramas, Fields and Metaphors: Symbolic Action in Human Society*, New York: Cornell University Press.

Ugur, M. and Mitra, A. (2017), 'Technology Adoption and Employment in Less Developed Countries: A Mixed-Method Systematic Review', *World Development*, 96(4): 1–18.

Vaid, D. (2014), 'Caste in Contemporary India: Flexibility and Persistence', *Annual Review of Sociology*, 40: 391–410.

Van Geneep, A. (1960), *The Rites of Passage*, Chicago, IL: University of Chicago Press.

Veblen, T. (1899), *The Theory of the Leisure Class: An Economic Study of Institution*, London: Unwin Books.

Water Digest (2022), 'Slower Flow of Ganga in Varanasi Worsens Sewage Problem', *Water Digest*, 8 March. Available online: https://thewaterdigest.com/slower-flow-of-ganga-in-varanasi-worsens-sewage-problem/ (accessed 14 November 2022).

Wax (1971), *Doing Fieldwork: Warnings and Advice*, Chicago, IL: University of Chicago Press.

Wax (1979), 'Gender and Age in Fieldwork Education: No Good Training Is Done by Any Man Alone', *Social Problem*, 26(5): 509–23.

Weber, M. (1958), *The Religion of India: The Sociology of Hinduism and Buddhism*, trans. and eds. H.H. Gerth and Don Martindale, Illinois: The Free Press.

White, H. and Nandini, G. (2001), 'Mapping India's World of Unorganized Labour', *Socialist Register*, 37: 89–118.

Wilson, M. (1954), 'Nyakyusa Ritual and Symbolism', *American Anthropologist*, 56(2): 228–4.

Wolcott, F.H. (1999), *Ethnography: A Way of Seeing*, Walnut Creek, CA: Altamira Press.

Index

About the Author

Sarita K. Kashyap holds a doctorate in Sociology from the Delhi School of Economics, University of Delhi. Her long-standing research interests include caste studies, the anthropology of death and the sociology of religion.